As Long as the Rivers Flow

The Stories of Nine Native Americans

**by Paula Gunn Allen
and Patricia Clark Smith**

SCHOLASTIC INC.

New York Toronto London Auckland Sydney
Mexico City New Delhi Hong Kong Buenos Aires

Photo Credits

p. 36: Army News Features; p. 204, 268: Associated Press; p. 237: Cherokee Nation of Oklahoma; p. 292: Nancy Crampton; p. 160: Culver Pictures Inc.; p. 7: Winson Trang (artist's conception of Weetamoo); p. 75, 121: UPI/Bettmann.

No part of this publication may be reproduced in whole or in part, or stored in a retrieval system, or transmitted in any form or by any means, electronic, mechanical, photocopying, recording, or otherwise, without written permission of the publisher. For information regarding permission, write to Scholastic Inc., Attention: Permissions Department, 555 Broadway, New York, NY 10012.

Library of Congress Cataloging-in-Publication Data available

ISBN 0-590-47870-2

12 11 10 9 8 7 6 5 4 3   3 4 5 6/0

Printed in the U.S.A.   40

First Scholastic paperback printing, October 2001

For Shaula, Max and Korinna

Acknowledgments

Our gratitude goes out to all who helped us with this book.

Twenty-nine pounds of dried salmon to Carla Gentry and Karen Wallace for their fine research.

Laurie Alberts, Rita Clark, Lia Cooper, Louis Owens, Pete White, Jill Williams, Mike Wolfe, Diane Wolkstein, and Hugh and Barbara Witemeyer all read various portions of the manuscript and offered sharp suggestions and comments, as did the members of our Writers' Group in Albuquerque: Barbara Byers, Nancy Gage, Janice Gould, Minrose Gwin, Margaret Randall, Ruth Salvaggio, Sharon Oard Warner, and Marie-Elise Wheatwind.

John Crawford and Tom Cummings read every word and saved us from many errors of style and substance, despite John's marathon strep throat and Tom's fractured vertebrae. They could always spot trouble ahead, like the misplaced phrase that made it seem as though Wilma Mankiller and the Spanish Conquistadores were sailing on San Francisco Bay at the very same moment.

Deborah Horsechief, a woman hero on many fronts, provided invaluable descriptions of Osage ceremonial dances and clothing.

Victor and Martha Garcia of All Indian Nations Book Store in Albuquerque gave freely of their bibliographic expertise, teasing, and friendship.

Our editor Ann Reit has been a wonderful guide for us. She and Lisa Papademetriou mushed us on through the last stages of writing while the blizzard of '96 howled about them and we basked in New Mexico and Southern California.

Thanks, above all, to the Native men and women we've had the honor to write about here.

Patricia Clark Smith
Paula Gunn Allen

Contents

Introduction

*A*s long as the grass grows and the rivers flow—

These words, and words like them, often appeared in nineteenth-century treaties made between American Indian nations and the United States government. The words were supposed to mean "forever." The problem is that they were not taken seriously by the government, which often went back on its promises. In spite of these ever-changing policies toward Native Americans, the unflagging strength of American Indians is indisputable.

The lives and work of the men and women whose stories are told in this book all reflect the importance that traditional American Indians placed on family and community. People like the Pocasset warrior Weetamoo and the Apache leader Geronimo worked not for individual recognition, but to improve the living conditions of their communities. In the spirit of these elders, today's leaders like Senator Ben Nighthorse Campbell of the Northern Cheyenne and Wilma Mankiller, the first woman to serve as Principal Chief of the Cherokee, work for the well-being of all.

Other Native Americans reaffirm traditional values in different ways. Laughter is a treasured part of Native life, and the mixed-blood Cherokee Will Rogers became one of America's best-loved humorists. Races and ball games have always been important in Native American ceremonial life, and Jim Thorpe, the Sac and Fox Olympic medalist, is considered by many to be the greatest athlete the United States has ever known. Michael Naranjo of Santa Clara Pueblo, although blinded in the Vietnam War, brings honor to his people with his beautiful massive sculptures. Through her novels and poems, Louise Erdrich of the Turtle Mountain Chippewa has helped thousands of readers to understand what it is like to grow up in American Indian and mixed-blood communities.

These Native Americans and countless others have succeeded in spite of the fact that American Indians have lost, over the years, more than 90 percent of their population and have the lowest life expectancy of any group in the United States.

American Indians have been displaced, dispossessed, and misunderstood, but the strong spirit and accomplishments of these nine men and women have helped to shape the face of our diverse nation.

1
Weetamoo

Weetamoo was probably born sometime around 1640 in the area now called Rhode Island, about twenty years after the Pilgrims landed and began to build Plymouth Bay Colony. Her father, Corbitant, the sachem or leader of the Algonquin-speaking Pocasset tribe, did not agree with other Algonquin tribal leaders who signed treaties promising to live peaceably beside the new arrivals. From the moment the English landed, Corbitant believed they would bring nothing but trouble. In the summer of 1621, the year after the Pilgrims arrived, Corbitant tried to persuade neighboring sachems to band together and drive the English away, but he had little luck. The Algonquins had seen what the muskets and cannons of the English could do, and they were cautious. Some thought the English would get discouraged by the harsh weather and hard work and go back where they came from. Others, guessing that these uninvited guests had come to stay, were determined to make the best of it. One way or another, most Indians in the early years of the English colonies were reluctant to start a full-scale war. Corbitant himself finally gave in and signed a treaty that said his people were the subjects of King James. He hoped that putting his mark on a paper would satisfy the English.

Corbitant's Pocasset tribe lived in the lands that lay north and east of Narragansett Bay in Rhode Island. In the winter months, they camped inland amid clearings in the woods and low-lying swamps thickly overgrown with oak, maple, pine, wild grapevine, and holly. There they were sheltered from the howling sea winds. On winter nights in smoky wigwams, Corbitant's daughter Weetamoo snuggled warm under beaver robes beside her little sister Wootonekanuske. But for most of the year Weetamoo lived within the sound of the sea at her father's favorite encampment, a plump neck of land called Mattapoisett that stretched about three miles into the bay. On late summer afternoons, she and the other children ran races and swam in the shallows, while they waited for clams and green corn to bake in pits dug deep in beach sand.

All year round, Weetamoo's days were filled with the tasks every Algonquin girl shared, even sachems' daughters. She dried fish on wooden frames and dug clams with her toes in wet muck.

She helped to plant and tend fields of beans and corn and pumpkins. Kneeling beside her mother, she ground corn and baked it in flat cakes flavored with berries and sweet woodchuck fat. As she grew older, she learned to sew fine beadwork. All her life, Weetamoo would be known for the richly decorated bright clothing she loved to make and wear.

Life wasn't all chores. Like children everywhere, Weetamoo and her friends played vigorous games that helped them grow strong and agile. But Algonquin boys and girls also played quiet games — games that could go on for hours and needed much patience — like seeing who could sneak up closest to an unsuspecting doe and her new fawns grazing in a meadow. The children knew these games were not only for fun. Weetamoo understood that she would need all the strength and skills these games taught her, especially if she became sachem after her father.

Algonquin women could be sachems. Rules were different from tribe to tribe, but among the Pocasset the office passed to the child or younger relative who seemed best fitted for it. The elders knew Weetamoo would be a good leader, not only because she was strong and intelligent and knew how to move through the woods, but also because she knew how to listen.

Weetamoo loved to sit quietly at the edge of the circle when her elders had gathered together talking. They talked about the weather and crops and births and deaths; they talked about curing

and hunting and their dreams. Best of all, they
told the stories that made them Pocasset, stories
they shared with other Algonquin — stories
about Kautantowit, the creator of human beings,
and Maushop, the giant who scooped out the
great shining Narragansett Bay and whose pipe
smoke was the thick wet fog that sometimes blan-
keted the coast. There were stories, too, about
Maushop's wife Squant, the protector of all
women, Squant with her beautiful long hair and
her strange square eyes.

And always throughout Weetamoo's childhood,
whenever she listened to the elders talking, she
heard them saying things about the English. They
recalled how for many years they had managed
to live at peace. At first, there was much trading
back and forth between the two peoples. The Algonquins made wampum belts from shells and
prepared fine beaver pelts. They exchanged them
for things made of metal and glass — cooking
pots, knives, axes, beads, lamp chimneys, and
buttons. It was against the law, though, to sell or
trade a musket to any Indian. The English did
not want the Algonquins to have firearms, just in
case a war should break out. Still, a good many
muskets found their way into Indian hands.

As time went on, matters had grown worse for
the Algonquin. The heavy horses and oxen the
English brought with them trampled Indian
fields, and when the Algonquins complained, the
English did nothing. Beaver hats and wampum
shells had gone out of style in Europe, and now

the Algonquins got very little in trade for them. No English court believed the word of an Algonquin if he or she spoke against an Englishman. The English called the Algonquin gods devils and urged the people to give them up. The English were taking over more and more land, often by getting the Algonquins drunk and making them sign papers when they were unable to think clearly. Every day the Algonquins had less and less land, and more and more of the English kept coming to settle. It began to look to many people as though old Corbitant had been right all along.

Weetamoo grew up knowing about her father's dream of a land where no English walked about noisily in their heavy boots or let their clumsy oxen trample young green blades of corn, a land where the people heard no clang of metal armor or jail doors and no voices preaching about how Kautantowit and Maushop and Squant were evil.

Many small Algonquin-speaking tribes in southern New England in the 1600s belonged to an alliance that the English called the Wampanoag Confederacy. When Weetamoo was a child, that alliance was led by Massasoit, the powerful sachem of the Pokanoket, who had given food and advice to the Pilgrims when they first arrived on the *Mayflower*. When the weather was clear, from Mattapoisett Weetamoo could look east across the bay to a peninsula crowned by a wooded green hill the Algonquin called Monthaup, where the soil was especially fertile and the sea air sweet. Monthaup was the particular headquarters of Massasoit, but it was a sacred place to all the Algonquin people of southern New England. On the hill rose a tall cliff of pale gneiss and quartz hung with honeysuckle and wild grapevines. The cliff formed a natural amphitheater, with one special niche like a throne. Someone sitting there could look across the lush slope of woods to the blue bay beyond. Massasoit took this seat when he presided over the great councils of the Wampanoag Confederacy at Monthaup.

Corbitant and Massasoit, the two neighboring sachems, did not agree about how they should behave toward the white people, but they had much else in common, above all, their love for their children. Massasoit had two sons named Wamsutta and Metacomet who were about the ages of Weetamoo and Wootonekanuske. The four children saw one another often when they were growing up, when tribes in the Wampanoag Confederacy came together for feast-days and councils. Sometime in their late teens or early twenties, Weetamoo married Wamsutta, the elder brother, and her little sister Wootonekanuske married Metacomet, the younger. By 1660 both Corbitant and Massasoit were dead, but the marriages of their children powerfully drew together the Indian people of southern New England. The leadership of the Pokanokets passed to Wamsutta, and Weetamoo became the sachem of the Pocassets. Weetamoo and Wamsutta had at least two sons.

Wamsutta continued in his father's path of

staying on friendly terms with the English. But he does not seem to have been as wise and careful as his father had been in dealing with them. He had a reputation for being proud, impulsive, and hot-tempered. He continued Massasoit's practice of selling Indian lands to the English, and he even tried to sell off land belonging to Weetamoo's people. From the time she was a child, Weetamoo had been taught by her father that Pocasset beaches, swamps, streams, and fields were never to be bargained away, and now her husband was trying to sell the very lands with whose care she had been entrusted!

Plymouth Colony court records show that Weetamoo appealed to English judges, who agreed with her that her husband had no right to sell the Pocasset land. History says nothing about what Wamsutta's and Weetamoo's married life was like, but this incident suggests that the young couple disagreed about some very important things.

Their marriage, in any case, was not destined to be a long one. In the summer of 1662, the Plymouth authorities heard rumors that Wamsutta was making alliances with the Narragansett, whose lands lay to the south, in what is now Connecticut and Rhode Island. This alarmed the colonists, who always feared that the various tribes of Algonquins might band together and make war on them. They ordered Wamsutta to appear before their general court in the town of Plymouth, Massachusetts Bay Colony, so they could question him about his dealings with the Narragansett. Wamsutta did not like being bossed around, so he ignored the summons and went off hunting with Weetamoo and several friends. The colonists sent two armed men to fetch him. When they surprised Wamsutta in one of his hunting lodges with Weetamoo, they thrust a pistol in his face and told him that if he "refused to go, he was a dead man." Wamsutta was furious, but he saw no choice except to go with his captors.

On the journey to the white settlement, Wamsutta came down with a high fever that continued to rage all the time he was being questioned at Plymouth. He was so sick the colonists allowed him to return home on a litter, but before he reached Monthaup he suddenly grew much weaker and died. The colonists just shrugged. They said it was probably Wamsutta's own bad temper that had caused his death. But Weetamoo and Metacomet, Wamsutta's surviving brother, and most of the other Algonquin peoples of New England were certain that the colonists had somehow poisoned Wamsutta in order to get rid of a strong Native leader.

After Wamsutta's death, Indians from many different tribes gathered on the slopes of Monthaup to honor him. Then they held a joyous celebration with feasting, dancing, and singing for Metacomet, the new sachem of the Wampanoags. During these ceremonial days when they were gathered to mourn the dead and honor the living, they spent much time talking about the growing numbers of white people, about broken promises and suspicions and fears. Nevertheless, a short time later Metacomet traveled to Plymouth and signed a promise to live in peace and friendship with the English, a promise he kept for many years.

What happened to Weetamoo after Wamsutta's death? Records of her are scarce for the next thirteen years. She continued to lead the Pocassets. As the mother of Wamsutta's children and as Metacomet's sister-in-law, she was a welcome and honored figure at Monthaup. Throughout his life, Metacomet greatly valued her ideas and sought her advice. At some point, she married a second husband, a Narragansett man named Petanennuit who was very friendly to the white colonists. This may seem like an odd choice for Weetamoo to make, but Algonquin women were free to choose their own partners, and something about this man must have pleased her, at least for a while.

By the early summer of 1675, Metacomet had just about given up living peacefully alongside the English colonists. Many things drove him to that, but most of all, it was the sight of wild forests and fields disappearing. The rich wilderness was being turned into square, muddy English villages and square English fields plowed in straight, thick rows. At a peace council called by the English authorities in Rhode Island, Metacomet recalled how his father Massasoit had tried

to help the English and had remained their friend
even as they grew greedier. He had tried, he said,
to continue that friendship, but it was no longer
possible in his generation:

> *My elder brother became sachem. . . . He was*
> *seized and confined, and thereby thrown into*
> *illness and died. Soon after I became sachem*
> *they disarmed all my people. . . . Their land was*
> *taken. But a small part of the dominion of my*
> *ancestors remains. I am determined not to live*
> *until I have no country.*

Metacomet felt he could not go on living in
peace while his people's land was disappearing
from under their feet. He had to do something,
and so, in alliance with other Alonquin tribes, he
began planning for war.

From her camp on the east side of the bay,
across the water from Monthaup, Weetamoo
watched events carefully and talked with the wise
people of the Pocassets. All her life, she had been
raised with the idea that the English did not belong in Algonquin country. Like Metacomet, she
had watched them grow more numerous, greedier for land, and less respectful of Indian rights.
They had even taken over Mattapoisett, her father's favorite site, and built the town there they
called Swansea. Corbitant's old dream of a land
without white people stirred in her heart.

She loved her brother-in-law Metacomet and
respected his judgment. But she was a strong

leader in her own right, and she did not like the
idea of being bullied into going to war by Metacomet or anybody else. She disliked even more
the English who kept coming to her and urging
her to join the English side against Metacomet,
should war come. Her husband, Petanennuit, was
also telling her to side with the English. But what
was best for the Pocassets? Could the Algonquins
really band together and win a war against the
English? Would they be able to continue living
their own way of life if they didn't fight? These
were the things a troubled Weetamoo thought
about in those June days as she gazed across the
bay at the thin smoke of council fires rising from
Monthaup.

Philip was the name the English called Metacomet, and the first shot in what became known
as King Philip's War was fired by a teenaged English boy at Swansea on June 24, 1675. The boy
had seen one of Metacomet's young Pokanoket
warriors trying to steal a cow, and he killed the
thief. Metacomet's people soon struck back and
killed nine Swansea men returning from church
services that same day. Now war had begun.

Metacomet and his Pokanokets swiftly moved
down the Monthaup peninsula to their stronghold. Plymouth Colony assembled an army to
chase them, but the English farmers and trades-
men made slow and clumsy soldiers. By the time
they reached Metacomet's headquarters on Monthaup, it was June 30, a full week after the shoot-
ings at Swansea. The English were sure they were

trapping Metacomet and his people on the little
peninsula, for the Pokanokets could not possibly
have enough canoes to evacuate the more than
two hundred men, women, and children who
lived there. But at the Monthaup encampment
the English found only dead fires and abandoned
wigwams.

It was not hard to guess what had happened.
On the night before, Metacomet had signaled
across the bay to Weetamoo that he needed her
help to evacuate his people, and Weetamoo at last
made up her mind. She sent boats across the
water to help in the evacuation. These boats were
probably not the slender birch-bark canoes of the
Indians who lived in the more northern parts of
New England, but sturdy dugouts made by hol-
lowing out huge white pine logs. The average dugout could hold from ten to twenty people. All
through the June night, the great shadowy dugouts paddled silently back and forth between
Monthaup and the Pocasset shores.

On the Pocasset side, the Pokanokets disem-
barked and were led quietly by their Pocasset
friends into hiding places deep in the tangled
swamplands that stretched inland for many
miles. As she watched boatload after boatload of
Pokanokets step ashore and melt into the soft
summer darkness, Weetamoo must have felt
some relief at making her decision. She had followed her heart, and she knew that now there
was no turning back.

Over the next week, war parties made up of

Pokanoket, Pocasset, and other Algonquin tribes struck at English towns in the area, using the Pocasset swamplands as their base. The villages of Taunton, Rehoboth, and Middleborough were all attacked. Finally, on July 8, the first English troop of about 36 people found their way to the outskirts of the swamp. There they camped, hoping to surprise a stray war party or two making their way back to the swamp. But one of them, a seasoned woodsman named Benjamin Church, noted with disgust that the English kept striking little fires so they could light their pipes. They simply could not last the night without tobacco, and so every Algonquin for miles around knew exactly where the English camp lay, just from the smell of their pipe smoke and the pinpoint sparks that lit the darkness.

Later, on July 19, more English joined that first troop, and together they decided to venture into the swamp to capture Metacomet and Weetamoo and their people. But the English didn't know how to move quietly and easily through the sucking mud, the sharp-edged reeds, and the tangles of vines. They soon discovered, as one of the Plymouth Colony ministers wrote:

> . . . how dangerous it is to fight in such dismal Woods, where their Eyes were muffled with the Leaves, and their Arms pinioned with the thick Boughs of the Trees, as their Feet were continually shackled with the Roots spreading every

*Way in those boggy Woods. It is ill fighting with
a wild Beast in his own Den.*

Safe in their hiding places, the Indians fired
muskets at the floundering English soldiers,
killing a few and wounding more. As dark approached, the English gave up and staggered out
of the swamp, muddy, mosquito-bitten, and discouraged. They decided it would be better just to
post guards around the swamp and wait to catch
Metacomet and Weetamoo. Surely several hundred people could not hide in a swamp forever.
This was not a bad plan, but the English were
not watchful enough. Ten days later, on July 29,
under the very noses of the English guards, Metacomet, Weetamoo, and their combined people
— more than three hundred men, women, children, and old people — stole silently out of the
north end of the swamp, crossed the Taunton
River, and headed northwest.

Great danger lay ahead of them, but as long as
they could travel through swamps or forests, they
had no need to fear English soldiers. The hiding
and stalking games they had all played in their
childhood served them well. But to reach the territories of sympathetic Algonquin tribes, Weetamoo and Metacomet now had to lead their
people on a long day's journey across Rehoboth
Plain, a wide area of open windswept fields
where trees were few and far between. Colonists
spied the long train of men, women, and children
making their way across the plain and sent for

the soldiers still patiently guarding the edges of the Pocasset swamp. Other soldiers were summoned from Providence, Rhode Island.

Early on the morning of August 1, the English army caught up with Metacomet and Weetamoo and their exhausted people at Nipsachuck, just northwest of Providence. The English opened fire, and at least thirty Pokanoket and Pocasset people were killed before Weetamoo and Metacomet could find shelter for them in a nearby swamp. There, the two leaders decided that the best plan would be to split up. Metacomet took fifty men and at least that many women, children, and elderly and headed northwest toward Nipmuc country in western Massachusetts.

Weetamoo led the rest southwestward, into Narragansett territory. About August 6, she was spotted on the coast of Stonington, Connecticut, where the excited settlers mistook her people for Metacomet's. They reported with satisfaction that the straggling band of people looked to be "starving & sick." No doubt they were, yet most of them made it to the protection of the Narragansetts, who took them in and treated them as honored guests. Over the beautiful bronze and gold autumn of southern New England, while corn and pumpkins came ripe, Weetamoo and her people were given time to heal and grow strong again.

We have no record of those days from the Algonquin side, but it was probably during these peaceful months that Weetamoo grew to love the

man who would be her third husband, a handsome Narragansett sachem named Quinnapin.
When she was married to her first husband, Wamsutta, the young couple had fought over his wish
to sell Pocasset lands. Her second husband, the
English-loving Petanennuit, had headed for
Plymouth to tell the authorities as soon as Weetamoo announced her decision to help Metacomet
escape from Monthaup. By that time there was
little love left to lose between them. It may be
that Quinnapin, whom she married in her middle
years when they were both committed to the
cause of Algonquin freedom, was the best partner
of all for Weetamoo.

The Narragansetts were brave in sheltering
Weetamoo and her people. They had signed a
treaty earlier in July agreeing not to harbor Indian refugees from English justice, but it soon
became plain to the colonial governments of Massachusetts, Connecticut, and Rhode Island that
Weetamoo could be hiding nowhere else but in
Narragansett territory. Besides, the English suspected the Narragansett were also helping Metacomet, who had safely reached his friends the
Nipmuc. With them and other allies, Metacomet
was now raiding and setting fire to English villages all over Massachusetts and northern
Connecticut.

By mid-December, when snows were falling,
one thousand armed English colonists set out to
track down the Narragansett in Rhode Island's
Great Swamp. There the Narragansetts had taken

refuge in a big fort they had built on an island. A palisade of logs surrounded by piled-up brush enclosed an area that contained many crowded wigwams. About a thousand Narragansetts and their friends, including Weetamoo and her people, planned to spend the winter safely hidden in the depths of the swamp.

In those short December days the snow and sleet were miserable, but because the water and mud of the swamp were frozen and could be walked upon, this English army had better luck than most in hunting down the Algonquins. When by accident they came upon the Narragansett fort, the English soldiers were astonished. They had not expected such a huge and complex structure in the middle of a swamp. They began by charging the fort, but in the end, they won by setting fire to the palisade, burning alive not only armed warriors, but defenseless women, children, old people, and the injured. The attack started at noon, as one contemporary English minister noted, just when the Narragansett had begun preparing their meal. By the late afternoon, he wrote gleefully, the English *"[made] their Cookrooms too hot for them at that Time, and they and their Mitchin [dinner] fryed together."* All told, perhaps 40 Englishmen died in the Great Swamp Fight. Anywhere from 300 to 600 Narragansetts and other Algonquin people died in the flames that billowed upward into a snowy December sky. As many as 300 were taken prisoner.

There are few stories from the Algonquin side. But it is known that Weetamoo and Quinnapin were two of the 400 or so Algonquin people who escaped the bullets and the burning at the Great Swamp Fight.

English soldiers' diaries tell how bitter the weather was that winter and what a hard time the English had getting back to their towns after the fight. The sufferings of the surviving Indians are not recorded. The fire not only took their loved ones, but it also devoured the stores of dried corn and beans and meat they hoped to live on through the winter. They needed to make their way through the snow to other Algonquin tribes who would help them. That is apparently what Weetamoo did, for by February of 1676 she and her husband Quinnapin were in Massachusetts with Metacomet's forces, attacking towns in the vicinity of Boston. At this point, the Algonquin were really winning the war. Out of 90 English towns, they had successfully attacked 52 and destroyed 12 of them completely.

Mostly, what is known about Weetamoo comes from histories and diaries written by English colonists. From mid-February to early May of 1676, it is known where Weetamoo was almost every day, thanks to an extraordinary document, *A Narrative of the Captivity and Restoration of Mrs. Mary Rowlandson*, written by an English woman. Rowlandson, a minister's wife, was captured when Metacomet's forces attacked Lancaster, Massachusetts, on February 10, 1676. It is not certain that Weetamoo herself took part in that raid, but Rowlandson was soon given into the keeping of Weetamoo and Quinnapin by the man who had captured her. One of Rowlandson's children, a toddler, was badly injured in the attack and died soon after. In the narrative, Rowlandson tells how she recovered from her shock and grief and gradually made a place for herself in the little Indian community on the march. Like Weetamoo herself, she was a skillful seamstress, and various Algonquin people paid her in food or money to sew shirts and caps for them.

During that winter and spring of 1676, Weetamoo and her people raided villages and kept moving, always staying ahead of the English army. The Algonquin traveled as far as ten miles a day, with all their belongings on their backs. They had only a few horses, and most traveled on foot. They carried very small children and anyone who was sick or weak. They ate whatever they could find — dried corn and peas, groundnuts, acorns, chestnuts, bear and deer meat, even horses' hooves.

In time, Rowlandson and many of her captors developed real respect for one another, and she grew to like both Quinnapin and Metacomet very much. But she hated Weetamoo! Weetamoo was the one who gave Rowlandson orders, and Rowlandson naturally resented her for that. But Rowlandson also thought Weetamoo was much too vain:

A severe and proud dame was she, bestowing every day in dressing herself neat as much time as any of the gentry of the land. . . . When she had dressed herself, her work was to make girdles of wampum and beads.

Rowlandson had no idea that Weetamoo was a sachem whose real work, in addition to sewing, was to lead her people. She just considered Weetamoo a very bossy person who didn't act meekly, as she believed women should. Rowlandson was not used to being among people who thought men and women were equally powerful.

Rowlandson describes many things that happened in the time between her capture and her ransom. She tells us that Weetamoo had a baby who got sick and died during that time, and how people came to "mourn and howl" with Weetamoo and Quinnapin for a night and a morning afterward. She tells us that every time Weetamoo caught her reading the Bible, she would snatch the book away and throw it outside the wigwam. After so many years of hearing white people say that Kautantowit and Maushop and Squant were evil demons, Weetamoo must have come to hate the English god. Once Rowlandson cooked a stew of peas and bear meat and invited Weetamoo and Quinnapin to dinner, but Weetamoo when served refused to eat from the same dish as Quinnapin. Perhaps it was taboo for Algonquin husbands and wives to share a plate. But Mrs. Rowlandson just thought Weetamoo had bad manners.

In early May of 1676, shortly before she was returned to her family, Rowlandson witnessed a great dance ceremony staged by Weetamoo and Quinnapin. They built a huge structure that held more than a hundred people, and Indians from all over New England came to their encampment. The dancing was done by four men and four women, including Weetamoo and Quinnapin. Rowlandson describes Weetamoo dressing for the dance:

> *She had a kersey [linen] coat and was covered with girdles of wampum from the loins upward; her arms from her elbows to her hands were covered with bracelets; there were handfuls of necklaces about her neck, and several sorts of jewels in her ears. She had fine red stockings, and white shoes, her hair powdered and face painted red that was always before black.*

Weetamoo loved to wear beautiful clothes and jewels, and since she was a sachem, her dressing well told others that the Pocassets were prosperous and powerful. But Rowlandson thought Weetamoo was just a "hussy," a bold woman who wore flashy clothes. Rowlandson also tells about the ceremony itself. While Weetamoo and Quinnapin and three other couples danced,

> *. . . there were two others singing and knocking on a kettle for their music. They kept hopping*

up and down one after another with a kettle of
water in the midst, standing warm upon some
embers, to drink of when they were dry. They
held on till it was almost night, throwing out
wampum to the standers-by.

By freely handing out wampum and food to the
crowd, Weetamoo and the others were spreading
goodness around, asking the universe to behave
generously to them in turn, and to send their people what they needed to survive. By May of 1676,
the Algonquins under Weetamoo and Metacomet
were beginning to be in need of such help from
the spirit world. With winter stores exhausted
and no chance to plant new crops, food was getting scarce. They had been on the run for ten
months now, enduring a bitter winter, and the
hard life was wearing people down.

A chance for the Algonquins to gather their
strength and replenish their supplies came in
mid-May, when the great runs of migratory fish
— silvery shad and alewife, and the big blue-
backed Atlantic salmon — began their annual
journey far up the Connecticut River to spawn in
quiet pools of fresh water. Every year, groups of
Algonquins traditionally put aside whatever dis-
putes troubled them to gather together at water-
falls along the New England rivers, where fish
trying to swim upstream could easily be trapped
or netted. This was always a wonderful, relaxed
time. Children ran about on the banks, laughing
in the blown spray, while everyone old enough to

help caught fish and prepared them to be smoked and dried.

Peskeompscut was one such waterfall on the Connecticut River where people gathered to fish. Here, the river ran between narrow granite banks before tumbling over a 50-foot drop in thundering foam. The steep gray cliffs above and below the falls were white with shadblow, the shrub that blooms just in time to tell people that the fish are running. In this wartime spring, when the Algonquin people needed rest so badly, they gathered again at Peskeompscut in the old way. The hundreds camped at the waterfall included members of Metacomet's and Weetamoo's forces as well as many Algonquin people who had never fought at all with the English. They went to Peskeompscut just as they always had done, because it was spring and the fish were running and it was good to be together.

On May 18, English people at the town of Hatfield, some miles down the river, learned of the big gathering at Peskeompscut from an English soldier who had escaped his Algonquin captors. They thought it would be a good chance for a surprise attack, especially since the escaped soldier reported there were few men at the encampment. A volunteer army of about 150 men led by Captain William Turner left Hatfield at sunset.

A heavy thunderstorm rolled through the Connecticut valley that night, but Turner and his company rode on through the driving rain and blue-white flashes of lightning, calming their

spooked horses. When they neared the sound of
the waterfall, the sky to the east was just beginning to turn pale. They tethered their horses and
crept near to the cliffs overlooking the falls. They
could see that the Algonquin people at the fishing
camp were still asleep in the shelters where they
had escaped the wet night. Just as reported, most
of the men were off on raiding or hunting parties,
leaving the work of catching and curing fish to
the women and children and elders. The Algonquins felt so safe at Peskeompscut they had not
even bothered to post guards.

The English lost no time. They climbed down
the cliffs, white with the blooming shadblow, and
crossed to the south bank of the river. There, they
spread out through the camp, and at a signal
began firing their muskets directly into wigwams.
The Algonquins instantly awakened to terror and
noise, blood and pain and confusion. Many were
shot in their bedrolls, and others were brought
down as they tried to struggle one by one out of
the wigwams. Some tried to make it to the dugouts drawn up on the bank, hoping to paddle to
the north shore of the river and lose themselves
in the woods. But the English marksmen just
picked them off, boatload by boatload, and Algonquin bodies tumbled in the swirling foam below the falls.

With most of the slaughter done, the English
turned to destroying the Algonquin stores of food
and ammunition. They also smashed two forges
they found there at the camp, which the Algon-

quins used for mending firearms and casting bullets. The English were so caught up in their work,
they noticed too late that large groups of Algonquin warriors, probably including Metacomet
and Weetamoo, had returned to the falls from
camps further up the river or from expeditions.
Suddenly, instead of an easy massacre of un-
armed and confused people, the English had a
real fight on their hands. In the end, about 40
Englishmen died, including their leader, Captain
Turner — nearly a quarter of the war party that
left Hatfield. Between two and three hundred Algonquin fell at Peskeompscut.

This slaughter, more than any other single
thing, broke the spirit of the Algonquin rebel
forces. Most of the dead were the Algonquin elders, the carriers of knowledge and stories. They
were the women, the bearers of life, the nurturers
and the healers. And worst of all, many of the
dead were children, the hope and the promise of
the years to come. The war would drag on
through the summer, but Philip and Weetamoo's
cause really died on that May morning, beside
the thundering waters of Peskeompscut.

It is very likely that Weetamoo lost children of
her own at Peskeompscut. From May on, throughout a summer when the weak and heartbroken
Algonquins suffered defeat after defeat, she and
Metacomet and Quinnapin and their straggling
forces made their way back to their own territories in the south. Many leaders were captured
or surrendered. Weetamoo's sister Wootoneka-

nuske, and her nine-year-old son were taken prisoner on August 1. Soon thereafter, Quinnapin was captured. He was put in prison and executed later that fall by Rhode Island authorities.

Weetamoo herself was ambushed with a number of her people on August 6 near the English town of Taunton, close to the swamps and beaches of her Pocasset land. Twenty Englishmen were enough to capture the sick and weakened Pocasset, but once again, for the last time, Weetamoo somehow escaped. On the banks of the Taunton River, she found a piece of a broken-up wooden raft, and tried to swim across the river clinging to it. Beyond the river lay the safety of the great Pocasset swamp, heavy with late-summer growth, whose trails and thickets she knew so well. She knew that if she could only make it there, she could hide and rest and get back her strength. But her exhausted body could not fight the swirling current of the tidal river, and she was swept under the water with her flimsy raft. The English found her naked body washed up on the beach of Mattapoisett, the same beach where she had laughed and run and dreamed as a child. For Weetamoo, the war was over. The English cut off her head and impaled it on a pole in Taunton where Algonquin prisoners could see it. They cried out in anguish for the brave and beautiful woman who had led them so many miles on such a fierce journey.

Metacomet himself was shot a few days later, on August 12, 1676, at Monthaup, in a little

swamp a few hundred yards from the cliffs where
he and Massasoit before him had presided over
so many councils and ceremonies and feasts. In
the end, both he and Weetamoo had found their
way home.

It is not known what happened to any of Weetamoo's children, but there are stories about her
nephew, the nine-year-old son of Metacomet and
Wootonekanuske. There was much debate among
the English about what to do with the little boy.
With the blood of Algonquin leaders from both
sides of his family flowing in his veins, the English
thought he might grow up to lead a new rebellion,
and many wanted him killed. Finally, judges decided to sell both Wootanakanuske and her son
into slavery in the West Indies. In March of 1677,
a Dutch trader sailed for the Caribbean with the
mother and son and other Algonquin prisoners.

History books say no more. But the descendants of the people who lived and fought beside
Metacomet and Weetamoo are still living in Connecticut, Massachusetts, and Rhode Island. They
are Pocasset and Pokanoket, Narragansett and
Nipmuc and Mashpee, and their families for generations have passed on the knowledge that there
is more to the story. They say that, according to
a plan worked out secretly among the Algonquin
peoples, the boy slipped overboard as the ship
passed near to the island of Martha's Vineyard,
just off the coast of Massachusetts, and swam
ashore, where the Mashpee were waiting for him
on the beach. They took him in and raised him

in safety, telling him that he must never forget
his heritage. Many people who are active today
in New England Native American treaty rights
and land claims proudly trace their descent from
him. Through him, they inherit the blood and the
spirit of Massasoit and Corbitant, of Metacomet
and Wootonekanuske, and Weetamoo. Algonquin
courage and independence live on.

2
Geronimo

In the 1880s, somewhere in the Mogollon Mountains of southwestern New Mexico, nine-year-old Marietta Palmer sat alone at her family's encampment. She was behind in her lessons, and so her parents had ordered her to catch up on schoolwork while they explored the nearby ruins of an abandoned Indian town. Staying in camp was supposed to be a punishment, but Marietta could always find wonderful things to do when she was alone, especially if she were outdoors. Today, when she was supposed to be studying her arithmetic and spelling, she had already plucked a batch of wild buffalo gourds from the gray-green vines that spread over the sandy soil. With four sticks for legs, one for a tail, and one for a neck with a baby gourd stuck atop for a head, each gourd became a fat pony or cow.

Marietta was so intent on making a twig corral

for her gourd animals, she didn't even notice the
group of strangers who had slipped quietly into
the camp until one of them rode his horse right
up to her. "Where is the water?" he asked in
Spanish. Marietta pointed downhill to the spring
and brought the buckets her family kept by the
cook-tent. She wasn't afraid of these people in the
least. She had enjoyed the time she'd spent with
her parents the year before in Navajo country,
and these folks looked a lot like Navajo to her.

The leader smiled down at Marietta while the
others watered the horses and mules. Her face
was deeply tanned and her long black braids glis-
tened in the sunlight. "You're an Apache girl,"
he said.

"No, I'm a white girl," Marietta told him.

The man laughed. "Awful dark for a white girl,"
he said. Then he looked around. "Where are your
people?" he asked. Marietta explained that her
family was nearby. The leader sent some of his
men to check, and they quickly reported back to
say yes, over the next hill they could see white
people poking around in some ruins.

The leader frowned. He seemed worried that
her family had left her by herself. Marietta assured him she was all right. "You're a nice big
girl, but you're an Apache!" he said. "You can go
to my camp. I'll give you a pony."

"I already have a pony," Marietta told him.

"You can play with my other Apache children,"
he said.

But Marietta just shook her head. "No, my

mother wouldn't like that," she told him. "She'd cry. I'm my mother's girl."

Now the other men motioned to the leader that they had to be going. He agreed, but he turned again to the girl. "Do they feed you well? Do you have fresh meat?" he asked. When Marietta told him they had only ham and bacon, he gestured toward the pack train of mules behind him. "Go cut some beef for my Apache girl!" he ordered. The men rummaged under the blankets thrown over one of the mules and tossed a big quarter of beef down on the camp table. Then the strangers all set off on the trail leading up to the mountains, quickly disappearing amid the piñon and juniper into the high timber.

When Marietta's family returned to camp, they were astonished to see a bloody slab of fresh beef lying there. They did not believe their daughter when she told them Apaches had left the meat for her. But soon, while steaks cut from that beef were sizzling in the fry pan, a detachment of cavalry rode into the Palmers' camp. They told Mr. Palmer he was foolish to take his family into the wilderness while the fierce Apache renegade Geronimo was on the rampage. Why, Geronimo and his men had just attacked a mule train loaded with beef that very day!

Now her family realized that Marietta's story was true, and suddenly everyone began to pay attention to her. The soldiers knelt down beside her and asked which way the Apache had headed. Marietta pointed down the trail, away from the mountains. "They went that way," she lied, and the soldiers all galloped off in pursuit. The secret of Geronimo's whereabouts was safe with Marietta.

Many years later, these two friends would meet again, far from the piñon-covered foothills of the southwestern wilderness they both loved.

Geronimo himself had spent a childhood more secure than many other nineteenth-century Apache children. Most Apaches were steadily warring back and forth with Mexicans in those days, but this was not true of the band Geronimo belonged to, the Bedonkohe Apache. Geronimo said that all the while he was growing up, "we never [saw] a missionary or a priest. We never [saw] a white man."

He was born sometime in the early 1820s in the mountains and canyonlands near the headwaters of the Gila River near the present Arizona–New Mexico border. The exact place of his birth is not certain, but he was raised in the shelter of steep canyon walls, where the rock is colored rose and gold and tall green cottonwoods shade clear rivers. At many places among those canyons, hot springs well out of the volcanic depths of the earth and form pools. It feels wonderful to soak in those warm waters. From time immemorial, people have known Geronimo's homeland as a place of great beauty and healing power.

Geronimo's family named him Goyahkla — "He Who Yawns." This seems a strange name for a person who would grow up to be known for his

tireless energy and courageous spirit. Perhaps he
was a baby who played so hard he wore himself
out. Or perhaps he was just resting up for the
long demanding life that lay ahead of him. As an
old man of nearly eighty, Geronimo looked back
on his babyhood as a time of harmony with the
natural world and the loving family who surrounded him:

> *As a babe I rolled around on the dirt floor of*
> *my father's teepee, hung in my tsoch [cradle-*
> *board] at my mother's back, or suspended from*
> *the bough of a tree. I was warmed by the sun,*
> *rocked by the winds, and sheltered by the*
> *trees . . .*

The elderly Geronimo also remembered how he
and his playmates used to pass the time:

> *Sometimes we played at hide-and-seek among*
> *the rocks and pines; sometimes we lingered in*
> *the shade of a cottonwood tree or sought the*
> *shuduck [a kind of wild cherry] while our par-*
> *ents worked in the field. We would practice*
> *stealing up on some object that represented an*
> *enemy. . . . Sometimes we would hide away*
> *from our mother to see if she could find us, and*
> *often when thus concealed go to sleep and per-*
> *haps remain hidden for many hours.*

Geronimo and his friends were learning skills
they would need as adults: how to sneak up on

game, how to gather food, and, above all, how to hide so perfectly they seemed to vanish into the cliffs, trees, and shadows. Hiding was an art the Apache were especially good at. When the Spanish conquistadores led by Coronado first passed through Apache country in the 1500s, they reported that the land was uninhabited. But Apache historians say their ancestors were there long before Coronado. The Apaches had been warned by the Indians of Mexico about the greed of these strangers from across the sea, and so they decided to keep an eye on them and not let themselves be seen. From behind rocks, from within tangled thickets, from high canyon ledges, Apaches watched as the pale men in clanking armor rode noisily through mountains and canyons. Meeting no one, and seeing nothing they wanted, the Spanish went on their way. Almost three hundred years later, the mischievous Apache children of Geronimo's generation who hid successfully — even from their sharp-eyed mothers — were practicing a skill that had long helped their people survive.

Even though the elderly Geronimo could look back on his childhood as easy and pleasant, Apache people always had to stay alert. One of Geronimo's earliest memories was of a woman who had gotten lost while gathering berries. The next day, Geronimo and the others in the berrying party found her. She had been attacked by a bear. She was very weak from infection and loss of blood, but she was alive. Back at camp, Apache doctors nursed her back to health. The Apache's knowledge of wild plants and herbs and rituals for curing was another great source of their strength. This incident deeply impressed the boy. In time, he himself would be given the Power of curing, among a number of other gifts granted him by Ussen, the Apache creator.

As Geronimo grew older, he learned to hunt small game with his bow and arrow, and he helped his parents more and more in the fields where they grew corn, beans, and squash. His training to be a warrior became more intense. To make them into strong runners with lots of lung power, Apache boys were taught to take in a big mouthful of water and then run for four miles before they spat it out. They also learned a special ritual way of speaking that Apache men still use in times of war and during ceremonies. Instead of saying "heart," for example, Geronimo was taught to say "that by means of which I live."

During Geronimo's early teens, some Nednhi Apaches from the south, near what is now the Mexico-Arizona border, traveled up to the Gila canyon lands to visit with the Bedonkohe. One sturdy Nednhi teenager named Juh kept tormenting the girls of Geronimo's family, spilling the baskets full of acorns they had worked hard to gather. Geronimo's mother ordered him to take the rude Nednhi boy aside and teach him a lesson. Perhaps Geronimo did, but whatever happened, he and Juh began a friendship that endured as long as both lived. A few years later, Juh married

Geronimo's favorite sister Ishton, one of the pretty acorn gatherers he had been teasing.

Sometime soon after, Geronimo's father died. His mother could have remarried, but she chose not to. In his middle teens, Geronimo suddenly became the oldest man of the family. That did not mean he had authority over his mother, for Apache women have always held considerable power in their families and communities. But Geronimo did have to provide for her and his brothers and sisters and cousins.

When he turned seventeen, after he had taken part in four required raiding or hunting expeditions, he was admitted to the council of warriors as a full adult. Now he could ask to marry Alope, a Nednhi Apache like Juh. She was beautiful and delicate, and the two young people had loved one another for some time. Alope's father thought a great deal of her, demanding many ponies in exchange for her hand. In his autobiography, Geronimo never says where he got those ponies, but he soon showed up with a whole herd of them.

The next years were the happiest of Geronimo's life. He took Alope to live near his mother and the younger brothers and sisters who still remained at home. Alope was not physically strong, but she was a loving wife and a good mother to the three children born to them. She was also an artist who enjoyed decorating the buffalo-skin walls of their home with her beadwork and drawings. Many decades later, the elderly Geronimo could still recall how good it felt to live in that tepee, his first adult home, with its walls covered with Alope's beautiful pictures of their world, their children playing around them, and his mother and the rest of his family nearby.

Despite the goodness of their lives, Alope missed her Nednhi people, and Geronimo and his mother missed Ishton, now married to their Nednhi friend and relation Juh. Apaches were a seminomadic people who moved about with the seasons and their own love of going places. Geronimo and his whole family often visited their Nednhi kin across the Mexican border in the states of Chihuahua and Sonora.

Northern Mexico was not a safe place for Apaches. Much raiding and skirmishing had gone on back and forth over the years between Mexicans and Apaches. In the 1830s, the states of Chihuahua and Sonora had offered bounties of up to $200 for every Apache scalp, even the scalps of small children. This was terrible not only for the Apaches, but for most of the people of northern Mexico. There was really no difference between the dried scalp of one black-haired person and another, and greedy bounty hunters murdered many Apaches and non-Apache alike to claim money for the scalps.

Even during the scalp-bounty years, Apaches and Mexicans had continued to meet to trade with each other at one traditional gathering place, the Chihuahuan fort of Janos. As people often do, they tried to find ways around harsh laws that restricted their coming together. Fi-

nally, in 1850, the state of Chihuahua withdrew
the bounty on Apache scalps and signed treaties
with three Apache leaders at Janos, though Sonora kept its bounty.

In the spring of 1851, Geronimo and other
Apaches under the leadership of the Chihenne
chief Mangas Coloradas made a trading expedition into Chihuahua. Their families went along,
for this was to be a pleasant peacetime adventure
in the season of desert wildflowers and fine spring
air. They camped by a river a little ways outside
the gates of Janos, and for several days in a row
most of the men ventured into town to trade. They
exchanged hides and furs, dried herbs, beadwork,
and baskets for Mexican metal goods, and woven
cloth and the alcoholic drink called mescal. The
Apaches left only a few men behind in camp as
guards. They feared no violence in this springtime of peace.

On March 5, 1851, as Geronimo and his friends
were headed back to camp after a full day of trading, they were met by terrified Apache women
and children, crying out the story that would
change Geronimo's life forever. Mexican soldiers
from another town had suddenly attacked the
camp, killing the guards and many of the women
and children, taking others captive to be sold as
slaves. General José María Carrasco, a newly appointed commander from the state of Sonora, had
heard of a large band of Apaches camped outside
Janos. Carrasco claimed that Apaches had stolen
some mules from a Sonoran town. It didn't really

matter to him whether the people camped outside Janos were the same ones who'd stolen the
mules. They were Apaches, and that was good
enough for him. Though he had no authority to
do so, Carrasco led his troops across the state line
into Chihuahua and attacked the camp outside
Janos.

Learning of the slaughter, Geronimo and the
others scattered and hid until dark. By moonlight, they crept into the silent field beside the
river. Geronimo found his mother, his wife, and
his children among the dead, lying together in a
single pool of blood. He was so stunned by the
sight that he could not speak or think. He felt
nothing — no grief, no anger, only emptiness. He
just turned away and walked toward the river.
He stood there for a long time, staring down into
the dark waters.

Later that night, still numb, Geronimo looked
on as Mangas Coloradas and the other Apaches
decided to retreat as quickly as possible toward
the Arizona border. They had too few warriors,
horses, and weapons to fight Carrasco. They left
their dead behind, determined to save those still
alive.

Back in the Gila canyonlands, the home seemed
to await the family's return. Toys lay scattered
about, and Alope's drawings and beadwork still
hung on the walls. Geronimo's feelings began to
flood back. In the Apache way, to discourage the
ghosts of the dead from returning to their earthly
home, he set fire to the family's tepees. He burned

all the family's goods as well. Every toy, every
tool, every blanket under which his loved ones
had slept reminded him too sharply of his loss.
His heart now began, as he said, to "ache for
revenge upon Mexico."

In the midst of his fresh grief, a great gift came
to Geronimo. He was sitting alone weeping when
he heard a voice call his name, *"Goyahkla!"* four
times. Then he heard it say, *"No gun can ever kill
you. I will take the bullets from the guns of the
Mexicans, so they will have nothing but powder.
And I will guide your arrows."*

Ussen, the creator, gave Geronimo a great
Power, invulnerability from bullets. Despite
many gunshot wounds, just as Ussen promised,
no bullet ever brought him down. Geronimo
would be granted other kinds of Power over his
lifetime — he could see into the future, cure bullet
wounds, and bring women through difficult child-
birth. But this first gift of Power from Ussen gave
him the heart to go on with his life after the
slaughter of his family.

Once the Apaches were safely back in Arizona,
Mangas Coloradas and other leaders began to
think about getting revenge on the Mexican
troops of Carrasco. They gave Geronimo a big role
in the planning because he had lost the most relatives in the attack. During the summer and autumn, he rode west and south to consult the
Chiricahua and the Nednhi Apaches. All agreed
that the Mexicans could not be allowed to continue to kill Apaches in cold blood.

The Apache expedition that made its way on foot across the border in the summer of 1852 was very different from the carefree, hopeful traders who had come venturing with their pack ponies and their families into Janos more than a year before. They were bent on revenge, and they left nothing to chance. First, the warriors made a hidden camp near the Arizona border where their relatives might safely wait for them. Then they headed south, stopping near a river outside Arizpe. Eight Mexican soldiers rode out of the town to ask the strangers what they wanted. Without a word, the Apaches killed them all. As Geronimo had hoped, this action drew all the rest of the soldiers out of the protection of the town. Geronimo recognized some men who had been among the raiders at Janos.

Geronimo himself was not a chief, but the other Apaches gave him the honor of planning the main battle. In thick brush by the river, Geronimo arranged his well-hidden warriors in a large circle with an opening in the direction of the approaching enemy. As the unsuspecting Mexican soldiers marched in their orderly lines toward the few Apaches they could see, the circle of unseen warriors quietly closed around them, trapping them.

In the two-hour battle that followed, Geronimo fought wildly. He kept seeing in his mind his slaughtered family, and he felt no fear because of his knowledge that no bullet could kill him. He seemed more than human as he dashed around the bloody woods, bringing down soldier after

soldier. Toward the end of the battle, after the
Apaches had shot all their arrows and thrust all
their lances into enemy flesh, Geronimo fought
on with only a knife and his bare hands. At last
the Mexican survivors fled to a nearby town.

During the fight, whenever the terrified Mexicans would point at the Apache leader who
seemed to leap up everywhere at once, they would
shout "Geronimo!" No one today is certain why.
Perhaps the Mexican soldiers were invoking the
help of Saint Jerome, *San Geronimo* in Spanish.
But Saint Jerome, who had lived the life of a
scholarly monk, was not a saint usually called
upon in battle. In any case, the name stuck, and
Goyahkla was ever afterward known as Geronimo
to both the Apaches and their enemies alike. The
young man had a new name to fit the hard new
way of life he had begun.

That name came to mean something far beyond
Apache country. Long after Geronimo's death,
when U.S. paratroopers in World Wars I and II
wanted to yell a single word that meant "Here
we come — look out!" as they jumped out of
planes, they would cry, *Geronimo!* Some probably did not know Geronimo was the name of an
Apache leader of the past. They just seemed to
know it was somehow a proud and brave American sound.

After Alope's death, Geronimo married again,
taking in time a number of wives, as befit his high
rank, and fathering many children, all of whom
he loved tenderly. But the victory at Arizpe and

new family ties were not enough to quiet his long-
ing for revenge. Over the next ten years, Geronimo often joined forces with other Apache leaders
like Cochise and Victorio in raids on the Mexicans
he hated so bitterly and on the Americans he was
coming to hate as well.

After the treaty of Guadalupe Hidalgo in 1848
ceded one-third of Mexican lands to the United
States, more and more whites began pouring into
New Mexico and Arizona. They came to prospect
for gold, to mine for copper, to ranch, and to farm.
They came to stay, and their presence altered
Apache life forever. Geronimo's people were
rapidly being squeezed out of their old ways by
Mexicans and Americans, but raids on their
settlements kept the Apaches provisioned. Skirmishing and raiding among Mexican villages became Geronimo's way of sustaining his people.
He made some foolish mistakes at first that nearly
cost him his life, but he soon became very skilled
at attacking small villages and pack trains and
escaping with livestock and goods.

Geronimo seemed nearly unstoppable, especially after he and his followers learned to use
rifles. In telling his life story, Geronimo remembered with pride what happened after he had
driven all the Mexican people out of one of the
first towns he raided:

When we discovered that all the Mexicans were
gone we looked through their houses and saw
many curious things. These Mexicans kept

*many more kinds of property than the Apaches
did. Many of the things we saw in the houses
we could not understand, but in the stores we
saw much that we wanted; so we drove in a
herd of horses and mules, and packed as much
provisions and supplies as we could on them.
Then we formed these animals into a pack train
and returned safely to Arizona. The Mexicans
did not even trail us.*

From Geronimo's point of view, he was being a
good provider for his people, getting further revenge on Mexican people, and having fine adventures in the bargain.

In 1861, the northern and southern parts of the
United States began to fight one another in the
Civil War. Though Geronimo's homeland lay far
from Fort Sumter and Gettysburg and the places
where most of the fighting was concentrated, the
war touched Apache lives deeply. In June of 1862,
Union soldiers from California led by General
James Henry Carleton set out for New Mexico,
determined to drive Confederate troops out of the
Southwest. Apaches did not like soldiers clad in
either blue or gray marching through their territory, and both Confederate and Union soldiers
despised Indian people. On July 14, 1862, Geronimo, Cochise, Mangas Coloradas, and about
200 Apache warriors armed with rifles banded
together to repel General Carleton's Union forces
at Apache Pass in Arizona. It was the first battle

between the Apaches and an army of the United States.

At first, well-hidden in the rocks overlooking the narrow mountain gap, Geronimo and the other Apaches were easily able to pick off the soldiers in an advance party. But then the men in blue rolled up two strange bulky machines on wheels and pointed them toward the rocks where the Apache lay hidden. The Apache had never seen cannons and did not understand what the soldiers were up to. Suddenly big shells whistled through the air and exploded all around the Apache, setting off rock slides and driving them from their cover. The Apaches fled, and Carleton's whole army marched unharmed through Apache Pass, where Carleton ordered a fort to be built. The Apache watched from hiding as the square stone walls of Fort Bowie arose. Now the army had an impregnable structure in the middle of Apache lands. From there, they would direct many costly campaigns against the Apache.

Once General Carleton had reached the Rio Grande, driving retreating Confederate forces before him, he assumed military command of all New Mexico Territory. One of his first orders concerned Apaches, whom he especially disliked because of the ambush at the pass. "All Indian men of that tribe are to be killed wherever and whenever you can find them," he wrote. "The women and children will not be harmed, but you will take them prisoners."

Though it was mainly Chiricahua Apaches who

had attacked his troops, Carleton's order applied to all Apache bands and to the related Navajo tribe. Many Indian people would suffer for that single failed attack on the Union Army at Apache Pass. Navajos from all over New Mexico and Arizona, and the Mescalero Apache of southern New Mexico, were rounded up like cattle and force-marched on the terrible Long Walk to the Bosque Redondo, a journey during which many died. General Carleton had talked about starting a reservation that would be a beautiful model village, where Navajos and Apaches would learn to live like white people. He did not consider that every people has its own vision of the best way to live. Besides, Carleton had made almost no real plans for large numbers of people to live on the open plains of Bosque Redondo. There was little firewood, no shelters, and no lumber to build them out of, and the crops the Indian people were forced to plant in the European way of farming failed miserably.

At this prison camp on the flat eastern plains, the Navajo and Apache lived in tiny dugout shelters covered with canvas. Here they endured four years of disease, malnutrition, and despair. Many people today still tell with pain the stories handed down from elders in their families about those terrible years from 1864 to 1868. After four years, even the government finally had to agree that their plan to keep Navajos and Apaches penned up was a costly failure, and it let the surviving people return to their homelands.

Geronimo himself did not go through that experience. By mid-1863, he was living mostly with the Warm Springs Apache band, near what is now Truth or Consequences, New Mexico. Other Apaches who had not been rounded up were also gathered there, including the Warm Springs leaders Victorio, Loco, and Nana. Victorio repeatedly tried to convince authorities that his people could live peaceably if they were guaranteed a certain fertile valley within their ancestral lands. But no one in the government wanted to take that land away from the white people who had already begun to settle there.

In the winter of 1869, Geronimo's favorite sister Ishton and her husband Juh, his boyhood friend, were living with the Chiricahua Apache in Arizona near Apache Pass. Geronimo heard that Ishton was pregnant and due to go into labor soon; Juh was gone, raiding across the Mexican border. Geronimo rode hundreds of miles to the Chiricahua camp to be with her, arriving just as her time came to give birth. Ishton was strong and healthy, but the women in Geronimo's family often had difficult childbirths. Ishton's labor went on for four days, and yet the birth seemed no nearer. Her baby, when he grew to be an old man, would tell the story of his own birth, and his uncle Geronimo's part in it:

Geronimo thought that [my mother] was going to die; he had done all he could for her, and was so distressed that he climbed high up the

mountain behind Fort Bowie to plead with Us-
sen for his sister's life. As Geronimo stood with
arms and eyes upraised, as our people do, Ussen
spoke. Geronimo heard his voice clearly, as
distinctly as if on a telephone. Ussen told Ge-
ronimo that his sister was to live, and he prom-
ised my uncle that he would never be killed, but
would live to a ripe old age and die a natural
death.

When the baby was born, he was named Daklugie, "He Who Forced His Way Through." Geronimo helped to raise and train him in Apache
ways. In Geronimo's old age, when he wished to
dictate his autobiography, it was Daklugie who
acted as his interpreter, and he would be at Geronimo's side when the old man at last died the
natural death Ussen promised him.

If Ussen kept his promises, the United States
did not. One problem all Native people had in
dealing with the whites was that the government
was always changing its mind and altering its
policies and going back on treaties it had made
with tribes. Government officials were always
coming up with some new scheme about dealing
with Indian people. Those plans seldom took into
account Native people's own ideas about what
would be best for them.

In 1871, the War Department and the Bureau
of Indian Affairs (BIA) chose a number of reservation sites for different southwestern tribes. In
late December, they announced that Indian peo-

ples were to be in place at their assigned reservations by mid-February of 1872. Few obeyed these new orders. General George Crook, who was in charge of the Apache operation, was about to round up the reluctant Apaches by force when, to his surprise, President Grant sent in General Oliver Howard instead. Howard's job was to try to get the Apache people to agree to settle peacefully on the land set aside for them. Crook was angry to have his military expedition halted. He thought he would lose face in the sight of the Apaches. But he had no choice except to wait.

Howard was a brave soldier. Though he lost an arm in the Civil War, he had insisted on returning to battle as soon as he had healed. He was also a very religious man who deeply cared about the well-being of the newly-freed Africans in the American South. In Arizona, he determined to talk to the Indian leaders themselves, to hear their points of view and to learn from them what terms they hoped to settle for. But many of the Apache leaders refused to come out of hiding. Howard knew he would have to do more than sit around forts waiting for Apache chiefs to come to him.

One bright blue October day in 1871, General Howard's small party set off from Fort Bowie at Apache Pass in Arizona Territory. They rode southwest across 40 miles of yellow chamisa and fragrant gray-green sage, heading for the Dragoon Mountains, where the Chiricahua leader Cochise had his stronghold. The party included

Tom Jeffords. Jeffords was the only white man
Cochise had ever agreed to deal with, and he and
Cochise had become close friends. Few — white
or Apache — dared to approach the stronghold
of Cochise uninvited. Cochise came to meet with
Howard not only because he trusted Jeffords, but
because he was impressed with Howard's courage. Also, Cochise was sick with the illness that
would soon kill him. Perhaps he felt he had little
time left to arrange matters with the whites before he must leave his people.

Cochise summoned other Apache leaders,
among them Geronimo, to meet with Howard. In
ten days' time, Apaches from all over New Mexico
and Arizona had gathered at Cochise's stronghold. Howard listened carefully to them. Together they agreed that the Apache would move
not to the barren San Carlos Reservation in Arizona Territory, which had been set aside for
them, but instead to a reservation that would be
created in the Apache Pass area, where Tom Jeffords would be the supervisor.

Like Cochise, Geronimo was impressed by this
one-armed man with the earnest face. He, too,
agreed to move onto the reservation with his family and followers. When the council broke up, he
announced he would ride double with General
Howard back to Fort Bowie and, without waiting
for an invitation, he sprang easily onto the back
of Howard's horse, clasping Howard around the
waist. As the two men rode together over the rugged miles, they got to know one another quickly,

as travelers do. When they neared Fort Bowie,
Howard felt a shudder travel through Geronimo's
body. Geronimo was a warrior, afraid of no one,
and certain that no weapon could hurt him. But
the sight of the fort made him tremble. It was
terrible for him to think of Apaches living inside
stone walls.

Nonetheless, Geronimo kept his promise and
took up a peaceful life on the new Chiricahua
Reservation at Apache Pass. The people began to
grow crops there and followed their old ways as
best they could, except that they were now discouraged from raiding across the Mexican border
both by the United States government and by
Cochise himself, while he lived. After General
Howard returned to Washington, General Crook
began rounding up the Apaches who refused to
accept reservation life, and he succeeded in getting many to come in. It seemed as though the
United States was winning its way, placing most
Apaches where it could keep an eye on them. But
in 1875, just three years after Cochise and Howard had struck their agreement at Cochise's
mountain stronghold, the Apache were forced to
deal once again with a shift in policy that angered
them deeply. Suddenly, the government announced that it no longer wanted to keep Apaches
on separate reservations for each major band.
Now it wanted something called "consolidation"
— that is, all the Apache would be moved to two
large reservations. The more westerly Apache,
like the Chiricahua, were told to go to the big

desolate San Carlos Reservation in the middle of
Arizona, where General Howard had promised
them they would never have to live.

San Carlos was a wretched place. There was
almost no sweet fresh water, no trees to soften
the harsh landscape and provide shelter and firewood, and no grass for game to graze upon. Crops
did poorly in the alkaline soil. The only kinds of
life that seemed to flourish were cactus and rattle-
snakes, and the great clouds of malaria-bearing
mosquitoes that bred in scummy pools of standing water. No Apache had ever chosen that place
as their homeland, and none wished to live there
now. About this time, Cochise died, leaving no
strong Chiricahua leader after him to protest the
new plan.

The agent in charge of the San Carlos Reservation was an arrogant and rather foolish young
fellow named John Clum. He had graduated from
an eastern military school, and he delighted in
training a "police force" of Apache men to perform precision-drill maneuvers while he barked
out commands. Clum also like to target-shoot at
saguaro, the eerily beautiful giant cacti that take
hundreds of years to grow. The Apache privately
called him "Turkey Gobbler" because of the
proud way he strutted and preened. Clum was at
least honest, as many Indian agents were not. But
he made the mistake of believing the Apache were
a simple people whom he understood very well.

White people with better sense of how Apache
liked to live, people as different as General Crook

and Tom Jeffords, warned that the different bands of Apache would not thrive if thrown all together on land too barren to support them. But Clum was cocky about his ability to make the consolidated reservation work. In July of 1876 he traveled south to the Chiricahua Reservation at Apache Pass to order the Western Apache, including the Chiricahua, Juh's Nednhi, and Geronimo's Bedonkohe, to move to San Carlos. Reluctantly, most agreed.

Clum always claimed that when he met separately with Geronimo and Juh, they both said yes to the move. He said Geronimo told him he just needed time to round up his followers. That done, he would bring them into San Carlos. It is not certain that Geronimo ever told Clum any such thing. To the end of his days, Geronimo swore that the only binding agreement he had ever made with whites was with General Howard. By the morning of the following day, Clum woke to find that Geronimo and Juh and their people had all disappeared from Apache Pass. The Turkey Gobbler was left behind, spluttering in frustration. Now Geronimo entered a new phase of his history. In the eyes of the United States Army, he was a renegade who had dared to defy their orders.

Geronimo and Juh hid for a while in Mexico with about 100 Apache who had followed them. They decided it would be best to split up. Juh took the Nednhi back to their homeland in the Mexican Sierra Madre, and Geronimo led the rest back across the border into New Mexico Territory, headed for Victorio's Warm Springs Reservation. Over 100 other Apache who had refused to move to San Carlos were also living there. The shortage of food turned the Apaches back to their old raiding way of life. Eventually, in April of 1877, Clum himself, accompanied by 100 of his Apache police, came marching down south to Warm Springs to round up these Apache holdouts. Clum especially wanted to capture Geronimo, who had made him look so foolish. Hiding most of his armed police in an abandoned adobe building at the Warm Springs agency, Clum sent a message asking Geronimo to come in and talk with him.

Geronimo went. When he saw the handful of Apache police scattered about, he probably figured Clum had set a trap. Still, he wanted to confront Clum. When the two men stood face-to-face, the 22-year-old army clerk began to scold the dignified middle-aged warrior for disobeying. An interpreter present on that day recalled how Geronimo screamed at Clum, "We are not going back to San Carlos with you! If you make any more mistakes, you and your two-faced Apaches will not go back to San Carlos either! Your bodies will remain to stink here at Ojo Caliente [Warm Springs] to make food for the zopilotes and lobos [buzzards and wolves]!"

Just then, Clum's 80 hidden police burst into the compound, surrounding Geronimo and disarming him. But Geronimo had kept his knife.

When Clum brought Geronimo onto a veranda, surrounded by the traitor Apache who had turned into police for the white man, Geronimo suddenly grabbed for the knife. It was better to die trying to slash one's way free than to be taken prisoner. But the knife was snatched away from him, and he and others were led toward the blacksmith shop, where the smith outfitted them with leg irons. Cavalry troops soon arrived to back up Clum and his police, and in May, Geronimo and about 450 Apache people were forced to begin their own long walk, a twenty-day journey of 400 miles on foot and wagon northwest to San Carlos.

At San Carlos, Geronimo and other men who were considered renegades were confined to the guardhouse. Clum was eager to bring Geronimo to trial for robbery and murder and hoped to see him hanged. Geronimo remained a prisoner until July, and then, without any explanation, he was released. He himself said he was never sure why. Some Apache say that Clum himself released Geronimo because Juh had come forward and threatened that if anything happened to Geronimo, a terrible Apache revolt would occur. In any case, Clum, who was always quarreling with his superiors in Washington, was soon forced to resign.

Now free of his chains, Geronimo could walk around San Carlos and see that life there was just as bad as everyone had feared. The other Apache brought in from Warm Springs who had not been imprisoned were told to camp wherever they

wanted on the reservation. After all the trouble
taken to capture the Apache at Warm Springs and
drive them to San Carlos, the white people did
not seem to bother much about keeping track of
them. Once Clum left, the reservation was run
mostly by dishonest agents who stole money and
sold off goods intended for the Apaches quartered
there. The people were starving and ill-clothed.
There were outbreaks of smallpox, and many suffered with malarial fever. Just as General Howard and Tom Jeffords had predicted, the different
bands of Apache did not get along. People blamed
their misery on one another as well as on their
white captors. Some Apaches especially blamed
Geronimo for getting them all into trouble
through his years of raids and his running away
from Clum. By late summer, the Warm Springs
leaders Victorio, Loco, and Nana broke out of the
reservation with about 343 of their people, leaving more than 140 of their friends and relatives
behind. That meant that Geronimo was the
strongest Apache leader still left at San Carlos.
For a time, Geronimo apparently thought it
would be unwise to try to break out. Even at
barren San Carlos, there were advantages to living in one place at peace. But one event seems to
have changed his mind.

To dull their despair, the Apaches at San Carlos
drank *tizwin*, liquor they brewed from fermented
corn. Geronimo got drunk one night in the spring
of 1878 and yelled angrily at a young nephew for
little reason. The Apache are traditionally gentle

with their children, and the boy felt so disgraced by Geronimo's tirade that he killed himself. When Geronimo realized what had happened, he knew he had to get away from the reservation that was stifling Apache souls. With a few others, he broke out of San Carlos. He met up with Juh in Mexico and resumed his old life of raiding for a year and a half, but in December of 1879, both men voluntarily returned to San Carlos. They had found life on the run very hard.

Back at San Carlos, Geronimo and Juh and many other Apache came under the influence of an Apache called Noche-del-Klinne, or the Dreamer, one of several American Indian spiritual leaders in the nineteenth century who preached that Indians should not fight against white people with weapons. If Apache would only be patient and dance a special wheeling dance the Dreamer taught them, Ussen would make the white people vanish from the land, and all the great Apache leaders who now lay dead would be restored to life. Many people witnessed the Dreamer call out of the earth the forms of both old-time leaders and recent ones like Victorio who had been killed by the Mexican Army.

For the time being, Geronimo was content to live quietly, as if he were thinking seriously about following the Dreamer's teachings, even though he, like Juh, never joined in the dancing. But then, in August of 1881, the Dreamer, who preached only peace, was brutally killed by United States soldiers, who were spooked by his quiet power

over the Apaches. After the Dreamer was slain,
Geronimo decided once again he could not bear
white people or reservation life any longer. In the
autumn of 1881, he and Juh and about seventy
Apache people once again fled San Carlos for
Mexico.

For the next few years, between 1881 and 1886,
Geronimo lived a life of running and raiding, with
occasional halfhearted surrenders and returns to
the reservation. It is not possible for Geronimo
and his followers to have done all the things at-
tributed to them and to have been in all the places
where people swore they had seen him during
these years. Anytime there was an attack upon a
settlement or a ranch or a supply train in New
Mexico, Arizona, or northern Mexico, people half
feared and half wished for it to be the dreaded
Geronimo they had encountered. It made a much
more exciting story that way. Besides, how could
anyone prove a raid *hadn't* been Geronimo's
doing? It was very hard for noisy soldiers on
horseback to catch up with a band of swift silent
Apache and confront them face-to-face so they
could learn whether they had been the ones who
had made a given attack. One soldier wrote that
hunting Apaches with army troops was like
"chasing deer with a brass band."

Still, some things Geronimo did are known for
certain. Most spectacularly, in the spring of 1882,
he successfully led a party from Mexico back to
San Carlos to set free many of the Apaches re-

maining there under the leadership of Loco. Those people, who had gotten used to reservation life, did not especially want to be set free, but Geronimo insisted, and they were afraid to oppose him. Reluctantly, they left behind their belongings and rode away with him. On their way back to the Apache stronghold in the Sierra Madre of Mexico, Geronimo killed plenty of guards and settlers to ensure that Loco and his people would be branded outlaws. Now they would not dare to go back to San Carlos or surrender to the pursuing troops. The journey was perilous for those softened by reservation life, and many died or were killed along the way. Nonetheless, Geronimo greatly swelled the numbers of free Apache by this daring rescue-kidnapping.

The end of Geronimo's freedom came finally in 1886. He was now nearing his mid-sixties, and most of the strong Apache leaders who had been his allies were dead or ready to give up fighting. For the last few years, his life had been a desperate one. "We were reckless of our lives," he recalled, "because we felt that every man's hand was against us. If we returned to the reservation we would be put in prison and killed; if we stayed in Mexico they would continue to send soldiers to fight us; so we gave no quarter to anyone and asked no favors."

In March, General Nelson Miles sent his lieutenant Charles Gatewood and two Apache scouts into Mexico with a message for Geronimo and the other Apaches hiding in the Sierra Madre. He could surrender now, or continue to fight to the death. Gatewood told Geronimo that most other Apaches had already surrendered and had been taken to new temporary quarters in Florida where the land was good and all would be given farms and livestock. In a few years, they would have a reservation of their own back in their own country.

Gatewood was lying, as General Miles had instructed him to do. In fact, although many Apaches had surrendered, none had been taken to Florida yet. It was true that the government planned to move them there, to Fort Marion, near Saint Augustine. However, what awaited them there in the tropical heat was not prosperous lives as farmers, but illness and despair. Reluctantly, Geronimo agreed to cross the border and meet with General Miles, who confirmed all that Gatewood had said. What mainly moved Geronimo and other war leaders to give in was the promise that they would all be reunited with their families and friends, as soon as a train could bring them to Florida. Geronimo surrendered, as he had several times before, but this time was the last. "I will quit the warpath and live at peace hereafter," he vowed.

Some days later, as the Apaches sadly boarded the train at Holbrook that was to bring them back to Florida, an army band played "Auld Lang Syne." The soldiers waiting around the station guffawed loudly. Geronimo and the other Apache were old acquaintances whom soldiers hoped never to see again, and they wished for the Apaches no "cup of kindness."

The years of Apache confinement are a long and terrible story in their own right. After a nightmare journey in barred-shut boxcars with no toilet facilities, the Apaches reached Fort Marion. Instead of being reunited with their families there, the male warriors, the "hostiles," including Geronimo, were imprisoned for eight months at Fort Pickens, 350 miles across the peninsula near Pensacola. Most children between twelve and twenty-two were taken from their parents and sent to boarding school at Carlisle, Pennsylvania, where a tuberculosis epidemic raged among them. The Apache who remained behind in swampy Florida began to die of malaria in great numbers. In the spring of 1887, the people were moved first to Mount Vernon, Alabama, where the climate was thought to be healthier for them, and then further west to Fort Sill, Oklahoma, in 1894. Twenty-seven years of exile would pass before Geronimo's people would be permitted to return to the Southwest. Even then they would not be returned to their homeland in Arizona but were sent instead to the Mescalero Apache Reservation in New Mexico, where many of Geronimo's proud descendants live today. Geronimo himself was never to look upon his beloved mountains and canyons again.

In the spring of 1904, all of the United States
and its territories were excited about hosting the
World's Fair in St. Louis, Missouri. Twenty-eight-
year-old Marietta Palmer Wetherill and her husband Richard had spent ten thousand dollars and
more than a year preparing their concession
booth. The Wetherills were traders to the Navajo
people, and they had amassed weavings, cradle-
boards, moccasins, and jewelry to sell. They were
also amateur archaeologists and ethnologists,
and they wanted their exhibit to be educational
as well as profitable. They had built a scale model
of a cliff dwelling such as the ancestors of the
modern Pueblo Indians once lived in. They
brought with them sixteen Navajo people who
were to demonstrate Navajo dancing, cooking,
weaving, and silversmithing.

Marietta was not eager to go to the World's
Fair. She had recently lost a baby, and she was
reluctant to make the long journey from Arizona.
But Richard thought the change would help her
cope with her loss. Besides, Marietta was a very
capable manager, and he needed her to help
with their large and complex exhibit, which employed thirty salespeople as well as the Navajo
artists.

On Marietta's first day at the fair, Richard
asked a cousin of his to show his lonely and confused wife around the fairgrounds. Marietta mar-
veled at an exhibit from Africa and another from
the Philippines. Suddenly, across the great hall,

she glimpsed someone who was not strange, but familiar. It was Geronimo, sitting all by himself in a tiny booth. He was supposed to be selling little beaded rings for ten cents apiece. The government of the United States had placed their great enemy, now in his eighties, on display. His eyesight was failing, but he stared straight ahead with great dignity. Marietta walked up to him and shook his hand. "You don't remember me," she said to him.

"I don't remember much," he answered her. "I've had too much trouble." Marietta recalled for him the story of their meeting in the 1880s, describing her gourd animals and his gift of the slab of beef. She also told him the part he had not known: how she had sent the soldiers riding hard in the wrong direction. At last Geronimo stroked her hand. "You do know me!" he exclaimed. "You are my friend from a long time ago."

The spring wore on. As often as she could get away, Marietta visited Geronimo in his booth, bringing him lemonade and ice cream. She would fetch an extra chair, and the two friends would sit in the little booth and talk for hours. Together, they recalled the canyons and the high country they both loved. By this time, Geronimo and his people were quartered at Fort Sill, Oklahoma, which was better than the swampy camps where they had lived in Florida or Alabama, but still he longed for the springs and canyons and ponderosa forests of his home. Once, when she asked him what treat she might bring him, he sighed. "I have plenty to eat," he told her, "but I want something for my heart, to keep me from thinking." Perhaps this was Geronimo's way of asking her for whiskey, but he was certainly thinking of some greater medicine as well.

Just before she was to return home, Marietta saw an article in a St. Louis paper that said the government would soon be returning Geronimo and his people to Arizona. Overjoyed, she rushed to tell the old man the good news. "Am I going to die in my own land?" Geronimo asked her. Marietta assured him he was. He ran his hands gently over her face and her hair. "Good-bye, my friend," he said, "but I still think you're an Apache."

Too late, Marietta learned the newspaper article had been wrong. Geronimo lived out his days in Fort Sill, Oklahoma. Marietta and Geronimo never met again.

As the elderly warrior lay dying of pneumonia at Fort Sill on February 17, 1909, his nephew Daklugie sat beside him and held his hand. Again and again, Geronimo murmured how sorry he was that he had ever surrendered. But even within the confines of army posts, Geronimo had kept his fighting spirit, continuing to use his powers to cure illness, to unite Apache, and to ensure that Apache ceremonies were still performed.

At his funeral, one old Apache woman cried loudly. "Everybody hated you! White men hated you, Mexicans hated you, Apaches hated you; all of them hated you. You have been good to us. We love you, we hate to see you go!" In a few words, this elder expressed the whole range of what Geronimo had meant to many people.

3
Will Rogers

One evening in the early years of the twentieth century, the sophisticated New York audience at Hammerstein's Paradise Roof Theater watched as a gangly cowboy with high cheekbones spun his rope, coaxing his lariat into a wide floating loop. Suddenly he called out "Right!" On cue, a handsome little bay horse burst out of the wings and raced across the stage. The cowboy threw his lasso, aiming to rope the horse by the nose—and missed! Carefully coiling his rope for another try, he assured the audience in his Oklahoma drawl, "There is hope." There was silence as he went on coiling, and then he added, "We are all chock full of hope." He paused, scratched his head, and squinted. "Of course," he added ruefully, "if there was a little better roping and less hoping, we would all get out of here earlier tonight." The audience roared with laughter and they came back for more. It wasn't for the roping. This Will Rogers fellow was talented with a lasso, certainly, but novelty acts like roping and knife-throwing were common on the vaudeville circuit. More and more, people were packing the supper show at the Roof to hear Will Rogers's wry comments about himself and the other acts in the show.

New York was a long way from the little town of Oologah in Oklahoma Indian Territory, where William Penn Adair Rogers was born on November 4, 1879, "in a log cabin next to the White House," as he sometimes said. The "White House" was what people around Oologah called the two-story ranch home built by Will's father, Clement Vann Rogers. The house was indeed big and white, with an elegant portico in the front. The nickname also slyly referred to Clem Rogers's reputation as a community leader and a politician, for he served as a judge and later as a five-term senator in the government of the Cherokee Nation. As for the "log cabin," Rogers explained that the White House was really

> *a big two-story Log House, but on the back we had three rooms made of frame. Just before my birth my mother, being in one of those frame rooms, had them remove her into the Log part of the house. She wanted me to be born in a Log House. She had just read the life of Lincoln.*

So I got the Log House end of it OK. All I need now is the other qualifications.*

Though Will's mother died while he was still a child, Mary America Schrimsher Rogers got her wish for a boy who would be great like Lincoln, though her son was destined to be famous in ways she could not have foreseen. Cherokee cowboy Will Rogers would go from cowboying, ranching, and a vaudeville roping act to become an internationally known and loved comedian, actor, radio personality, newspaper columnist, and political commentator. His humor would help give Americans the heart to survive World World I, the Great Depression, and the dark beginnings of fascism in Europe. Many people today do not realize that Will Rogers was Native American. But Rogers himself was fiercely proud of his Cherokee heritage, and his gentle, pointed ribbing of people like politicians and "experts" in all fields is thoroughly American Indian in style and spirit.

When young Will was growing up, Oologah, like most of Oklahoma Indian Territory, was beautiful bluestem prairie under wide skies, open country that made people feel free and alive. As a grown man revisiting it in 1932, Will was swept by memories:

---

* Will Rogers's own grammar and spelling are kept here to give the flavor of his writing.

We was driving over a Country where 36 years before as a boy 18 years old I had helped drive a bunch of cattle from that very place to Western Kansas and there wasent a house or a chicken in the whole county. That plains was the prettiest country I ever saw in my life, as flat as a beauty contest winner's stomach, and prairie lakes scattered all over it. And mirages! You could see anything in the world — just ahead of you.

This rich and hopeful country was full of displaced people with hard histories behind them. Many of them were Indian, and a number of heroes profiled in this book — Geronimo, Jim Thorpe, Rogers himself, Maria Tallchief, Wilma Mankiller — began or ended their lives there. The Cherokee Nation, from whom Will was descended on both sides, originally were a farming people, inhabiting what are now the states of Tennessee, North and South Carolina, Georgia, and Alabama. More than other southeastern tribes, they adopted white ways, including the owning of African-American slaves. They were eager for education and developed their own system of writing, published their own newspaper, and ran their own school system. By 1827 they had written their own constitution and adopted a representative form of government. None of this made any difference to the land-greedy white people for whom the Cherokee were simply in the way.

In 1829 Will's paternal grandfather Robert

Rogers, a quarter-Cherokee then living in Georgia, was one of a few Cherokee people who agreed to give up their land in the east in return for land in Oklahoma Indian Territory. Robert Rogers and others thought that they would not be able to fight the government and that they might as well go to Oklahoma while there was still good land to choose from. As it turned out, Rogers guessed right. In the following year, under President Andrew Jackson, Congress passed the Indian Removal Act which said that all southeastern Indian people must be resettled in Indian Territory. By 1838, most of the rest of the Cherokee were also forced into removal. Under leader John Ross they had resisted attempts to take over their land, but now their lands and their belongings were seized, and Cherokee families were force-marched to Indian Territory with a U.S. military escort. At least one quarter of the 16,000 Cherokee on that march died of hunger, cold, and disease along what came to be called the Trail of Tears.

Meanwhile, Robert Rogers and his three-eighths Cherokee wife Sallie Vann Rogers had comfortably settled in the Going-Snake district of the Territory, where Robert farmed and ranched. Will's father, Clement Vann Rogers, was born there in 1839. A lot of bitterness lingered between the "Old Settlers," southern Cherokees like Robert Rogers who had deeded Cherokee land over to the government and moved to Oklahoma Territory, and "Ross's people," those Cherokee familes who had stayed behind and tried to make a brave stand beside John Ross, only to find themselves herded like animals along the Trail of Tears. When Robert Rogers died in 1842, while Clem was still a toddler, there were rumors that he was murdered by Trail of Tears survivors who scorned him for being an early sellout. His last words were, "See that Clem always rides his own horse." Perhaps he meant, "Bring Clem up to be his own man."

Clem Rogers grew up to be an extremely successful rancher and farmer. He dropped out of school in his early teens, but in 1855 when he was just 16, he and five other cowhands drove 500 steers from Going-Snake all the way to St. Louis, Missouri, losing only one animal along the way. At 17, with two slaves named Rabb and Houston and a small herd of cattle, he started his own ranch outfit near the present-day town of Talala, Oklahoma. Two years later, in 1858, he married Mary America Schrimsher, a member of the Paint Clan of the Cherokee Nation whose people had come over the Trail of Tears from Alabama. Both were mixed bloods. Clem about one-quarter and Mary about three-eighths Cherokee. Later, their son Will would say that while he didn't have the arithmetic to figure just how much Cherokee he was, he sure enough was Cherokee.

In many ways the 19-year-old couple were very different from one another. Clem looked like his Scots-Irish, English, and Welsh ancestors, while Mary's features were strongly Native American. Clem hated school, while Mary was an honor student, a graduate of the Female Seminary at Tahlequah. Clem was all business, and people respected him; but everyone loved Mary America. She was known for her warmth and her lively sense of humor, which she often used to turn aside her husband's all too quick temper. She was a fine musician who treasured her grand piano and made the family home bright and welcoming. Just because they were out on the prairie far from the nearest town, Mary saw no reason not to have music, lace curtains, bright rugs, and well-tended flower beds around her.

Clem was a slaveholder who fought in the Civil War on the side of the Confederacy, like most other Old Settler Cherokee. His legendary Cherokee commander, a brilliant military strategist named Brigadier General Stand Watie, refused to surrender for a full two months after Robert E. Lee himself had given up the Confederate cause at Appomattox. After seeing a good deal of action, Clem rose to the rank of captain.

The Civil War destroyed Clem Rogers's ranch, for his slaves were now free and his cattle had been run off by Jayhawkers, gangs of Union sympathizers from Kansas who raided Confederate farms and ranches. By renting farmland and raising crops, Clem was able to earn enough money to start ranching again at Oologah, near Claremore, where in 1875 he built the "White House." Together Clem and Mary had nine children, though only four lived past childhood. By 1879, when Will Rogers was born, Clem was a senator in the Cherokee National Congress and one of the powerful citizens of the emerging Oklahoma Territory. At the request of the Cherokee Chief William Penn Adair, with whom Clem had served in the Confederate Army, the boy was named after him.

As a child, Will was very close to his mother. He was her only surviving son, and she and his three older sisters doted on him. There is a family story about how as a toddler Will once put his bare foot right into a pan of dough his mother had placed on the floor to rise, imagining how good the squishy stuff would feel between his toes. Instead of scolding him, Mary just smiled and said it would make the bread taste all the sweeter.

The Oklahoma Will grew up in was extremely varied. It was at once southern and western and made up of many Indian tribes, many varieties of mixed-blood people. In Indian Territory, Native Americans, European whites, and freed African-Americans worked side by side and often intermarried. After the Civil War, Rabb and Houston, Clem Rogers's former slaves, had stayed around and continued to work as ranch hands for the Rogers family. Their children and the Rogers children were playmates. It was important for Will Rogers's later life that he grew up with many different voices in his ear, many different faces before his eyes. As an adult he would become one of the great American speakers on behalf of tolerance and understanding between peoples.

From his earliest years Will loved ranch life. With tools of Civil War vintage, Indian Territory cowboys worked hard, long hours in the summer's heavy, humid Oklahoma heat and the winter's cold bluster. The livestock in those days was wilder and rangier by far than the cattle that ranchers raise today, but the ranchers did not have modern veterinary skills, and the animals were more likely to suffer ailments and injuries that resulted in heavy losses to the ranch.

Like most ranch children, Will probably took what part a small boy could in roundup and branding, maybe assisting at the birth of a foal or calf. But for the most part he played cowboy, dreaming of riding the range from Texas to Kansas to Chicago on the longhorn cattle drives. Will especially enjoyed the riding and roping, which remained his two favorite pastimes all his life long. One of his best friends during those years was Dan Walker, an African-American cowboy whom Will called "Uncle," who worked for Will's dad. Uncle Dan showed the child over and over how to make a lariat and how to throw a rope, and as the boy grew more skilled, Uncle Dan taught him some rope tricks to impress his sisters. Will took to roping anything that moved. There were some wary dogs and cats on the Rogers spread!

His beloved mother Mary America died on May 28, 1890, when Will was ten. At the time of her death, he was ill with measles and could not attend her funeral services. "My folks have told me

what little humor I have comes from her," he once
said. "I can't remember her humor, but I can
remember her love and understanding of me."
Years later Will's wife Betty would say he never
got over that death, which "left in him a lonely,
lost feeling that persisted long after he was successful and famous." When his friend the cowboy
artist Charlie Russell died in 1926, Will imagined
his friend had gone to a sort of Oklahoma heaven,
where he would be sure to run into Mary America
Rogers.

> . . . *you will pop into some well kept ranch house*
> *under some cool shady trees and you will be*
> *asked to have dinner, and it will be the best one*
> *you ever had in your life. Well when you are*
> *thanking the womenfolks. You just tell the*
> *sweet-looking little old lady that you knew her*
> *boy, back on an outfit you used to rep for. . . .*

After Mary America died, Clem hired a house-
keeper to take care of the children and run the
household, and later married her. Will didn't
much like this stepmother, who was also named
Mary, Mary Bible. But the boy had his own dif-
ficulties to deal with. School had never been very
appealing to him. He didn't care to be cooped up
in a classroom where he had to sit still, remain
quiet, and recite memorized lessons only when
the teacher called on him. He longed to be outside
with Uncle Dan, chasing hapless poultry with his

snaking lariat, riding horses beneath the Oklahoma skies.

Will spent his younger years moving from
school to school, often because his irrepressible
energy and sociable nature got him into trouble.
His earliest school was Drumgoole, a one-room
log cabin attended mostly by full-blood Cherokee
youngsters. As a mixed blood, Will recalled, "I
had just enough white in me to make my honesty
questionable." Of the schoolwork itself he remembered little, and only one thing seems to
have seized his imagination. "We had a geography [book] around there," he recalled, "but we
just used it for the pictures of the cattle grazing
in the Argentine and the wolves attacking the
sleighs in Russia."

In later years, Will himself would travel to
Argentina to try to find ranch work, and he would
twice visit Russia to report on the massive
changes happening there under Communism. If
nothing else happened at Drumgoole, perhaps
those pictures in the geography book awakened
his lifelong passion for travel to faraway places.

He was soon moved to the Girls' Seminary
in Muskogee, where his beleaguered parents
thought his older sisters could keep him in
line. Instead, fun-loving Will devoted his attention to making his sisters laugh. His skill as a
comic surfaced early on, as his sisters found
great delight in his imitations and the hilarious
expressions into which he could twist his small
face.

After the Girls' Seminary, he attended Willie
Halsell College — not actually a college, but
rather a private secondary school. There he
earned the nickname "Rabbit" because of his big
ears and his speed. In 1893, after his first year at
Halsell, Will and Clem attended the Chicago
World's Columbian Exposition, an enormous fair.
There Will rode a camel, and he admired the first
giant Ferris wheel America had seen; it stood 300
feet high. But above all, he was thrilled with Buffalo Bill's Wild West Show, particularly the performance of the Mexican *vaqueros*, or cowboys.
One performer, Vincente Oropeza, billed as the
world's greatest roper, brought tears to Will's
eyes. Around a ranch, roping was a practical skill
for catching horses and cattle, but vaqueros like
Oropeza had made it into a fine art. Oropeza
could spin a big vertical loop, have a horse run
through it as though it were a stable door, and
then catch a second horse by the nose or the tail
with the same loop. He could spin a horizontal
loop around his ankles and dance gracefully in
and out of the circling rope. Whatever he did with
his lariat, he made it look completely effortless.
Will watched wide-eyed as for a finale Oropeza
spelled out his last name in the air with his sinuous rope. Will's destiny was pretty much sealed
— he was going to be the fanciest roper anyone
had ever seen!

At Will's next school, Scarritt College in Mississippi, he did pretty well in some subjects —
especially elocution — but he kept getting into

trouble with the rope that now never left his side. One time he roped a statue on the Scarritt campus: "I lassoed the stone gal — goddess of something — off the top of the water fountain and broke all her limbs." Clem paid for the statue rather than have Will sent home, but soon after, Will tried to rope the headmaster's horse and succeeded only in throwing the mare into a panic. She dashed madly through the backstop of the school's tennis court and crashed through a picket fence, and Will was returned to the White House in disgrace.

In January 1897, when Will was nearly 18, his exasperated father sent him to Kemper Military Academy in Boonville, Missouri. Clem never seemed to remember that he, too, had hated the confinement of school. Now he hoped that in a military atmosphere his fun-loving son would settle down and develop the skills Clem thought he needed to become an influential rancher, politician, and businessman. Will adjusted almost satisfactorily to life at Kemper. He was proud of the uniform the cadets wore. He took an interest in history, in which he made good grades, and he also continued to show quite a flair for public speaking, a skill he shared with his senator-father.

Still, life at Kemper didn't seem to quench Will's mischief. Disguised in blackface, he used to sneak out of the school dormitory to see as many vaudeville and traveling shows as he could. Later, back at school, he would entertain his classmates by reenacting the shows and practicing the face-making skills he first developed at the Girls' Seminary. He took a real delight in entertaining his fellow students. One of his classmates later recalled how Will would

> *torture his face till it looked like a wrinkled*
> *saddle blanket and make funny motions with*
> *his hands and roll his eyes and, some way or*
> *other, manage to make us laugh. I never saw*
> *him get up in front of a class without making*
> *them laugh before he sat down.*

In spite of his willingness to please his fellow cadets, he continued to be enormously proud of his Cherokee blood. That was not a joking matter, and he never hesitated to confront the students who openly ridiculed Indians. Once, he grew very angry when a student referred to a certain Indian chief as a "thoroughbred." He told the student that "full-blood" was the right word and said it spoiled his whole afternoon to hear a human being described like an animal.

Another time he stood before a print depicting "Custer's Last Stand." "You know," he said to another cadet, "I like that picture." When his friend asked him why, he replied, "It's the only time my people got the best of it." Will's comic abilities entertained others, but he also used humor as a pointed way of quietly establishing his fearlessness and integrity.

With one year in the military school left to finish, Will decided that he had had enough and ran away from Kemper to strike out on his own. Unknown to his father, Will set out to find work as a cowboy. He made his way to a big ranch a fellow student had told him about in Higgins, Texas, owned by a man named Perry Ewing. When Ewing discovered that Will had run away from school, he wrote to Clem to tell him of his son's whereabouts. Clem wrote back to say that if Ewing could get any decent work out of Will, it would be more than he'd ever managed to do.

In fact, Will worked hard for the ranch. That spring of 1898, Ewing's son Frank, Will, and five other hands were given the job of driving 400 head of cattle from Higgins to Medicine Lodge, Kansas, where they would be fattened for market. Much like the cattle drive the young Clem Rogers had ridden on to St. Louis in 1855, this was a journey that changed the boy Will into a man. All his life, Rogers would look back on that summer of shimmering heat, lowing cattle, and sudden prairie storms as one of the best times of his life. They made about six miles a day, alternately letting the cattle rest and graze, and then driving them ahead for two or three miles. As an old man, Frank Ewing remembered vividly how well the young cowhands ate on the journey.

Once in a while we'd pass a little ranch and buy butter, milk, and eggs and have us a feast. There was lots of wild plums in those days, and we'd gather 'em in our hats while on horseback, or just eat 'em off the bushes. Once in a while the cook might gather 'em in a dishpan and make us a cobbler in the Dutch oven.

Shortly before his death, Rogers still loved to recall how "I et out of a chuckwagon and slept on the ground all that spring and summer of '98."
Will liked the cattle drive so much he tried to get on another one as soon as possible. He spent the rest of the summer driving cattle for big Texas ranches and was delighted to watch and learn from cowhands with experience handling the big herds. He was taking part in a way of life that was rapidly disappearing, as more and more rangeland became fenced in, and more and more cattle were shipped to market by train instead of being driven across great open expanses. Rogers's brief time of cowboying came at the end of an era.
After that idyllic summer and early fall of 1898, he went home to visit his father. Between boarding schools and cowboying, it had been some years since Will had spent much time at home, and he was shocked by the signs of change in Indian territory. There were more and more white people around, and the big ranches were beginning to be broken up. The United States government, in the name of progress, was forcing most of these changes. As it had during Removal and the Trail of Tears, the government was about to betray the Cherokee once more.
Like Clem Rogers, the Cherokee Nation as a

whole had prospered in the 60 or 70 years since Removal. Like most tribes, the Cherokee just let people work as much land as they could use. Whoever wanted to run a small or large spread could begin working any unoccupied land. Will's father had developed a large, prosperous ranch — some 60,000 acres at its greatest. The system seemed to work pretty well for most people. By the closing years of the nineteenth century, the Cherokee boasted 98 percent literacy through the use of the Cherokee syllabary developed by the great leader and teacher Sequoyah. The Nation's fields flourished, yielding abundant crops. Housing was comfortable and adequate in rural areas as well as in the small towns where people traded for needed tools and goods. Medical care was also available for all members of the Nation.

Despite all this, Henry Dawes, head of the Federal Dawes Commission which oversaw the Cherokee and other Indian Territory tribes, maintained that the Cherokee system of tribally owned land was not a good one. Like many white people, he believed private ownership was the only key to progress. Talking about the Cherokee way in a speech in 1885, he made the astonishing claim that

. . . under [it] there is no enterprise to make your home any better than that of your neighbors. There is no selfishness, which is at the bottom of civilization. Till this people will consent to give up their lands, and divide them

*among the citizens so that each can own the
land he cultivates, they will not make much
more progress.*

In 1898 Congress passed the Curtis Act, also
called the Allotment Act, which took back much
of the land originally assigned the Cherokee and
other Native nations when they were compelled
to move to Indian Territory decades before. Now,
under the allotment system, tribally held lands
were redistributed to single nuclear families, 160
acres to each family. Single people were given 80
acres, an amount far too small for the kind of
cattle ranching that had enabled Clem Rogers,
and most of the Cherokee nation, to prosper. The
Curtis Act not only stripped the Cherokee and
other tribes forcibly of their lands but caused an
avalanche of new white settlers called home-
steaders or Boomers. Will Rogers would observe
years later:

*Every time the government moved the Indians,
they gave 'm the same treaty: "You shall have
this land as long as the grass grows and the
water flows." But finally they settled the whole
Indian problem. They put the Indians on land
where the grass won't grow, and the water
won't flow!*

In the wake of the Curtis Act, by 1903 the Rogers's holdings would be reduced to a spare 148
acres, which was all that Will Rogers and his

father, Clem, could get allocated. Clem, always
looking ahead, saw the changes coming. He had
tried to fight against allotment. But seeing it was
no use, in 1898 he sold his livestock, bought a
hotel, and moved into the town of Claremore,
renting the old Rogers spread to tenants from
Illinois. Soon he became a banker and ran a livery
stable. Those were smart business decisions. But
Clem Rogers, whom his son remembered respect-
fully as "a real cowhand," would never live on a
ranch again. After his cowboy summer, Rogers
returned to a businessman father and an Old
Home Place that was sadly run down and tended
by strangers.

   At his father's urging, Rogers remained in the
Territory to look after the much-diminished
ranch, living in the White House with the tenants
and his old best buddy, Spi Trent, a cousin he
had been close to since childhood. After a while,
not caring for the tenants, he, Spi, and a black
ranch hand named Hayward built a separate
cabin for themselves. But his stay on the farm
didn't last long. The restricted operation, the
growing Boomer population and their accom-
panying fences, houses, and small towns lacked
the free challenge Rogers had so loved during his
cowboy days. However, he found an outlet for his
excess energy in his roping, and he entered a
number of local contests, sometimes winning and
always learning ways to perfect his skills. Restless, he made a number of trips to adjoining
states, once even all the way to New York, and

he enjoyed parties, dances, and playing practical
jokes on friends. Modern ranching was clearly not
where his heart lay.

In the fall of 1899, he traveled to a fair in St.
Louis to participate in a steer-roping contest
sponsored by a man named Zach Mulhall. Ever
after, Will Rogers would credit Mulhall with giving him his start in entertainment: "That gave
me a touch of show business, in a way," he said,
"so I was ruined for life as far as actual employ-
ment was concerned." Rogers continued making
the rounds of the state fairs after his stint with
Mulhall's troupe ended, returning to Oologah
from time to time.

Will may not yet have had a clear idea what
he wanted to do, but he had gotten a very clear
idea about whom he wanted to marry. In the autumn of 1899, he went into the Missouri-Pacific
Railroad station at Oologah to pick up a banjo
he had mail-ordered from Kansas City. A young
woman with short brown hair and bright blue
eyes whom he had never seen before was tending
the station agent's counter. She was Betty Blake
of Rogers, Arkansas. While recovering from ty-
phoid fever, Betty was visiting her sister and her
brother-in-law, the Oologah station agent. Will
was so struck by her that he couldn't think of
anything to say. He just turned around and
walked out the door, completely forgetting to ask
for his parcel. It may have been love at first sight,
or it may have been that her hair — cut as short
as a boy's during her illness — scared him off.

A few evenings later they were both invited to supper at the Oologah hotel owned by mutual friends. Rogers was shy at first but warmed up after the meal when everybody gathered around the piano in the parlor to sing the latest songs from the sheet music he had brought back from Kansas City. He himself never learned to play any instrument well, and his voice was untrained, but all his life he loved music. On this frozen prairie night, the rollicking strains of "Hello, My Baby, Hello, My Honey, Hello, My Rag Time Gal" helped break the ice between the dark young man with the cowlick and the lively visitor from Arkansas. For the rest of Betty's visit, the two spent a lot of time together. After she returned to Arkansas at Christmas, they wrote to one another. Soon Will's letters began to express his feelings for her more and more strongly, but Betty kept insisting that they should just be good friends. There were many reasons why she hesitated. She was white, he was a mixed-blood Cherokee, and mixed marriages were still not accepted easily outside of Indian Territory. Perhaps most important, Betty's genteel widowed mother had struggled to raise her eight children on very little money, and financial security was important to them. For a long time it didn't seem to Betty as though Will Rogers had much direction in life, compared with the young lawyers and railroad men who came courting her.

Will and Betty were both 20 years old when they met, and it would take him nine long years of letters and off-and-on-again meetings to convince her to marry him. In the end, their marriage would be remembered as one of the happiest and most devoted in all American show business. But Rogers had long years of loneliness to endure, and he continued to fill his time with roping contests and trips.

In the fall of 1900, Will almost got killed by a newfangled invention in San Francisco where he was sharing a room in a small hotel with another cowboy. When they went to bed, Will's roommate blew out the light just the way he would blow out a candle or a kerosene lamp back home. As it happened, their room was lit not by kerosene but by gas, used even in small hotels in the sophisticated city by the bay. A gaslight continues to send off gas even when the flame is out unless a valve that cuts off the gas flow is closed. The young men didn't know about the valve, and as they slept, gas fumes filled their room. They were found in their beds unconscious, and taken to a hospital where the doctor on duty abandoned Will Rogers for dead. Luckily, some medical students who happened by decided to use him for an experiment. They tried out various unorthodox methods of reviving the young man, and he eventually recovered consciousness. When he was better, Rogers returned to his father's spread in Oklahoma. He was still quite ill and, at his worried father's insistence, finally agreed to stay home for a time. With Will Rogers, though, such promises never held for long.

Rogers still longed to become a cowboy in some place where the land wasn't being fenced in. Even as a little boy leafing through the geography book, he had dreamed of the Argentine pampas and of the free life of the gauchos, the Argentinian cowboys. In the spring of 1902, at the age of 23, Will left home for good after his father bought out his share of their cattle herd for $3,000. He convinced his friend Dick Parris to join him on a trip to Argentina where he'd heard that large-scale ranching was thriving. Neither was sure where Argentina was, but figuring it lay to the south, they set out — logically enough — for New Orleans. There they were told they must go to New York, and in New York they heard that they could catch a boat to Argentina much faster if they went to England and sailed from there.

When at long last the young men got to Argentina, they discovered to their discouragement that jobs on the big ranches were few, and the competition for them was fierce. They had spent most of their money enjoying the sights in England and buying first-class passage on the ships they had sailed on; now they barely had enough money between them for one ticket back to America. Rogers sent his friend Dick Parris off to the States laden with presents for Clem and his sisters. He had bragged so steadfastly about what a wealthy rancher he would become in Argentina that he didn't want to go home broke. Parris agreed to deliver the gifts and report glowingly on Will's success on the pampas. Rogers finally swallowed his pride and asked Clem for the passage home, but this time his father refused to bail him out. His reckless son would have to find his own way home. Clem's stubbornness hurt Rogers deeply.

Eventually Rogers secured passage on a cattle boat headed for South Africa, where he stayed for a time working for the cattleman he'd shipped out with. He tired of that job, tried mule-skinning, and found his way back into show business. By 1903 he had landed a job doing rope tricks with Texas Jack's Circus in Ladysmith, South Africa, one of a number of traveling shows that crossed Europe, Africa, Australia, and the Orient with acts drawn from every continent. These shows combined European circus acts like jugglers and acrobats with Australian and African tribal dancers, American Wild West shoot-'em-ups, and American minstrel shows, featuring white actors dressed up in blackface as African-Americans. Native African audiences watched in disbelief as Rogers and other performers presented the crude minstrel-show routines — what in the world were these strange white people with their faces smeared with black cork supposed to be doing?

Billed as "The Cherokee Kid," Rogers created a riding and roping act that was a success across South Africa. Restless after several months, and homesick for Indian territory, he decided to head for Oklahoma by way of Australia and New Zealand, where he enjoyed public acclaim with his

act. In New Zealand, the *Auckland Herald* wrote
"The Cherokee Kid is a gentleman with a large
American accent and a splendid skill." With such
reviews to back him, Will Rogers soon earned
money for passage to California and a train ticket
back to Oklahoma. By the time he found his way
back to Claremore, he had traveled 50,000 miles.
The love of long journeys that would mark his
adult life was well established.

Back in the States, Will's old restlessness soon
caught up with him. He traveled the fairs with
his rope act and soon hooked up again with Mulhall, who was headed for the 1904 St. Louis
World's Fair. If gate receipts are trustworthy,
nearly a quarter of the population of the United
States visited this giant exposition that celebrated the hundredth anniversary of the Louisi-
ana Purchase. The Mulhall troupe was booked
to be part of a giant Western exhibit and performance called Cummins's Spectacular Indian
Congress and Life on the Plains. The great Apache
leader Geronimo was also a part of the show.
Geronimo was by now in his eighties, but nonetheless he participated ably in the steer-roping
contests, showing the skill that had enabled him
to survive and keep his people fed with good beef
during so many years on the run. Even though
he was Cherokee, Rogers himself was cast as a
doomed white soldier in a reenactment of Custer's Last Stand, dying very dramatically at each
performance. He also did a trick roping act,
though he did not receive billing in the program.

Life was never boring around the fair. One day, for instance, Rogers's boss drew a gun on a disgruntled employee and when some of the shots hit bystanders, Mulhall was arrested for reckless endangerment. But the highlight of Rogers's stint at the fair was the day he received a note from Betty Blake, whom he had not seen in four years, asking if he would like to meet with her. He invited her to that afternoon's show, and she came with one of her sisters and a friend. To Betty's horror and her companions' amusement, Will Rogers stepped out into the arena decked out in a gaudy skintight red velvet costume ornamented with gold braid, a costume that he'd worn in New Zealand as the "Mexican Rope Artist." Betty's companions did not think entertainment was a respectable profession to begin with, and his get-up convinced them that Will Rogers was a country bumpkin with garish taste. Their giggling made Betty's face flame. But after the show, the two stole off alone. They ate dinner and strolled around the fair while they caught up on one another's lives. That evening they listened to the great Irish tenor John McCormack sing at the fair's Irish Village. Though it would still be years before Betty would agree to get married, from this time on the two would stay in touch, even if Betty did not quite approve of Rogers's choice of profession.

By 1905, Rogers was in New York City performing in another of Mulhall's Wild West shows. During the troupe's engagement at the New York

Horse Fair in Madison Square Garden, a huge steer broke loose and rampaged around the arena. He headed up the stairs and made it all the way into the balcony, causing pandemonium among the audience. Then, as The New York *Herald* reported:

> . . .*the Indian Will Rogers . . . ran up the Twenty-seventh Street side and headed the steer off. As it passed the corridor again into view of the spectators he roped the steer's horns. Alone and afoot he was no match for the brute's strength, but he swerved it down the steps. . . . Immediately the ropes of a dozen cowpunchers fell over it from all sides and it was brought down with a quick turn and led from the track.*

Will made sure to send the clipping to Betty.

As the popularity of Wild West shows started to fade, Rogers began to perform exclusively in vaudeville, the variety shows staged in indoor theaters. He got the idea of training his horse Teddy to dash across the stage so he could show off his roping skills with a fast live animal. Rogers said that the bored New York audience would have paid him no attention if it weren't for Teddy:

> [*They*] *seemed to think, well this fool is a long way from home, so don't seem to know what he's doing floundering around there. But that's such a nice little pony and seems to be the only one knows what he is doing, and if we don't*

*help him out he will get rode plain back to
Oklahoma. So for the ponys sake, they laid their
papers down . . .*

At first Rogers's was a "dumb act," with him
simply performing his rope tricks and not speaking. But very soon another performer suggested
that he ought to try announcing a rope trick before he did it, letting the audience know what to
look for. The first time, he said shyly, "I want to
call your sho 'nuff attention to this little stunt I
am going to pull on you, as I am going to throw
about two of these ropes at once, catching the
horse with one and the rider with the other. I
don't have any idea I'll get it, but here goes." He
was astonished and hurt when the audience broke
into laughter. He thought they were laughing at
him, not with him, and he vowed never to speak
on stage again. Very gradually, others were able
to convince him to keep on talking, and soon the
roping became less important than the talking in
his act. Will Rogers the comedian, Will Rogers
the cowboy-philosopher, had gotten his start.

Within ten years, Rogers had become the most
popular entertainer in the United States, which
pleased him no end. But to his way of thinking,
the most important thing that happened to him
was that Betty Blake, whom he had courted all
but hopelessly for nine years, finally said yes to
his proposal. They were married in November of
1908, soon after Rogers' twenty-ninth birthday.
On their twenty-fifth wedding anniversary, Will

would write affectionately, "The day I roped Betty, I made the star performance of my life." The young couple made their home in New York, where Rogers tried to find steady theater work. Earlier Betty had frowned at having a husband in show business, but once they were married, she began to relish the exciting life they led. Now, neither thought seriously of going back to Oklahoma to settle down, though both missed their families.

When the Rogerses' first child, William Vann Rogers, arrived in October of 1911, no one could have been prouder than his grandfather Clem. In the two years since the marriage, Betty had managed to build a bridge between Will and his father, soothing her husband's pride and assuring the gruff old man how much they both loved him. When Clem heard of the baby's birth, he immediately mailed off a tiny pair of beaded moccasins to his grandson. Within nine days, one of his daughters found Clem had died in his sleep.

Three other children would follow — Mary, in 1913; James, in 1915; and Fred, in 1918, who would die as a baby. As a very popular entertainer, Rogers was gone a lot, but when he was around, he was a devoted father. Unlike his own father, he never pushed his children, and he tried to help them find the things they wanted to do in life. It was really only when it came to riding and roping that Rogers had a hard time keeping his patience with his children. When one of them bungled a rope trick, he would point at the tangled lasso and scream, "What are you trying to do — kill snakes?"

By 1915, with two children and a third on the way, Will and Betty were eager to get him work that would be steady. He got his big break from Florenz Ziegfeld, a flamboyant showman and promoter. In his younger days, Ziegfeld was not above charging people admission to view an exhibit of "invisible Brazilian fish"; inside the exhibit tent sat a large glass tank filled with clear water. In 1907 he had started producing a yearly New York show called the Ziegfeld Follies' in imitation of European shows like the Parisian Folies Bergère. The Follies used vaudeville-style variety acts, but most people came for the lavish production numbers featuring the glamorous "Ziegfeld Girls" who sang and danced in daring costumes of satin, feathers, and sequins. Ziegfeld insisted his shows were also "educational." Sometimes the Ziegfeld Girls would pose floodlit in a *tableau vivant*, a "living picture" of a famous painting or scene from history.

Soon Ziegfeld starting putting on the Ziegfeld Midnight Frolic, a smaller after-hours revue staged on the roof garden above the theater. Here the patrons could drink, dine, dance, and watch a much more informal show with a lot of sassy give-and-take between the performers and the audience. The out-of-town tourists came to the regular Ziegfeld Follies, but the sophisticated New Yorkers crowded this late-night show.

When Rogers began performing in the Midnight Frolic, he saw right away the difference between this kind of show business and vaudeville. With vaudeville shows, people almost never came back to catch a show a second time, especially if the show was on tour. But the Midnight Frolic was like a nightclub, and many of the regular crowd came almost every night. That meant Rogers needed fresh material for every single show.

Thanks to Betty, Rogers realized he had an unfailing source of new material. She pointed out how he was always reading items from the newspapers out loud to her and their friends and making hilarious comments about world and national events. Why didn't he make that part of his act, instead of joking around about the other performers and members of the audience? He started doing just that. Today, 70 years later, hosts of late-night TV usually start their opening monologue asking if the audience noticed such and such an item in the newspaper. As they make joke after joke about things that have happened that very day in the news, we are watching the legacy of Will Rogers's style of comedy.

In 1915, when Rogers began making comments on everyday events part of his act, the United States was uncertain about whether to enter World War I (1914–1918), already raging in Europe. Rogers joked about how unprepared the United States was: "We are the only nation that waits until they get into a war before they start getting ready for it," he observed glumly. On the other hand, he thought, maybe there was hope:

"There is some talk of getting a machine gun —
if we can borrow one," he reported.

Rogers's jokes about current events were such
a hit in the Midnight Frolic that in January of
1916 Ziegfeld put him into the regular Follies
production earlier in the evening as well. Since
people often went to the Follies and then took the
elevator up to the theater roof afterward to catch
the Midnight Frolic, that meant Rogers had to
have two fresh routines each night. But he insisted it wasn't hard. The latest edition of any
newspaper gave him more than enough comic
material.

When the United States did enter World War I
in 1917, Rogers worried that joking about it
might be in bad taste. But audiences needed
laughter to help them cope with their fear and
grief. When at last the troops came home, Rogers
called attention to all the victory parades being
staged across the country. "If we really want to
honor our boys, why don't we let them sit on the
reviewing stands and make the people march
those fifteen miles?" he wondered.

In 1918, Will Rogers got his chance to break
into movies in a silent film called *Laughing Bill
Hyde*, produced by Samuel Goldwyn, a major
filmmaker of the time. The movie, based on a
popular novel of the day, tells the story of a good-
hearted escaped convict making his way across
Alaska. Rogers's folksiness seemed just right for
the role, even if moviegoers wouldn't be able to
hear his country drawl. The Goldwyn studios

were then located in Fort Lee, New Jersey, just across the Hudson River from New York City. Will acted before the cameras during the day and appeared onstage in the Follies at night. *Laughing Bill Hyde* was a big success, and soon Rogers signed a contract with the Goldwyn studios to begin making motion pictures in California starting in June of 1919. This was a big decision for the Rogers family, for it meant giving up at least for a while both Will's career on the stage and the family's life in New York. But the move would mean a bigger salary and a return to the west that Will and Betty both loved. There, they could look for a house with lots of room for their children, dogs, horses, and other assorted pets. Rogers made a series of movies that were well-reviewed but not big hits at the box office. In them he usually played a good-hearted country bumpkin who got unfairly blamed for something and at the last minute was proven innocent.

Goldwyn did not renew Rogers's contract in May of 1921 because the company was losing money and had to cut back. But Will Rogers decided he wanted to form his own company and try making his own short low-budget films starring himself. One of these, *The Ropin' Fool*, is invaluable because it shows wonderful footage of Will doing rope tricks. For the movie, he whitened his ropes with shoe polish to make them more visible and filmed some of the stunts in slow motion, so the audience could see the beautiful sinuous motion of the rope and the roper. The story is a simple one about a man who can't resist roping anything he sees. When he asks a woman to marry him, he ropes the third finger of her left hand with a miniature noose.

All in all, Rogers made three interesting short pictures, but the problem was that Will Rogers Productions had no way to get its movies placed in theaters. For the first time in his adult life, Will Rogers had tried something and failed. To pay his debts, he went back to New York in 1922 to work again for the Ziegfeld Follies, leaving his family behind in California. This was especially hard because the Rogers's baby Fred had died of diphtheria in June of 1920 while Will was away on business. He hated leaving his wife and children, but he needed money fast. Between the New York stage appearances and many after-dinner speaking engagements, Rogers managed to make up his losses. He signed a two-year movie contract with Hal Roach in 1923, though he didn't much like the cowboy slapstick pictures Roach put him in. He grumbled that all he ever seemed to do in a Hal Roach picture was run around barns and lose his pants.

At the same time that Rogers was beginning his movie career, he also had begun to write for the public. In 1919 he published *The Cowboy Philosopher on the Peace Conference* and *The Cowboy Philosopher on Prohibition*, collections of his political jokes from the Follies shows. In 1922 he began to write a weekly column for the McNaught

Syndicate that he continued until his death in 1935. In 1926 he also started doing a much shorter daily column of about 200 words, usually a series of little "squibs" about current events and observations from whatever place he happened to be visiting. Probably more people in the United States got to know Will Rogers through that daily column than any other way. Millions of readers of the 600 newspapers that carried Will Rogers' daily "telegram" depended on it to start their day. Rogers took his writing seriously. Whether he was traveling or at home, he would telegraph his column to the newspaper syndicate six days a week. Even when he had serious gall bladder surgery in 1927, he dictated his daily column to Betty just before he was wheeled into the operating room. By the late 1920s, because of that column, he had become a real political force in the United States.

Rogers was also reaching people's homes by radio. In January of 1928, *The Dodge Victory Hour* variety radio program aired a special segment featuring Rogers broadcasting directly from his home in Beverly Hills. After Rogers had done a few minutes of monologue, he said solemnly, "I want to introduce a friend of mine who is here and wishes to speak to you." Then he screwed up his face and started imitating the high-pitched New England voice of President Calvin Coolidge, who had just been talking with unhappy farmers in the Northwest:

*Farmers, I am proud to report that the country
as a whole is prosperous. I don't mean by that
that the whole country is prosperous, but as a
hole it is prosperous. That is, it is prosperous
for a hole. A hole is not supposed to be prosperous, and you are certainly in a hole. There
is not a whole lot of doubt about that.*

Amazingly, many of the people who heard this
wonderful nonsense were sure it was President
Coolidge himself talking. Rogers felt bad because
even though he disagreed with the president a
lot, he liked him personally. Coolidge urged him
to forget about it.

Will Rogers was always on the side of tolerance
and fairness, but when it came to politicians he
didn't spare anybody. His humor wasn't cruel,
but it could be cutting, and it almost always fell
on both sides of most issues. As a mixed-blood
person, he'd spent his whole life seeing both sides
of many questions. He might start by making fun
of the Republicans, but he'd be sure to give the
Democrats a poke, too. As for his own politics, he
liked to say, "I belong to no organized party. I'm
a Democrat."

Rogers assured people, "I have joked about
most of the prominent men of my day, but I have
never met a man I didn't like." Yet there was at
least one man for whom he seems to have held
only cold fury. Will Rogers, to be sure, had never
met him, for the man was Andrew Jackson, the
nineteenth-century president who had betrayed

the Cherokee people into Removal. On a 1928 lecture tour, a reporter named Ben Dixon McNeil watched disbelievingly as the usually genial Rogers addressed a large audience of Oklahoma Cherokees. The speech started as usual. But then, McNeil wrote, "Suddenly, he became furious. His transformation was terrifying, and for three minutes his astonished audience was treated to a demonstration of what primitive, instinctive hatred could be." While Rogers denounced Andrew Jackson and recalled for his audience the horrors of the Trail of Tears, "The Indians listened, and then the quiet was ripped by the screaming war cry of the tribe, while Rogers stood white, trembling, and actually aghast at himself. Afterward, he said wonderingly that he didn't know what had got into him." Usually Rogers kept a tight rein on his emotions. But on that evening in 1928, as he stood among the Cherokee people so reduced by the Allotment Act and other Indian policies, for once he let go and spoke with all the anger he felt.

By the time the Great Depression that began in 1929 was in full force, Rogers's humor had become both darker and more compassionate. He hated human suffering. All his adult life he had given freely to charities, and he was always glad to appear at benefits for good causes. Now he directed a great deal of his writing and speaking toward encouraging Americans to get behind relief efforts. Herbert Hoover, the president who succeeded Coolidge, was following a policy of not

doing much of anything about the Depression.
The government didn't like the idea of giving
away food, Rogers speculated, because "they
think it will encourage hunger. The way things
look, hunger don't need much encouragement.
It's just coming around naturally."

He got impatient with all the politicians who
liked to theorize about what had brought about
the Depression, instead of trying to figure out how
to keep poor people fed and sheltered. "There is
no reason to know where all this depression
comes from," he said. "If a snake bites you, you
ain't going to stop and study out where he come
from and why he was there at the time, you want
to start figuring on what to do with yourself right
then."

Rogers himself always tried to help people in
practical ways. In 1933, when the Gulf Oil Company signed him for a weekly Sunday night radio
program called *The Good Gulf Show*, he divided
the $50,000 the corporation paid him for the first
seven shows between the Red Cross and the Sal-
vation Army.

Rogers got back into making movies again in
1929 with the Fox Film Corporation studios. Now
that there were "talkies," movies with sound,
Will Rogers's real gifts of comic timing and in-
flection could come through to a film audience.
His first round of moviemaking had not turned
out too successfully, but in the last six years of
his life he came into great fame and wealth
through movies. In 1934 he was the most popular

star at the box office, ranking over Clark Gable
and Mae West. In 1935, the last year of his life,
only the child star Shirley Temple topped him.
In the 1930s Rogers's movies were far more popular than any other comedian's. People today love
the Marx Brothers and W.C. Fields movies because they make outrageous fun of stuffy people
and stuffy values. Will Rogers films often seem
corny now. They are mostly about an honest
simple person, played of course by Rogers, who
makes everybody see where the plain and sensi-
ble course of action lies.

The main problem about Will Rogers movies
is that Will didn't get to write the scripts. People
still read Rogers's collections of columns to hear
his fresh voice, but often the movies seem very
dated. Back in the thirties, he often threw aside
the script and made up his own dialogue on the
spot. He would change speeches to make them
shorter and less flowery. Once, for example, he
was playing a horse trainer talking to another
man about what would happen if a horse named
Emperor won a race. The script read, "If Emperor
wins, I'll see to it that you get that strip of land,
without any further trouble — in any event, we'll
call off the feud. What do you say?" Will changed
it to say, "Well then, if Emperor wins you get the
land and the old man drops the feud." It was
much better dialogue, but it was hard on the
other actors waiting for their cues. Sometimes
Rogers would secretly arrange to nudge a fellow
actor to cue the next speech. In his spontaneous

approach to acting, Will Rogers was way ahead of his time.

Rogers never got caught up in being a movie star. To him, it was only a job for which he was overpaid. He did his work well, but at four-thirty every afternoon he wanted to be done for the day and on his way home. By the 1930s, home was a 300-acre ranch about an hour's drive from the studio. From the patio, the family could look out across the beautiful foothills of the Santa Monica Mountains to the Pacific. There they built a huge U-shaped barn to house their string of some thirty horses, a riding ring, a roping pen, and a polo field. The center of the rambling main house was a large room with a huge stone fireplace. It was furnished with bright Navajo rugs and Mexican baskets and all sorts of mementos of Rogers's life — old saddles, pictures from Western artists like his friend Charlie Russell, even a stuffed calf mounted on wheels so he could practice roping inside. Often a live calf, a gentle purebred Brahma named Sarah, joined the family in front of the fire.

Together Rogers and his children practiced roping and trick riding. Mounted on four horses, they would tear madly around the riding ring four abreast, all standing on their saddles. When Mary grew more interested in boys and clothes and acting than in horses, Rogers observed sadly that his daughter "went social on us."

The ranch was the scene of many lively gath-

erings. Politicians, scholars, writers, artists, and
down-on-their-luck cowboy actors were all part
of the Rogerses' circle of friends. They would
gather in the Santa Monica hills for hard-riding
polo games and barbecues. Parties at the Rogerses' were neither very wild nor very fancy. Will
Rogers was never a drinker, and all his life his
favorite food was beans — "kinder soupy navy
beans soaked with plenty of real fat meat."

With all his love for his home and family, Rogers had a lifelong case of wanderlust. He always
had enormous energy and a great love of adventure. Perhaps the losses he suffered early in his
life — the deaths of his mother and brother, the
dwindling of the Cherokee Nation and his family's high place within it — affected him strongly,
making it difficult for him to stay in one place for
very long. Whatever it was that made Rogers
want to roam, Betty Blake Rogers understood his
need to be frequently on the road. Sometimes he
would take her along, and those were some of her
happiest memories:

*If Will had a free day he liked to hop in the car
and drive off without any plans. He would call
to me, "Come on, Blake, let's get going," and
away we'd go. . . . We were alone; I had him
all to myself. There was no reading, no calf
roping, no hundred and one other things he
always seemed to be doing. . . . Sometimes we*

would spend the night in a little town off the main boulevard. Will liked the small country hotels and liked talking to the people he met in out-of-the-way places.

At other times, it was his male friends he wanted for company, and with no warning they might find themselves packed in Will Rogers's car, aiming across the border for Mexico or on a train headed for a big rodeo in Cheyenne, Wyoming.

Sometimes Rogers made his wanderlust fit right in with his work. He traveled the globe as a reporter, cabling back to his newspaper syndicate his observations of life in Russia under Communism; of Managua, Nicaragua, after a terrible earthquake; of China and Japan during the Sino-Japanese war. Franklin D. Roosevelt, one of the string of American presidents he counted as his friends, said, after Rogers returned from a 1926 trip to Europe, "Will Rogers' analysis of affairs abroad was not only more interesting but proved to be more accurate than any other I had heard." Rogers was an open-minded observer who liked to appreciate a country for what it was, rather than criticize it for not being like the United States. He was skeptical about Communism, for example, but after his 1934 trip to Russia, he wrote, "The question arises: How is Russia getting along? Well, to be downright honest with you, it's getting along better than we want it to. Think that over."

As a traveler who had a terrible time with sea-
sickness, Will Rogers became an early and pas-
sionate fan of aviation. With foresight, he kept
insisting that air power would be important in
any future war, and he loved hanging around
with famous pilots like Charles Lindbergh, Billy
Mitchell, and his great friend and fellow Okla-
homan Wiley Post. With a copilot, Post set an
around-the-world flight record of eight days in
1931, and in 1933 he made a solo flight around
the world.

Moved by his usual restlessness and quest for
fresh adventure, in the summer of 1935 Rogers
agreed to join Post on a flight that would take
them north from Seattle, Washington, across
Alaska and Siberia and on into Europe. Rogers
planned to keep writing his daily column
throughout the trip, radioing it in along the route.
His family would meet him in Europe at the end
of the journey. Betty was anxious about the no-
tion of her husband's flying over Siberia, but he
was as stubborn at 56 as he had been as a young
man. He had gotten a glimpse of the place the
year before from the Trans-Siberian railway and
loved its wildness. He wanted, as Betty remembered, "to see it in the only way one can really
see such a vast country — from the sky."

On August 8, 1935, Wiley Post and Will Rogers
flew out of Seattle in a secondhand Lockheed Orion plane to which Post had added a new engine,
new wings, propeller, fuel tanks, and heavy pontoons for water landings in the Alaskan coastal

wilderness. The pontoons made the little plane nose-heavy and hard to handle, but Rogers had confidence in his friend. "No danger with this guy!" he wired Betty. He was in his element, sending back his column about the fine adventure they were having. "Was you ever driving around in a car and not knowing or caring where you went?" he wrote. "Well, that's what Wiley and I are doing. If we hear of whales or polar bears in the Arctic, or a big herd of caribou or reindeer, we fly over to see it."

In this joyful fashion, they were heading from Fairbanks to Point Barrow. "Furthest point of land north on whole American continent," he wired his daughter Mary. At the time, Mary was acting in a summer stock theater in Skowhegan, Maine, where she was appearing in a play called *Ceiling Zero* in the role of a young woman whose father is killed in an air crash. On the way to Point Barrow, Post and Rogers encountered ceiling zero conditions due to heavy fog. Post had not checked for a weather report, and soon he was lost.

About seven o'clock on the evening of August 15, an Alaskan Native named Clair Okpeaha and his family were fishing on a small coastal lagoon fifteen miles southwest of Barrow. They heard an engine, then watched as a small red plane touched down. The two men in the plane asked the way to Barrow, and the Okpeahas gave them directions. They chatted awhile about how good the walrus and caribou hunting had been, while Post and Rogers stretched their legs. Then the men returned to the plane and took off. The Okpeahas watched the plane climb toward the cloud banks and turned back toward their fishing. A sudden noise "like the sound of a shotgun" made them look skyward again. What they saw horrified them. The plane seemed to stand on the air for a moment as its engine abruptly cut. Then it somersaulted downward, wing over wing, and landed on its back in the shallow waters of the lagoon. Will Rogers and Wiley Post, badly mangled in the crash, died instantly. Mr. Okpeaha called out to the men; getting no answer, he started to run all the way to Barrow to summon help.

By dawn of the next day, the two bodies, wrapped in sleeping bags, were loaded gently into oomiaks — boats made of skin stretched over wooden frames — and white and Native rescuers began paddling north toward Point Barrow. Sergeant Stanley Morgan of the U.S. Army Signal Corps, in charge of the operation, reported that while the Alaskan Native people who helped retrieve the bodies did not know who Post and Rogers were, they felt a sense of great loss. On the journey northward, "one of the Eskimo boys began to sing a hymn in Eskimo, and soon all the voices joined in his singing until our arrival at Barrow." Back in the States, there would be many grand memorial services and lengthy obituaries for both men, but the chorus of Inupiaq voices rising in the Arctic dawn seems a most fitting elegy. Will Rogers, who had begun his life in Indian Territory, died among Native people who were there at the end to sing him home.

4
Jim Thorpe

People everywhere have always admired swift runners for their power, endurance, and grace. But to American Indians, runners weren't merely fine athletes. They carried news from one place to another and bound the scattered settlements of the people together. They carried word of births and weddings and deaths; they told of upcoming councils and feasts or warned of impending danger. They reminded people that no matter how far apart they might live, they were one.

These messengers needed to be in superb physical condition. But they also had to be intelligent people with good hearts who could be counted on to speak the truth. In many Native American tribes, the best runners have held special ceremonial offices and responsibilities. They have often been trusted with important political errands.

Stories are told all over the Americas about old-time runners who had unusual powers. Ceremonial runners often didn't allow others to watch them when they were traveling at their top speed. But there are tales among many tribes about people examining the tracks these runners left behind in sand or snow or soft earth. The astonished trackers would find that the space between footprints increased from 5 feet, to 10, to 50 feet, until the tracks vanished altogether, at a place where the runner apparently took flight. Other stories tell of runners able to make themselves invisible to enemies who might try to interfere with their errands. Whether or not one believes those stories, it is true that long before the coming of Europeans and their horses, news traveled very rapidly across thousands of miles of North and South America by relays of messengers on foot.

The allied Sac and Fox tribes of the upper Midwest were spread out over a wide range of territory. To keep in touch, they had a special group of runner-messengers called *a'ckapäwas*. These men lived lives of strict physical and spiritual discipline, like the monks of Europe and Asia. They were not allowed to marry. Early in his training, a young Sac or Fox man who hoped to become a runner carved for himself a wooden bowl and spoon. He ate only from them for the rest of his life, no matter whose house he was visiting. Each man who succeeded in becoming

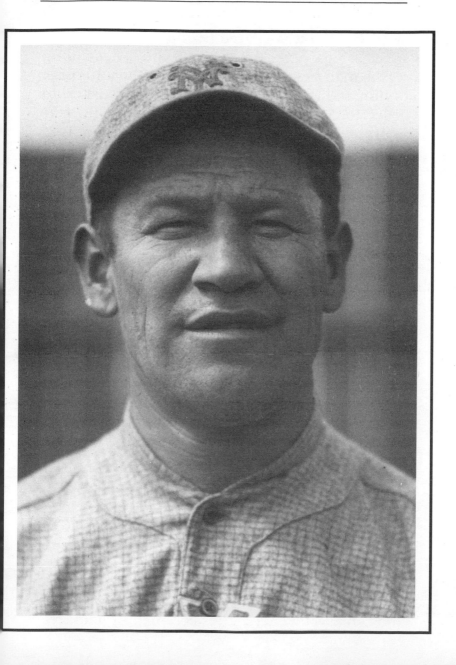

an *a'ckapäwa* was visited by a particular animal spirit — bear, deer, or hummingbird, depending on the man's clan. The animal spirit would come to him and tell him certain things he must do in order to become a fast runner who would fear nothing, a person able to meet all he experienced with good humor and a tranquil heart.

In the 1860s, the last known *a'ckapäwa* ran four hundred miles from what is now Green Bay, Wisconsin, to warn allies around present-day St. Louis about an enemy attack. Just before his death, he predicted what it would mean for the Sac and Fox people if they did not keep up their tradition of ceremonial runners:

> *Later on you will have no one who will go about telling anything that happened to you. You will have a hard time. Even whenever you die you will not know that of each other if no one goes about reporting it, if you lose the ceremonial runners.*

About twenty years after that last ceremonial runner died, just as dawn broke on May 28, 1888, twin baby boys of Sac and Fox heritage were born in a one-room cabin in Indian Territory a little north of the present-day town of Shawnee, Oklahoma. One of the boys was named Wa-tho-huck, Bright Path in the language of the Sac and Fox. That proved to be a well-chosen name. There were no longer any *a'ckapäwa* left to teach Sac and Fox youngsters the ceremonial runners' ways, but this baby must have carried some of their old-time power in his blood. Wa-tho-huck would grow up to blaze his own particular bright path across the stadiums and playing fields of the world. Under his English name, Jim Thorpe, he is celebrated to this day as the single greatest athlete the United States has ever known.

By the time Jim Thorpe and his twin brother Charlie were born in Oklahoma, the Sac and Fox had fallen onto hard times. Throughout the nineteenth century, white settlers eager to farm the rich soil of the prairies and bottomlands gradually squeezed the Native people from their tribal lands in Wisconsin, Iowa, and Illinois. They forced the Sac and Fox into small areas of Iowa and Kansas.

Jim Thorpe's great-grandfather, Black Hawk, had tried to stop the newcomers from taking over. With a tiny band of allies, this valiant Sac leader began attacking forts and settlements in 1832 to protest unfair treaties and the seizure of Indian lands. Militia and federal troops were called out against Black Hawk. Two future United States presidents, Colonel Zachary Taylor and Private Abraham Lincoln, and Lieutenant Jefferson Davis, future president of the Confederate States of America, all served in the Black Hawk War. (Lincoln, thinking back on his war experience, said he could not remember meeting any enemy except mosquitoes.)

Unlike United States troops, Sac and Fox armies traveled with their families. Black Hawk's actual fighters numbered only about forty people. Still, throughout the spring and summer of 1832, Black Hawk and his people were often able to drive back the militia and the federal troops who pursued them. It was only a question of time, though, before this small rebellious group of people became worn down by lack of supplies and life on the run. By August, Black Hawk was ready to surrender, but the troops ignored his white flag. On August 3, 1832, about 1,300 federal troops and militia attacked Black Hawk's people in Wisconsin where the Bad Ax River enters the Mississippi, just above present-day Prairie du Chien. Some 300 Sac and Fox men, women, and children were slaughtered.

After the fleeing Black Hawk had been captured, the United States government released him on condition that another Sac leader named Keokuk be made the sole chief of the Sacs. Unlike Black Hawk, Keokuk was an easygoing man who had always argued against warring with the white people. United States government agents had showered him with presents and promises and given him a free trip to Washington. Keokuk was peace-loving, but he also loved profit. Soon after becoming chief, Keokuk sold off all but forty acres of the remaining Sac lands in Iowa. In 1869, the Sac and Fox who still lived on their small reservations in Iowa and Kansas were told they must move once again. The United States Government was now trying to confine as many Indian people as possible to land it had set aside as Indian Territory in what is now Oklahoma.

Jim Thorpe was born into a hard-living family of Indian Territory mixed bloods. His father was a grandson of the great Black Hawk himself. His father's mother, a Sac and Fox woman named No-ten-o-quah, or Wind Woman, married Hiram G. Thorpe, a strapping Irish blackmith on the Sac and Fox reservation in Kansas. Their son — Jim's father Hiram P. Thorpe — was born about 1850. His early years were spent on the Kansas Reservation, where Sac and Fox people intermarried freely with whites. Otherwise, the Sac and Fox were determined to live as much in the old way as possible. More than many other tribes, they resisted schools and missionaries and even refused the offer to have a flour mill built in their community. When the Sac and Fox were ordered to move yet once more, this time to Indian Territory, Hiram P. Thorpe and his family were among those who made the journey under military cscort. They walked south to Oklahoma through the early winter cold beside great rumbling ox-drawn wagons that carried their household goods.

Hiram P. did not grow up to live a very settled life. A big powerful man, he loved the outdoors, dogs, whiskey, and the horses he bred, raced, and traded. He had a reputation as a two-fisted brawler in the fights that were always breaking out in what local people called "The Seven Deadly Saloons" of nearby Keokuk Falls. One time, in a saloon named The Black Dog, a drunken

man shot another man dead. Then he waved his
gun around at the silent crowd, daring anyone
else to come forward. Hiram P. quietly rose from
his table. He walked over to the dead man, stuck
his finger in the fatal wound, and then shook the
finger in warning at the killer, splattering him
with drops of blood. Awed, the man backed off.
No one could beat Hiram P. for raw courage.

Hiram P. was a superb hunter and fisherman
who always returned from a day in the woods or
on the river with fresh game or fish for the family
table. He farmed his allotted 163 acres only as
much as necessary to feed his family and livestock. On Saturdays, men would gather in the
pasture by the Thorpe cabin and compete against
one another in different sports. "My father was
the champion in sprinting, wrestling, swimming,
high jumping, broad jumping, and horseback riding," Jim recalled proudly. Hiram P.'s rough
ways and hot temper alienated his children, but
nonetheless Jim admired his father's strength, his
way with animals, and his ability to live off the
land.

Hiram P. loved at least five women and fa-
thered a good many children over the course
of his life, though his most enduring relation-
ship seems to have been with Jim and Charlie's
mother, Charlotte Vieux. She was a strong
woman of French, Potawatomi, and Kickapoo descent who had been raised as a Potawatomi. Like
many Potawatomi, she was deeply Catholic, a
faith she passed on to her children. She needed

to be strong to live with Hiram and to endure the early deaths of five of their children.

Much of the land reserved for the Sac and Fox was flat and sandy, but the Thorpes lived in the more fertile bottomlands of the North Canadian River. The name "Oklahoma" means both "red earth" and "red people" in Choctaw. Where Jim Thorpe grew up, the red earth gave the people pasture grass and good garden soil. Deer and squirrel, quail and rabbit abounded among the forests of shady cottonwood and gnarled blackjack oak. The river yielded fish and wild duck aplenty.

For active boys like Jim and Charlie, the hardships of their early lives were outweighed by the fun and the freedom. As a grown man, Thorpe remembered how exciting an ordinary game like follow-the-leader could be when a long line of boys ducked under the bellies of draft horses, jumped off barn roofs, and waded fast creeks. Hiram P. taught his boys to fish, hunt, trap, and break wild horses. Charlie was quieter than Jim, and not quite as strong or as fast, but the twins were inseparable. No game or adventure was fun for Jim unless Charlie was part of it, too.

The U.S. Indian Agency records have Hiram P. down as one of only thirty Sac and Fox tribal members who could read and write English, and he seems to have believed strongly in education for his children. For six-year-old Jim and Charlie Thorpe, that meant following their elder brother George and their half brothers and sisters to the

Sac and Fox agency boarding school, some twenty-three miles north of the Thorpe ranch. It also meant a new life of rules and bells, lines and schedules, and itchy uniforms. Cheerful, obedient Charlie didn't mind school very much, but Jim detested the routine. He would not enjoy school until he was much older.

The schools run by the government for American Indian children were a combination military academy and vocational school. Girls were taught white people's methods of housekeeping, and boys were taught some trade that would fit into the white world. At the Sac and Fox agency, school boys were taught how to farm. The children studied some reading, writing, geography, and basic arithmetic. But above all, these schools aimed to "civilize," that is, to de-Indianize their pupils. The frightened, homesick children were assigned an English name if they didn't already have one. They were given white-style haircuts and uniforms and were punished if they were caught speaking their native language. They were made to learn hymns and study the Bible. They were discouraged from having much contact with home, especially if their families were "blanket Indians," people who held on to their traditional ways. At most such schools, the goal was not to make these boys and girls into American Indian doctors, lawyers, artists, or professors. Instead, the schools tried to turn out docile Indian workers with white values and manners. When the students were grown, they would have low-paying jobs in the white world and they would raise their children to do the same. The school administrators hoped the students would lose all sense of themselves as Indian people.

In his early school years, the "incorrigible" Jim was always compared by his teachers with gentle Charlie. Jim had plenty of brains, but he hated being ordered around and cooped up inside. Probably he was also uneasy about the way things were going at home. At about the time Jim and Charlie began school, their parents separated for a while, and Hiram P. took up with another woman. Once, in second grade, Jim tried running away from school, but when he showed up at the ranch, Hiram P. whipped him soundly and brought him right back. Still, however much he hated school, for the first two years Jim did not protest very much, probably because he had Charlie to keep him from being too homesick.

But the year Jim turned eight, tragedy entered his life. Epidemics took a big toll every year throughout Indian Territory, and in the spring of 1896 Charlie came down with pneumonia. His parents were summoned to the agency school to help nurse him, but Charlie, whom everyone loved for his sweet nature, died before they arrived. Jim had lost his twin, the person closest to him in the world. The once-boisterous, fun-loving boy became quiet and withdrawn. He left school for the rest of the term. In those first months of raw grief for his brother, he often took a friendly hunting dog for company and went camping alone. He returned to school the following fall, but now all the drudgery and strictness seemed unbearable without Charlie. Jim began to rebel in earnest.

Rebelling mostly meant running away from school. Jim wasn't the only student who bolted, for many of the students were homesick and hated the rigid ways of the school. Once, when a fellow runaway hid out at his own home near the Thorpe ranch, he was startled by an unearthly noise. Peeking out, he saw the agency police wagon, used to gather up the truants, rolling up his lane. The racket was coming from Jim Thorpe, tied up in the back of the wagon and howling his defiance with all his might.

When Jim turned eleven, Hiram P. grew weary of dealing with his stubborn son, and he tried to solve the problem by sending Jim to a school, as he put it, "so far you will never find your way back home." That school was Haskell Institute in Lawrence, Kansas, 300 miles north of the Thorpe ranch.

Today, Haskell Institute is Haskell Indian University, the largest institution of higher education for American Indian people. It offers excellent academic and vocational curricula. In 1898, as at the much smaller Sac and Fox agency school, the emphasis at Haskell was on military discipline and learning a trade. The students spent most of their time marching and drilling and working in the school's bakery, tailor shop, or wagon shop or on the school farm.

At Haskell, Jim Thorpe did not learn much more academically than he had back at the agency school. But Haskell was the place where he first saw people playing football. One of the disciplinarians showed the smaller boys the rules of the game. The older boys wore padded shirts and helmets and played with a real pigskin football, but the smaller boys like Jim made do with their regular clothes and a knotted sock stuffed with grass. With their makeshift ball, they practiced drop-kicking, passing, and scrimmaging.

The Haskell varsity team had one real star, Chauncey Archiquette, whom Jim quickly came to admire. Instead of playing with the boys his own age, Jim began to hang around the football practice field, studying how his hero moved on different plays. Archiquette couldn't help noticing the intense youngster who watched him from the sidelines. He had seen this same boy running all by himself with surprising speed across the field after the team was through practicing. One day Archiquette stopped to talk to Jim. He could see how Jim yearned to touch the real football he carried, and he let him hold it. Then Archiquette brought Jim over to the school wagon shop where he worked. He made Jim a ball of his own by stitching together harness leather scraps and stuffing them with rags.

Armed with his new ball, Jim organized games among the boys of his own age group. He began to display the qualities of leadership he hadn't shown since Charlie's death. His schoolwork also began to improve a little.

On January 12, 1900, the football team of Carlisle Industrial School in Carlisle, Pennsylvania, the best known of all the Indian schools, got off the train at Haskell. With their coach, Glen "Pop" Warner, they were returning from a winning game against the University of California at Berkeley for the East-West championship. This trip marked the furthest distance any football team in the country had ever traveled to play a game. Players from the Carlisle squad were regularly chosen as all-Americans. Jim never forgot seeing that well-trained team of young men who moved with such ease around the campus of Haskell during their brief visit. He wondered if he would ever grow to be that tall, that confident, if he could ever be part of a team that good.

One day in 1900, Jim's time at Haskell came to an abrupt end. A classmate whispered to Jim that he had seen a letter in the school office saying that Hiram P. had been hurt in a hunting accident. Jim didn't wait for the school officials to get around to notifying him. He just headed straight for the railroad yards in the clothes he was wearing. All he could think about was getting home. He slipped into an empty boxcar, hoping to hitch a ride as far as he could. Unluckily, the train he chose was headed in the wrong direction, northeast toward Kansas City instead of south toward Oklahoma. Jim jumped the freight and began his long trek toward home.

It took Jim two weeks to reach his folks' ranch. He was relieved to find Hiram P. alive and pretty well recovered from his wound. His parents were living together again, and expecting another child. But instead of welcoming his son, Hiram P. beat him. Perhaps he was angry that Jim hadn't waited for the school to pay his train fare, or because he knew that this episode of running away would make it hard to get Jim back into Haskell. Jim began working on the ranch for his father, but this was not to be a peaceful or long-lasting homecoming. In January of 1901, his mother gave birth to her eleventh child, a boy who lived only three days. A few weeks later, Charlotte Thorpe herself was dead. About the time of these deaths, which must have saddened him deeply, Jim again made his father angry by neglecting his chores. Hiram P. whipped Jim once more. "I deserved it, but I didn't feel like taking it," Jim remembered when he was a grown man.

Jim took off again, this time for the Texas Panhandle. Exactly when he left and how long he stayed away are not certain. But he was now a 13-year-old, big and hardy enough to do ranch work for hire. He worked until he had earned the money to buy himself a fine team of horses and drove them proudly back from Texas to the family ranch, uncertain what welcome he would get. As he remembered, "My father took a look at the horses and decided to let me stay."

At his father's insistence, Jim enrolled in the local public school he attended for the next three

years, helping his father on the ranch the rest of
the time. At the end of the 1903 term, a recruiter
from Carlisle visited the little schoolhouse, looking for new students, particularly those with
promise of being athletes. By February, 1904, Jim
was on a train heading north and east to Carlisle,
where he would begin to blaze the bright path
his name promised.

Carlisle was founded in 1879 on a site that had
been used as a fort where the citizens of the Pennsylvania town could be safe in case of Indian attack. During the Civil War, it became a Union
cavalry post that was attacked and burned by the
Confederacy. At Carlisle, as at other Indian
schools, manual training and military drill were
taught, but here there was far more emphasis on
academic subjects. Good students could participate in a debating society or put on productions
of Shakespeare's plays. A number of Carlisle
graduates went on to careers in law, teaching,
business, and other professions. Carlisle athletic
teams were in the top rank of school sports, regularly playing well-known private colleges and
state universities.

Jim did not stand out during his first two years
at Carlisle. There were some early disappoint-
ments. He had wanted to study to be an electri-
cian, but the school didn't offer such a course,
and so Jim was assigned to the tailor shop instead. Ever since he had seen the Carlisle football
players at Haskell he had dreamed of making the
varsity team, but at 16 he stood five feet five

and one-half inches tall and weighed only 115 pounds. Even though he was quick and agile, he did not qualify for any varsity team. He settled for working at the tailor shop and playing intramural sports.

Jim was just growing used to his new school when word came in August that Hiram P. Thorpe had died of blood poisoning, perhaps from a snake bite. The bad news that Jim seems to have dreaded hearing most of his young life had come at last. Trains were too slow to get him back to Oklahoma in time for the funeral. Jim grieved by himself through that Pennsylvania fall for the father he had both loved and hated. Now he was an orphan, alone in strange dormitories and classrooms far from the blackjack oaks and river bottomlands of his childhood.

Carlisle authorities worried about Jim's withdrawal and sadness. They decided to send him on an "outing," where he would be placed with a white family. The idea behind the outing system was that a young American Indian would be sent out to work and board in white people's homes, where the student would be treated like a member of the family. He or she would learn white manners and values in a loving home while doing useful work. Some Carlisle students did have good outing experiences. But often they were treated like servants by the white families, working hard for a lower wage than a regular servant or farmhand would get.

Jim was placed first with a Quaker family. He

might have enjoyed doing farmwork, but this family kept him inside doing household chores. He felt even more depressed as he worked at an endless round of washing dishes, peeling vegetables, and scrubbing floors. Eventually he was sent to a different farm in New Jersey, where he gardened. He remained there until the spring of 1907, when he decided he had had enough of planting and hoeing vegetables. He wanted to be back at Carlisle, where he could play sports, and so he ran away from the farm. At Carlisle, the runaway was punished by being sent to the guardhouse for a while. When he emerged from detention into the April sunlight, a new phase of his life began.

During his outing time, Jim had grown. At 19, he was almost five feet ten, and he weighed 144 pounds. Farmwork had kept him in shape. The other boys who had played intramural games with him knew he was stronger and faster than any of them. But the varsity coaches at Carlisle still hadn't discovered the natural athlete in their midst.

One soft spring evening, as Jim and his friends were walking to an intramural football game, they passed the varsity track team practicing the high jump. The bar was set at five feet nine inches, and no one was able to make it over the top. Jim gauged the height. He felt in his bones that he could clear that bar, and he asked the team if he could try. They nodded, grinning. They were waiting to see this eager boy go sprawling in the dirt. But sure enough, just wearing his regular work clothes and heavy shoes, Jim took a running start and easily cleared the bar. Word spread quickly, and Jim soon found himself on the track team.

Pop Warner, the firm-jawed head coach at Carlisle, was used to cursing and scolding and driving his players hard. When he came to Carlisle, Warner learned that if he were going to be a successful coach, he would have to stop swearing at his players and insulting them. The American Indian players had pride and dignity, and those methods did not work with them. They would rather skip practice than put up with insults. Warner found if he treated Carlisle players with respect, they were willing to work very hard for him.

Jim was no exception. On Arbor Day, April 26, 1907, he competed in his first official meet. He won the high jump and the 220-yard and 100-yard hurdles, and came in second in the 100-yard dash. Before Carlisle let out for summer, Jim had competed in his first intercollegiate meets against Pennsylvania State College and Bucknell, and scored enough points to win his school letter. One extra reward was that Jim would not be faced with another dreary outing summer of doing farm work for low wages. "Pop's boys," as the good athletes were known, were allowed to stay around the sleepy green campus, doing light work like painting the dormitories, keeping in shape, and playing pickup baseball games.

At first, Warner wanted to keep Jim only on the track team. He didn't think Jim was hefty enough for football, and he was afraid his new track star would get hurt on the gridiron. But football, real football, had been Jim's dream for too long, and he wasn't about to give it up. He pleaded so hard that Warner let him suit up as a kicker. Jim could boom a football a long distance, and Warner thought Jim would be safe from burly tacklers if he just kept him on the kicking team. But Jim persisted. Warner decided to teach Jim a lesson. He handed him a football and ordered him to run against a field of players waiting to practice tackling. About forty hulking young men were scattered all over the field, their eyes glued to Jim and the ball he carried. Warner figured Jim would get tackled so often by the big linemen that he'd soon get discouraged. But Jim, running at top speed, eluded tackle after tackle. Pushing other players easily aside, he snaked across the whole field. No one had been able to bring him down. Warner was stunned. Was his tackling squad as slow and clumsy as that? No, it was just that this rookie was so untackleable. Warner had to face the fact that Jim belonged on the 1907 varsity football team.

In 1907, new rules had just been made for intercollegiate football. Football had been getting a bad reputation as a game in which gangs of thugs beat each other to a pulp. The new rules tried to ensure that only real students would be allowed to play. New plays like the forward pass were now allowed. The officials were trying to change the game so that there would be more passing, kicking, and catching and less time on the field with two opposing teams slamming into one another. Pop Warner himself invented a lot of things people nowadays take for granted as part of football, including numbered jerseys and thickly padded uniforms. He also was a master of devising clever plays that made it hard for the opposing team to tell who had the ball. Some of them are still used today. But Warner's most famous invention, called the "hunchback play," is no longer legal. One player pretended to have the ball while another teammate, with the ball safely hidden down the back of his bulky jersey, sneaked across the goal line and scored. The crowds loved it.

That first season of 1907, Jim did not get to play very much. He still had a lot to learn about the game. Warner appointed one of his best players and brightest students, the Cherokee-Delaware Albert Exendine, to be Jim's mentor. Pop Warner always said he thought American Indians learned quickly because they had been taught to stand by and study carefully how their elders did something before they themselves gave it a try. Now Exendine worked with Jim on how to block, tackle, and handle the ball. Jim did learn swiftly, and he was allowed to play in four games at the end of the 10–1 winning season. He was impatient to play more, and he would jump up and down restlessly on the sidelines while he watched the Carlisle Indians score again and again.

Just being part of a proud winning team gave Jim confidence in other parts of his life. His typing and business skills teacher, Marianne Moore, who became a famous American poet, always remembered him as a hardworking dependable student whose handwriting was as "firm and clear as a clerk's." She also remembered his politeness. Once, when she chaperoned a group of Carlisle students to the circus, Jim gallantly offered to carry her parasol. But by 1908, Jim was not merely hardworking and polite. His grades shot up to "excellent" in his academic subjects. When one of his teachers had to be gone for a day, she asked Jim to take over, and his classmates all said later they thought he would make a good teacher. Jim Thorpe was no longer the withdrawn, lonely boy he had been for much of his youth. For a time, it seemed as though the pride and discipline of the old-time Sac and Fox runners had come to live in him.

During the spring 1908 track season, Jim was the only Carlisle student who qualified for the Penn Relays, which are still one of the most important meets in the United States. There, he tied for first place in the high jump, clearing the bar at six feet one inch. The referee flipped a coin to decide which contestant would be declared winner. Jim won the toss and was presented with his first gold medal.

That summer of 1908, Jim decided to travel

back to Oklahoma for the first time in four years. He must have been dismayed by what he saw there. It is hard for most people to return to a place where they grew up after they have been away for a long time. Nothing is ever the same as in memory. It was even harder for Jim Thorpe. He was not returning to a real home, but only to visit the graves of his mother and father. Besides, Oklahoma was changing rapidly in those first years of the oil boom. More and more Native people were selling off their allotments and losing their land. More and more white people were crowding into the little towns, and many of them detested Indian people.

Jim saw, too, what was becoming of the other Thorpe children, his siblings and his half brothers and sisters. Some of the younger children were rebellious, escaping from boarding school at every chance they could get, just as Jim had. His half brother Frank, trying to grow cotton without good machinery, was married with four children. The Sac and Fox agency would not lend him money to buy better machinery because they said Frank was "unreliable." Mary, the sister Jim was closest to, already had lived a hard life. As a child, she had fallen off a wagon onto some sharp cornstalks that punctured her throat so harshly that she could barely speak. Only her brothers Jim and George could understand what she said. She kept falling in love with men who were lazy or heavy drinkers, and now, at nineteen, she had a little boy to care for. Mary inherited the great strength that ran in the Thorpe family, and she had been known to throw a full-grown man to the ground. With her strange noises and her fierce look, she was beginning to get a reputation as something of a witch, or at least as someone who could do harm if she wanted. Mary didn't mind. She would use that reputation to protect herself. Mary was a real fighter, and Jim loved her spirit. He would always try to take care of her.

When Jim returned to Carlisle later that summer, he must have been thinking a great deal about how life would have been different for him if he had never gone away to school in Pennsylvania. In any case, this was the year he began to shine as a football player. At 175 pounds, he was no longer a lightweight. He started at halfback, and the team had a great season of ten wins, two losses, and one tie. After the season, Jim was named to the third-string all-America team. In the spring term, Jim played basketball and also distinguished himself in track. Jim was not the only star of the Carlisle Indians track team, but his power and his versatility were truly astonishing. In one meet against Lafayette, he won six gold medals for the 120-yard high hurdles, the broad jump, the high jump, the 220-yard low hurdles, the shot put, and the discus throw.

It may be that in that triumphant year of 1908–1909, success was going to Jim's head. Pop Warner was strict with his "athletic boys" in some ways, but he also gave them a lot of special treatment, and they were hero-worshipped by nearly everyone on campus. Often, misbehavior or slipping grades were overlooked. Jim began to cut classes. Also, he began to drink, a problem that would grow worse through his life. Things might have been different if he had had a wiser mentor — say, one of the old-time *a'ckapäwas*, who trained the young Sac and Fox to be great runners and taught them how they must learn to live in balance.

That summer of 1909, Jim did something that seemed like harmless fun at the time, but would cost him dearly in years to come. With some other Carlisle athletes, he traveled south to North Carolina and signed up for the summer with the Rocky Mount Railroaders, a semipro baseball team. He was paid about $25 a week to play as an infielder and a pitcher. Many college athletes spent their summers in this way, but they usually signed up under false names. They knew that to compete in the Olympics and other big contests, they were supposed to be amateurs who had never been paid for playing a sport. Their aliases protected them. James Thorpe signed up under his own name. Maybe he knew nothing about the amateur athletic rules, or maybe he just didn't think losing his amateur status would ever again matter to him.

That summer's taste of freedom seems to have made him determined never to return to Carlisle and its restrictions. At 21, he was becoming a heavy drinker. As the team traveled around to little towns in the East Carolina League, stories grew up about Jim. He was not a real brawler like his father Hiram P., but he was hard to manage when he was drunk. Once, legend has it, he stuffed a deputy upside down in a trash barrel. But athletes were treated as special in rural North Carolina, just as they were at Carlisle. The law tended to look the other way for the baseball players who gave the people of these sleepy tobacco-growing towns so much excitement and pleasure.

In September, Jim Thorpe headed back to Oklahoma and his family, helping his beloved and fierce sister Mary on her farm, and hunting, fishing, and drinking with his brothers. He missed the excitement of Carlisle and intercollegiate athletics, just as the students and the coaches missed his presence. But he was also angry at the school, and he had good reason. Carlisle refused to refund money deposited in his account there until he explained why he had not returned for fall term. Jim may have been in his early twenties, but he was not an adult in the eyes of Carlisle.

Still, he was drawn back to the school. At Thanksgiving, when the Carlisle Indians played at the University of St. Louis, he traveled there to watch his old team triumph. He spent Thanksgiving with them, promising to return for spring term. After the holiday, he brought Pop Warner back to Oklahoma with him to hunt for deer and turkey. At Christmas, Jim showed up at Carlisle in time for the annual student party. Again, he promised to come back to Carlisle when the new term started. But winter turned to spring, with no Jim Thorpe showing up on the Carlisle fields. Instead, he signed up for another season of semi-pro baseball in North Carolina.

Halfway through the summer, the entire East Carolina League went bankrupt, and Jim headed back for Oklahoma. He hung around Mary's and his brothers' homes for a while. Then he began drifting from town to town, picking up work here and there. It must have seemed to him that the really exciting part of his life was over, though he was just 23. In the summer of 1911, on the streets of Anadarko, Oklahoma, where he had been doing some drinking in the bars, he heard someone call out, "Jim! Jim Thorpe!" He looked into a warm familiar face. It was Albert Exendine, his old mentor at Carlisle, back in Oklahoma to visit his own relatives.

Albert Exendine was one of Carlisle's success stories. He had gone on from Carlisle to get a law degree, and now he was coaching football at Otterbein College in Ohio. He was delighted to see Jim. "Why don't you go back and finish school?" Albert asked him.

"They wouldn't want me back there now," Jim said. But Albert assured him Carlisle did want Jim Thorpe. Albert knew that Pop Warner was putting together the strongest Carlisle football squad ever and that Warner missed Jim. Albert also knew that Warner had already tried to write to Jim. The coach wanted to tell his former star that if he'd come back, he would train Jim in track-and-field events for the 1912 Olympic games to be held that next summer in Stockholm. At Albert's urging, Jim agreed to telegraph Pop Warner. By September, 1911, after being gone for more than two years, Jim was back at Carlisle.

That fall of 1911, the Carlisle football team racked up an 11–1 winning record, with Jim as the hero of many of those games. He was chosen to be a first-team all-American halfback. Some of his old confidence and warmth seemed to come back in all his success. At Christmas he played Santa Claus and handed out presents and candy to a number of Indian children. He began to get a reputation as a good waltzer. He especially liked dancing with one of the most popular women students at Carlisle, Iva Miller, who was part Cherokee. When they were first introduced, Jim told petite, bright-eyed Iva, "You're a cute little thing." At first Iva thought Jim was impolite, but she was soon won over by his good-heartedness and his campus fame. Jim Thorpe had grown into a good-looking man, with a shambling walk and a wonderful grin that spread across his broad face when he was pleased. Two years later, in October of 1913, Jim and Iva would be married.

All that spring of 1912, Pop Warner began training Thorpe and another student, a short, sinewy Hopi runner named Louis Tewanima, for the Olympics. After a winning Carlisle season of track meets, both men qualified for the U.S. Olympic team. In the excitement of preparation for the big

contest, another event happened that Jim should
have been part of. In late April, the class of 1912,
Jim's class, graduated. Jim was not among the
graduates. He had missed too many classes.

At the Olympic trials, Louis Tewanima made
the U.S. team for the 10,000-meter run, and Jim
Thorpe for the pentathlon and the decathlon. Before he sailed for Sweden, Jim wrote to the Sac
and Fox agency back in Oklahoma to request that
they release $100 of the money kept in trust for
him to help with his trip. The agent refused to
send the money. He said he thought Jim would
be better off at school or farming instead of "gal-
livanting." He did not think Jim was able to handle his own money or to make decisions about
his own life. Jim Thorpe had been chosen as a
member of a team that would represent the entire
United States at an important international
event, but once again he was reminded that the
government saw him as a child. Somehow, Carlisle Indian School and Pop Warner together
found enough money for Jim to make the trip.

Thorpe would always recall how awed he was
at the sight of the big ocean liner, the S.S. *Finlandia*, that would carry the U.S. team to Sweden.
He was a 24-year-old who had never seen the
ocean, and he always vowed that the transatlan-
tic voyage was the most exciting part of his whole
Olympic adventure. Over the years, a legend got
started that on that whole voyage Jim just slept
and ate and sat in deck chairs and hardly trained
at all because he was such a "natural athlete."

This may sound like a compliment, but it really was not. In a way, it was saying that American Indian people were so big and strong they could afford to be lazy. But fellow members of the U.S. team remember Thorpe's doing calisthenics and practicing for his events just like the rest of them. There is even a photo of him running laps on the deck of the ship. He was in superb condition, and he had worked hard to be.

Both of Jim's events were grueling tests. They demanded excellence at a number of sports. The Scandinavian people were thought to be best at these multisport events, and the host country of Sweden was certainly hoping that they and other northerners would carry off the prizes. In 1912, the decathlon athletes competed in ten events over three days — the 100-meter dash, the 400-meter race, the javelin and discus throws, the 1,500-meter race, the 110-meter high hurdles, the shot put, the high jump, the running broad jump, and the pole vault. The pentathlon events were the 200-meter and the 1,500-meter races, the running broad jump, the javelin throw, and the discus throw. All five pentathlon events were held on the same day.

The pentathlon came first, on July 7. One by one, Jim Thorpe won four out of the five events and came in fourth in the javelin throw. The European crowds, always curious about American Indians, began to follow him around from event to event. He seemed so big and natural to them, and so strong and speedy, they started calling him "The Horse." Jim liked that. He would gallop around the decks of the docked *Finlandia*, where the American team slept, shouting, "I'm a horse! I'm a horse!"

A few days later, Thorpe's Hopi teammate Louis Tewanima finished second in the 10,000-meter race. He was beaten by a Finnish runner whose time was so fast it would not be broken until the great Sioux athlete Billy Mills shattered it in the 1964 Tokyo Olympics. Even more important, people in Stockholm were paying attention to the American Indian competitors at this 1912 Olympics.

The three-day decathlon competition began on July 13 in a heavy rain. Jim placed third in the 100-meter dash and second in the running broad jump, leaving him in second place overall. But on this first day of competition, he was determined to walk off the field in the lead. When it came his turn at the shot put, he hurled the heavy iron ball a good two and a half feet farther than anyone else, putting him well ahead.

On July 14, Jim placed first in the high jump, fourth in the 400-meter run and set a record that lasted for more than thirty years in the last event of the day, the 110-meter hurdles. He had doubled his lead. On the fifteenth, the final day of the Olympics, Jim finished second in the discus throw, third in the pole vault, and third in the javelin throw. Only the 1,500-meter run remained. People thought that after the three days of relentless competition, Jim might begin to weary. But he ran the 1,500 in an even faster time than he had in the pentathlon. "The Horse" had not only speed but astonishing stamina. Jim's point total in the decathlon would stand as a record for the next sixteen years.

At the presentation ceremonies, while the crowds roared, King Gustav of Sweden presented Jim with two laurel wreaths and two gold medals. He also gave Jim a bronze bust of his kingly self and a gold and silver model of a Viking ship, a gift from the czar of Russia to the decathlon winner. Then the king clasped Jim's hand and exclaimed, "Sir, you are the greatest athlete in the world!"

"Thanks, King," Jim answered. Oklahoma born and bred, he did not know what else to say to this elegant European royal person in his frock coat and shiny top hat. But he always vowed that that was the proudest moment of his life.

After the Olympics, there was plenty of celebrating, and huge welcome-home parades and ceremonies for the American team once they were back in the States. Among them they had won sixteen gold medals, but it was Jim who was singled out for attention. He was stunned by the cheering that greeted him everywhere. "I heard people yelling my name," he remembered later, "and I couldn't realize how one fellow could have so many friends." But perhaps Jim did not have that many real friends, after all. The cheers would pretty much die away within six months of his triumph.

That fall of 1912, Jim returned to Carlisle and had one more winning football season, scoring 198 points, the most that had ever been scored in a single season by any collegiate player. He was again named to the all-American team.

The highlight of the season was probably the game against West Point. Pop Warner roused his team by reminding them that the fathers and grandfathers of these Army cadets were the cavalry soldiers who had mistreated their own Native forebears. Dwight David Eisenhower, who would go on to be a five-star general, the Supreme Allied Commander in the European theater in World War II, and the President of the United States, was a starting player for Army in that game. Long afterward, despite a full life of commanding vast international armies and governing a nation, Eisenhower remembered vividly how no one could seem to stop Jim Thorpe from running the ball that day. Finally, Eisenhower and another player brought Jim down hard. Watching Jim lying dazed on the grass, flat on his back, Eisenhower figured the big ball carrier was through for the game. Then, to his astonishment, he saw Jim stagger to his feet and trot right back into formation. Carlisle beat Army, 26–6.

Before basketball became popular, January was a slow month for sports news, falling as it did between football and baseball seasons. In that January of 1913, a sports reporter on the Worcestor (Massachusetts) *Telegram*, poking around for a story, broke the news that Jim had played base-

ball for pay. If that was true, then Jim Thorpe
was not an amateur athlete, and he had not been
eligible to compete in the Olympics. Suddenly,
papers all over the United States and Europe
were running the story. The Amateur Athletic
Union (AAU) demanded a written statement from
Thorpe. He apologized and said he hadn't realized at the time that he was doing wrong, but the
AAU demanded Thorpe's medals and prizes back.
His name and scores were erased from the record
books. It was as if there had never been a 1912
Olympics for Jim Thorpe. Throughout his life he
would almost never speak about being stripped
of his medals. Thorpe's silence was probably a
sign of his deep hurt.

Without having graduated, Thorpe left Carlisle
in February of 1913. He had spent most of his last
nine years there. Now he felt it was time for something else. He signed up to play major league
baseball with the New York Giants, who were
eager to have a big name on their roster. But
baseball had never been one of Thorpe's true
sports. He had not spent that much time per-
fecting baseball skills, and he spent much of the
next three years unhappily watching better Giant
players field balls and score runs. Thorpe said
later, "I felt like a setting hen, not a ballplayer."
When he married his Carlisle sweetheart Iva
Miller in October of 1913, as a publicity stunt the
Giants sent the young honeymooning couple on
a world tour. The money and the privileges were
fine, but after Thorpe's contract ran out, he began

to look around for something he would like better. That something, for a while, seemed to be pro football.

In 1916, Thorpe signed with the Canton Bulldogs of Canton, Ohio, where the Pro Football Hall of Fame is now located. That year, the Bulldogs won the national championship. In 1919, while playing for Canton against the Massillon Tigers, Thorpe kicked a 95-yard field goal. The wind was blowing in the right direction to aid the ball, but still, that kick is often spoken of as the greatest kick in football history.

In 1920, Thorpe was named president of the American Professional Football Association, which two years later became the National Football League. That was a big honor, but Thorpe was no administrator. He was not cut out to handle money, shuffle papers, and resolve quarrels between players and management. He soon gave up that job, but he kept on playing football. In 1922, he organized the Oorang Indians, a new team made up entirely of full- or mixed-blood Indian men, some of whom he had known back at Carlisle. That team lasted two seasons. Thorpe played professional football off and on until 1926 and baseball until 1929, when he retired at 41. It was the beginning of the Great Depression, and Thorpe had few real skills except his athletic ability.

In his personal life, bad luck, bad decisions, and drinking kept Jim Thorpe unstable. The hardest blow of all was the death of his and Iva's first

child, three-year-old James, Jr., in the terrible
influenza epidemic of 1918. Iva and his friends
believed that that death was what turned him
into a real alcoholic. Over the years, Thorpe was
to have two more marriages and seven children
— three daughters by Iva and four sons by Freeda
Kirkpatrick, his second wife, whom he married
in 1926 and divorced in 1941. He lived at various
times in Oklahoma, California, and Michigan,
making a spotty living as a laborer and a movie
bit-part player and sometimes giving lectures or
exhibitions. Like many athletes, he had not been
encouraged to think much about what he would
do when he grew too old to play ball. There were
always reporters eager to write stories about how
the mighty athlete was now digging ditches and
down on his luck. Sometimes he got into trouble
because people knew of his reputation for size and
strength and were always taunting him or challenging him to fight. He was generous with what
money he did have and often gave it away to
anyone who had a sad story to tell.

Jim Thorpe had some happiness in his later life.
He dearly loved his children, his hunting dogs,
his old cars, and hunting and fishing. He cared a
great deal for American Indian causes. He had
good friends who always stood by him. Those
friends say he would seldom talk about his glo-
rious past wins, and never about the Olympic
medals that had been stripped from him, but
when a 1950 Associated Press poll of sports-
writers and broadcasters named Thorpe "The

Greatest Athlete of the Half-Century," he was delighted. In the next year, Hollywood came out with a movie called *Jim Thorpe, All-American*, starring Burt Lancaster. Since the 1940s, people had been asking whether Jim should have been stripped of those Olympic medals in the first place. The President of the International Olympic Committee, a man named Avery Brundage, would not listen to any appeals. Some thought it was because Brundage, too, had competed in the 1912 pentathlon and decathlon. He had been favored to win, but he had come in sixth, far behind Thorpe. Perhaps he never lost his bitterness over that defeat.

The restoration of Thorpe's medals had to wait until 1982, when he had been dead nearly 30 years. By then, many people were working to get Jim Thorpe's name back in the record books. They discovered that the Olympic committee had broken its own rule, which clearly said that any challenges or objections to an athlete's win had to be filed within 30 days of the awarding of the prize. The newspaper story about Thorpe's baseball summers had not come out until about seven months after the Stockholm games. His honor was restored. Back in 1913, Thorpe's gold medals had been given to the men from Sweden and Norway who had come in second to him. When these men were tracked down, it turned out both medals had long ago been stolen! Some thought the medals had been trying on their own to find their way back to their rightful owner.

Thorpe had had heart trouble for some time, and he died of a heart attack on March 28, 1953, two months before he would have turned 65. He had asked to be buried in Oklahoma, and his children wished to give him proper Sac and Fox ceremonies. But Thorpe's third wife, whom he married in 1945, had other ideas. Patricia Thorpe was a white woman who did not get on well with his children or his old friends. While he lived, she seemed determined to use her business skills to turn Jim Thorpe into a moneymaker. She arranged for lectures and personal appearances for him, charging high fees. Now she wanted to see to it that even in death he was profitable. She wanted Oklahoma to put up a fancy memorial for Thorpe. She planned to build a motel next door and call it Jim Thorpe Tepees. When the deal fell through, she contacted the small town of Mauch Chunk, Pennsylvania, where Thorpe had never even set foot. If the town would change its name to Jim Thorpe and build a monument, she'd bury him there. That is exactly what happened. His body rests far from his native blackjack oaks and red soil.

Jim Thorpe's children grew up to be more traditional Sac and Fox than he had been, closer to their roots. His daughter Grace has worked tirelessly to keep nuclear waste dumps off the Sac and Fox reservation, and his son Jack has served as chief of the Sac and Fox tribe. The Thorpe children believed their father's body should have been buried in the old way, and returned to its native earth between sunrise and noon on the third day after death. "Dad's body was sold as a tourist attraction," his son Richard has said bitterly.

In the summer of 1981, Thorpe's children gathered the clan in Oklahoma for a Ghost Feast to appease the wandering spirit of their father. Perhaps on that summer day, in some way, the great athlete came home at last to his Sac and Fox ancestors, *a'ckapäwas* and all.

5
Maria Tallchief

In the early 1930s, a little girl named Betty Marie sat beside her Osage Indian grandmother Eliza on one of the rough wooden benches ringed around an outdoor dance ground near Fairfax, Oklahoma. Drumbeats, music, and dancers pulsed through the arena, dance after dance, song after song. The gatherings Eliza and Betty Marie attended were religious ceremonies, connecting the dancers and the audience to the spirit world. But they were also social occasions bringing families and friends together. The rhythm and the movement of the dancers was very slow and stately, while low voices chanted in the background. Through it all, Betty Marie could hear the steady *tunk-thunk*, *tunk-thunk* of the heartbeat drum.

As she stared wide-eyed at the dancers, drummers, and singers, the child recognized grown-

ups she knew from her everyday life in Fairfax.
She saw men and women her parents would greet
as they passed on the street and people who came
to do real estate business with her Osage father,
buying and selling buildings and plots of land in
booming Osage County.

At ceremonies, these ordinary folks looked very
different from their usual selves. Men whom
Betty Marie was used to seeing in business suits
or in overalls were now resplendent in long
broadcloth leggings decorated with ribbon-work
designs, finger-woven wool sashes, and beaded
moccasins. Their bright calico shirts were draped
in bandolier beads. They strapped sleigh bells
about their knees and wrists, so even their slight-
est movement resounded with jingling. Soft pelts
of otter hung at their backs.

Women whom Betty Marie usually saw sweep-
ing their porches or shopping in plain cotton
housedresses now walked elegantly about in
silken and sateen blouses of plum and emerald,
crimson and turquoise. Their heavy broadcloth
skirts were decorated with wide bands of ribbon
work. The faces of the women and men alike were
alive, intent, and full of energy. The people were
not different just because they were wearing different clothes. On days like this, they were performing the ceremonial dances that said they
were Osage.

Back in the 1880s, the United States had forbidden the Osage tribe and other Native Americans in Oklahoma Territory to dance together in

the old way. Native ceremonies, especially ones that involved dancing, made government and military officials nervous. They wanted to make all American Indians who had been deprived of their land and sent to live in Oklahoma Indian Territory forget their heritage. They rightly suspected that ceremonies and dancing brought Native people strongly together. But even during the government ban on dances, the Osage had disobeyed and gone on holding ceremonies in secret.

The child seated beside her grandmother did not know all these things. She knew only how her whole small body responded to the *tunk-thunk* of the heartbeat drum and the sight and sound of her people dancing. For the most part, Betty Marie would not be raised in Native American ways, and her life would soon take her very far from the Osage world of otter pelts and drums and dusty Oklahoma dance grounds. As Maria Tallchief, she would become one of the world's greatest ballerinas, excelling in a European style of dance. Still, she would never forget going with her grandma Eliza to the ceremonies and the proud, transformed faces of her neighbors when they gathered together and moved once again in the centuries-old patterns of Osage dances. Long before Betty Marie could put her feelings into words, she understood that dancing comes from a place very deep in the heart.

Betty Marie's father, Alexander Tall Chief, was brought up mostly as an Osage. Until he could walk, his mother Eliza laced him snugly into a cradleboard and carried her baby around on her back. As a child, Eliza herself had lived in a circular Osage lodge of hickory saplings covered with buffalo skins. Eliza's father was an Osage chief named Peter Big Heart. By the time of Betty Marie's birth, most Osage would no longer be living in snug lodges, but rather in fancy mansions of many rooms. Osage history, and especially the part her great-grandfather Peter Big Heart played in it, greatly shaped Betty Marie's early life.

Before the coming of white people, the Osage had commanded a vast area that covered parts of what are now the states of Missouri, Arkansas, and Oklahoma. By 1825, the government had pushed the Osage north and west onto a small reservation in Kansas. In 1870 they were ordered to move once again, this time to Indian Territory in what is now northeastern Oklahoma. Indian Territory was supposed to be set aside as homelands for a number of Native nations, including the Osage. There, they were supposed to be allowed to govern themselves. The Native nations were to hold those lands as their sovereign nations "as long as the grass grows and the rivers flow."

The Osage made some especially smart decisions in their years of being moved about. When they sold their Kansas reservation land back to the government in 1870, they received the unusually good price of $9 million. They deposited it all in the U.S. Treasury, where it drew five percent interest. Then they used the money to buy back one and a half million acres of what had once been Osage land that lay within the newly created Indian Territory. The Osage carefully chose a rocky and hilly sector of the northeastern part of the Territory. They reasoned that white people would very likely leave them alone there because the country wouldn't make good farmland. But it was full of deer and buffalo, and the Osage were great hunters. Here, they thought, they could live well and enjoy peace.

Wise as they were, two things the leaders could not foresee would soon change Osage life forever. They did not know that the great herds would soon vanish because the United States government was determined to kill off the buffalo, whose meat and hide enabled Plains Indian people to live in their old ways. And in 1870 no one, white or Osage, suspected that beneath the rocky hills of Indian Territory lay vast reservoirs of thick crude oil, the "black gold" that would soon make the local economy boom.

In those early years of the twentieth century, the U.S. government was trying to change the old Indian ways of life by means of the allotment system. Traditionally, Indian people in a tribe owned land and hunting and fishing rights communally. Sharing the land and caring for it drew people closer together. The government wanted to force Indian people to own land privately, the way whites did, with each family allotted 160 acres that was theirs and theirs alone. What land was left over would be settled by white people.

The allotment system was disastrous for Native Americans. Many could not read, and many were confused about white ways of dealing with property and money. It was easier for greedy whites to cheat individual property owners than to cheat a whole tribe governed by wise councillors.

Once oil was discovered in 1897, tribal leaders feared that Osages might grow rich quickly and become very easy prey for crooks. In 1906, Peter Big Heart, Betty Marie Tall Chief's great-grandfather and other leaders worked out a compromise with the government. They reluctantly agreed that the Osage would own their land as individuals. But the Osage would own in common and share as a tribe whatever wealth lay *beneath* the surface of the earth, such as minerals and oil. The government, impatient to get on with allotment so more white people could start moving into Oklahoma Territory, hastily agreed. When the oil money began to roll in, all Osage families shared in it equally. Even if Osage had lost their land, they could still collect their oil payments four times a year at the tribal council house. Thanks to Peter Big Heart and other wise leaders, the small Osage towns of Pawhuska, Hominy, and Fairfax were for a while among the wealthiest communities in the United States.

Many Osage people did not know what to do with their sudden money. All across the United States, newspapers made fun of "rich Osage" who would build a mansion outfitted with velvet draperies and grand pianos and then choose to spend most of their time in mild weather in an old-fashioned brush shelter in the backyard, where the family could catch the breezes and see the stars wheeling overhead at night. Stories were told of families who would replace their Cadillac with a brand-new one if the first car got so much as a flat tire, and of children sent to school with hundred-dollar bills for lunch money. Like many people who find themselves suddenly rich, the Osage didn't find the paper dollars very real.

Non-Indian people didn't just make fun of the rich Osage — they bitterly envied them, too. In the 1920s, while Betty Marie was growing up, Osage County was marked not only by wealth but by bloodshed. According to the agreement worked out with the government, Osage people's oil rights could be inherited by any relative or named heir, even if the person was non-Indian. This provision was important because there were many mixed-blood families among the Osage, but it had some terrible consequences. Many greedy white men set out to marry Osage women for their oil rights, and corrupt lawyers and businessmen schemed to become the "guardians" of Osage people who were thought unable to understand complicated financial affairs. If those Osage people died, their rights would pass to their conniving husbands and guardians.

Suddenly, in the early years of the 1920s, many mysterious and sudden deaths of Osage people began to happen in Indian Territory. As many as sixty wealthy Osage were murdered during what came to be called "The Osage Reign of Terror." Coroners who were supposed to determine how people had died were bribed to cover up the facts. If an Osage man or woman had been poisoned, for example, the coroner would claim the dead person had died from drinking bad bootleg liquor. By 1925, murder was so common that the FBI conducted a special investigation in Osage County, but the agents' presence did not put a stop to the killings.

Betty Marie Tall Chief was born into the wealth and violence of Fairfax, Oklahoma, on January 24, 1925. Her father, Alexander Tall Chief, had inherited a substantial income from his family's oil rights, and he also seems to have inherited good sense and caution from his mother Eliza and his grandfather Peter Big Heart. The Tall Chiefs did not go in for lavish spending, and no white person schemed to become Alexander's guardian. The family did well not only on their oil money, but also from the ways Alexander himself invested it. Betty Marie's economic situation was unusually good for a young Native American in the first half of the twentieth century. Without her father's money from Osage oil shares, it would have been nearly impossible for her to make a career of ballet, no matter what superb talent she possessed.

Betty Marie's mother, Ruth Porter Tall Chief, was also a big factor in her daughter's success, but in a very different way. She did not care a great deal about Osage history and did not even consider bringing up her three children in Osage ways. This proper young woman of Dutch and Scots-Irish heritage had come on a vacation to Oklahoma and fallen in love with good-looking, good-natured Alexander Tall Chief. In later years, he would remark jokingly to his children that Ruth Porter married him because of his oil allotment money. Maybe there was some truth in that joke, but in any case, different as they were, the Tall Chiefs seem to have enjoyed a happy marriage.

Alexander liked making leisurely real estate deals while playing golf with his cronies, and he enjoyed dropping in on the movie theater and the pool hall he owned on the dusty main street of Fairfax and passing the time of day with the patrons. There was nothing leisurely about Ruth Porter Tall Chief. She was a strict parent to Betty Marie and her younger sister Marjorie. Ruth resigned herself to letting her oldest child Gerald follow his father's easygoing ways, but she was determined that her daughters be raised as refined young white ladies. Eager to make them cultured and graceful, she enrolled them in piano lessons and dance classes while they were still very young. They both excelled in their studies, even as small children.

Even though Betty Marie and Marjorie were both highly gifted, they were not very much alike. Marjorie, the baby of the family, was more like her father and brother, fun-loving and outgoing. Betty Marie was shyer, a very serious little girl who wanted more than anything to win her mother's praise. She kept much to herself, practicing both piano and ballet with a fierce concentration. A teacher came twice a week all the way from Tulsa to Fairfax just to give Betty Marie and Marjorie their dance lessons. By the time each child turned four, the teacher had them dancing in toe shoes, and soon the Tall Chief girls were performing as a sister act, in spangled costumes, at Fairfax events. They looked so sweet and precocious as they danced and played the piano together, no one thought to wonder if they were allowed enough time just to be little girls.

The Great Depression began in 1929 when Betty Marie was four years old. The stock market crashed that October, and millions of investors went bankrupt. Thousands of banks closed, leaving people without any of the money they had deposited. The stock market crash was followed by a severe drought that affected the midwest and southwest. The drought particularly devastated Oklahoma. Many banks, ranches, and businesses in the small towns of the Osage Reservation failed. Desperately poor people from Oklahoma, scornfully called "Okies," began packing up their belongings and heading for California, where rumor said there was easier living and plentiful farmwork in the lush fields and orchards of the central valley. Fortunately, Alexander Tall Chief had invested his oil money in real estate as well as in stocks and local businesses, so his family continued to live comfortably.

Even though the Tall Chiefs were not hard-hit by the Depression, they, too, were dreaming about California. Ruth was worried that her talented daughters had gone about as far as they could go with Oklahoma teachers. If Betty Marie and Marjorie were to become real musicians or dancers, they would need the sophisticated teachers only a big city could offer. At Ruth's urging, the family moved to California in 1932, the year Betty Marie was seven. Alexander Tall Chief made the move cheerfully. He had gradually grown away from his Osage heritage. Whatever Ruth wanted was all right with him.

The Tall Chiefs settled in Beverly Hills, and soon Betty Marie and Marjorie were studying with the stern ballet master Ernest Belcher. When Ruth first brought her daughters to audition for his class, Belcher was horrified to see the little girls dancing *en pointe*, on the tips of their toes. Their young bones were not fully grown yet, and their feet might easily have become permanently deformed. He told their mother he would accept the Tall Chief sisters only if they would enter his beginning classes and forget all they had learned from their Oklahoma teacher. No more were Betty Marie and Marjorie to perform flashy popular routines in spangled costumes before adoring local audiences the way they had in Oklahoma. Under Belcher's guidance, the Tall Chief girls solidly developed their ballet skills until he felt they were ready to perform in public.

Belcher designed a performance in which Betty
Marie and Marjorie danced in buckskin skirts and
feathered headdresses, doing what he thought
looked like an "Indian Dance." Neither the costumes nor the dance were authentic to any Native
nation. Betty Marie could remember the actual
Osage ceremonial dances she had attended with
her grandma Eliza, but she was an obedient child
who did what her teacher told her. Soon, she
would learn to say no when she was asked to do
anything that seemed to her to exploit her Osage
heritage.

When Betty Marie and Marjorie were a few
years older, Belcher realized that both girls had
grown beyond what he could teach them. He
helped Mrs. Tall Chief get them admitted to the
school of Bronislawa Nijinska, a world famous
Russian ballerina and choreographer. With her
lithe figure and slanting eyes, Nijinska closely
resembled her brother, Vaslav Nijinsky, who is
still considered one of the finest dancers of this
century. Once, when someone asked how he could
jump so spectacularly on stage, he replied "I
merely leap, then pause." Rumor had it that Madame Nijinska had sometimes danced in her
brother's place when he was ill, and no one in the
audience had spotted the difference.

Nijinska made a powerful impression on young
Betty Marie. She was an elegant, intense woman
whose circle of friends included Hollywood ce-
lebrities as well as European aristocracy. She was

extremely demanding of her students, requiring
that they show dignity and composure at all
times, not only during classes. She expected them
to be very committed to the ballet. Bubbly Marjorie still took it all as a lark. Dancing was something she did because she found it fun, but Betty
Marie dedicated herself deeply to becoming the
best ballerina she could be. Belcher had taught
her all the basic movements and techniques, but
now she began to work with Madame Nijinska
on subtler things. Madame knew that what separated good dancers from great dancers was
heart. She worked hard to get her students to
express their individual styles in their dancing.
Just performing the motions perfectly was not
enough. "Puppets!" Madame would sniff if she
saw dancers moving mechanically.

Betty Marie's own discipline and unstinting ef-
fort to live up to Madame's requirements helped
her grow into an erect, elegant, dignified ballerina of exceptional quality. By the time she entered Beverly Hills High School, she was
becoming a beautiful young woman, with a
strong, lithe body, masses of shining black hair,
smooth olive skin, high Osage cheekbones, and
thoughtful dark eyes. She was too shy to be one
of the most popular girls at school, and dancing
and piano practice took up most of her spare
hours. But Mrs. Tall Chief insisted that her
daughters have normal social lives, and Betty
somehow squeezed in time on weekends for
dances and beach picnics with her friends. Dave,

the boy she dated most during high school, was
fun to be with, but Betty's real passion was only
for ballet.

Nijinska was a teacher who insisted that her
students know more about the world of dance
than just the different steps and positions. When
famous people in the dance world passed through
town, Nijinska introduced her students to them.
She took them backstage at ballet performances,
wanting them to be familiar with costumes,
makeup, lighting, sets, and all the people besides
the dancers who joined together to make a ballet
performance. She also insisted that they learn
from other dance teachers besides herself. She
made the Tall Chiefs take classes with David
Lichine, a choreographer and former dancer who
had once danced with the great Anna Pavlova,
the most famous ballerina of all time.

Lichine was married to Tanya Riabouchinska,
a ballerina much younger than he, and not very
much older than Betty Marie and Marjorie.
Warmhearted Tanya quickly took the adoring
Tall Chief girls under her wing. Tanya had begun
to dance with the Ballet Russe de Monte Carlo as
a "baby ballerina," playing children's roles, and
she and David had fallen in love while they
danced as partners. Betty Marie sighed when she
thought about this handsome couple. Their story
was so romantic it almost seemed like a ballet
come true. How wonderful it must be to share
your work and your life with someone you loved!

The three best dancers in Madame Nijinska's

classes were the Tall Chief sisters and Cyd Charisse, the spirited daughter of a ballet teacher. In 1941, when Madame Nijinska was invited to stage a program at the Hollywood Bowl, she chose a dance she had choreographed to Chopin's Piano Concerto in E Minor. The ballet would feature her three prize pupils. Cyd would grow up to be a Hollywood actress who would star in many glamorous musicals, just as Betty Marie and Marjorie would one day both become world-famous ballerinas. But on that starry evening as they waited in the wings of the giant outdoor arena, they were just three anxious Los Angeles teenagers with sweaty palms and butterflies in their stomachs.

As the first notes of Chopin cascaded through the air, Betty Marie danced gracefully onto the stage — and tripped before an audience of thousands! Quickly recovering her balance, she found the beat and continued smoothly with her performance. Inside, she wanted to die, but she knew she must go on for the sake of Madame and the other dancers. Tears spilled down her cheeks as she came offstage, certain that Madame would scold her for her clumsiness. But Nijinska, usually so stern and demanding, put her arms around the trembling 15-year-old. She soothed her and told her stories of the worst moments famous ballerinas have lived through onstage. Why, one time during a Royal Command Performance Irina Baranova had gotten a bad start on making a leap and landed right on her head before the royal

family. When another dancer's shoulder strap
broke during a romantic *pas de deux*, her alert
partner snatched some trimming from her costume and covered her up, and the two danced
bravely on. What mattered, Madame said, was
having the heart to keep dancing, to rise above
mistakes and accidents. Betty nodded. She
understood, but she was still miserable. To her
surprise, the papers the next day did not even
mention her mishap. Instead, they praised the
performance.

Ballet dancers, choreographers, and company
directors from all over the world knew and respected Madame Nijinska, and when they visited
Los Angeles they often dropped in on her school
to observe her classes. Among them might well
be one or more youngsters who would become
the stars of the next generation of dancers. Sergei Denham, the manager of the Ballet Russe de
Monte Carlo, came by one afternoon when his
company was on tour. He watched as Betty
Marie, now sixteen, danced with her class. Then
he took her aside and had her perform a solo
while he watched her critically.

Denham had observed hundreds of aspiring
young dancers, and he recognized the promise of
this lithe youngster with the great dark eyes. If
the Tall Chiefs would grant their permission and
pay for her tuition and traveling expenses, he
would take Betty Marie on tour with the Ballet
Russe as a student! It would be a wonderful way
for her to prepare to join the company as a regular

dancer. Her heart soared with hope — perhaps her real career was about to begin. But when Madame Nijinska put Denham's offer before the Tall Chiefs, Ruth's answer was a firm no. Betty Marie was too young to leave home and tour with a company, no matter how well-chaperoned she would be. She needed to stay home and finish high school and then carry through with the family's plan for her to go to college at UCLA. There would be plenty of time later for her to become a professional dancer, if she wished.

Betty Marie knew it was useless to argue with her mother. She was sure that she had seen her one golden chance slip away. Perhaps for that reason, in her senior year she eased up on the demanding schedule of piano and ballet practice she had set for herself and allowed herself more time for friends and activities at school. By her graduation in June of 1942, she had to admit that perhaps her mother had been right. It would have been sad to miss this last year of being young and carefree among family and friends. But now she faced an uncertain future. World War II had begun, and many of the boys she knew were going straight from classes in algebra and senior English into military training camps. Soon, they would be fighting overseas, and some would not return. Many of her girlfriends were training as nurses or taking jobs in the various businesses that flourished under the demands of wartime.

Betty Marie herself would be starting college at UCLA in the fall, but somehow she couldn't seem to get very excited about classes and sororities and football games. More and more, she was sure that all she really wanted to do was to dance. Early in that long, slow summer, she was hired as one of a group of dancers for the Hollywood musical *Presenting Lily Mars*, starring Judy Garland. When she proudly announced to her father that MGM would pay her for her work, Alexander Tall Chief laughed and said she'd be the first Osage in a long time to actually earn her living. Dancing on the movie set was fun, but the work lasted only a short time and soon Betty Marie was again faced with endless hot summer days. Her beloved Madame Nijinska had closed her school for the summer and gone off to New York to choreograph for the Ballet Russe.

Los Angeles seemed empty of all life until one day Tanya Lichine stopped by the Tall Chief house to pay a visit before joining her husband David in New York, where he had taken a job with a ballet company. When she saw how low-spirited Betty Marie seemed, Tanya suggested she come to New York and see if Sergei Denham was still interested in her for the Ballet Russe. To Betty Marie's surprise, Ruth Tall Chief agreed to the plan. Perhaps she thought her daughter might be more willing to settle down to being a normal college girl if she understood firsthand how hard it was to succeed as a ballet dancer in New York.

Betty's first weeks in New York were as discouraging as Ruth Tall Chief might have wished. Day after day, Sergei Denham's secretary informed her coldly that Denham was too busy to see her. But Tanya and Madame Nijinska kept her spirits up. Tanya brought Betty Marie to rehearsals of the Ballet Russe and introduced her to various figures in the ballet world. One young dancer, Helen Kramer, was so open and warm to Betty Marie that the two became instant friends. Helen helped the newcomer to find a tiny room at a nearby hotel where many dancers stayed, and Betty Marie began to feel a little more at home in New York.

One night, Betty Marie and the Lichines were having dinner at the Russian Tea Room, a favorite gathering place for Europeans who had fled from a continent torn by depression and war. The many intellectuals, artists, and professionals who were coming to New York to build new lives brought with them a cultural strength and power this country had previously lacked. A few years earlier, it would have been unthinkable for New York to be the great center for ballet theater it was becoming now in the early 1940s, thanks to gifted European *émigrés*.

Amid the dark wood and red velvet of the restaurant, Tanya whispered to Betty Marie to look over at a nearby table. There with a party of friends sat George Balanchine, the brilliant Russian *émigré* who directed the School of American Ballet, where Betty had enrolled in classes until she could find a job. Balanchine! Everyone in the world of ballet seemed to love him or hate him. Some thought he was ruining ballet with his strange dances. Unlike *Swan Lake* or *Sleeping Beauty*, many of Balanchine's ballets told no story and were simply dancers moving to music. Other people thought he was pouring bold new life into an art form that had become too stuffy and rigid. People gossiped about Balanchine's reputation for training young ballerinas and then losing interest in them for newer, younger dancers once they were well-started on their careers. Already he had married two such women and trained many more, all known as "Balanchine's ballerinas." He insisted that the young women he trained put themselves utterly under his direction and do exactly as he told them. When he and his party got up to join the Lichines, Betty was surprised to see how short he was. But as he spoke with the others in Russian, his black eyes burned in a way that made her forget all about his height. She could not follow the conversation, but she knew that he was taking notice of her.

But Balanchine was not destined to enter Betty Marie's life just yet. Soon after the evening they met, she received a call from Sergei Denham. The Ballet Russe was about to go on tour in Canada, but because of wartime restrictions none of the company's dancers who held Russian citizenship were allowed to enter that country. Denham had to find substitutes quickly. Suddenly, Betty Marie found herself on a train speeding toward Ottawa for the opening engagement of the tour. She was very proud to be employed as a member of the Canadian touring troupe of the Ballet Russe de

Monte Carlo, even if it was mainly wartime regulations that got her the job.

Her elation was somewhat dimmed by the cold reception she got from many of the other dancers in the company. Several times Betty Marie was allowed to dance roles that ordinarily would have been saved for a more experienced dancer. She learned roles very quickly, so it made sense to substitute her if someone fell sick. But that explanation didn't suit the jealous dancers in the company. They could see that Betty Marie was Native American, and when they found she was Osage, they remembered the outrageous stories in the press about the "rich Indians" and the royalties the Osage people received from their oil rights. They began to whisper that her parents must have bought her a position with the Ballet Russe de Monte Carlo. It didn't help that Betty Marie was naturally reserved or that it took her a while to realize that ordinary company dancers all traveled in the coach car rather than in the more costly Pullman sleeper. The others mistook her shyness for snobbery, even after she began to ride in the coach cars along with them. Through it all, Helen Kramer remained her loyal friend. But the spiteful remarks and the long train rides across the chilly Canadian plains were hard on the young dancer who had grown up in friendly, sunny Los Angeles.

When the tour was over, Denham invited Betty Marie to join the Ballet Russe de Monte Carlo as a member of the *corps de ballet*, the group of dancers who dance supporting roles or form the background chorus. There was only one catch. Denham also asked her to change her name. Like most companies, the Ballet Russe wanted its dancers to have Russian-sounding names because Russia was the home of the Bolshoi Ballet, one of the most prestigious ballet companies in the world. Even if the dancers were really from Oklahoma or New Jersey, the Ballet Russe wanted to suggest that they were Russian with long years of Bolshoi training behind them. Many of the made-up names sounded rather silly. Poor Helen Kramer had to call herself Elena Kramarr. The company officials asked Betty Marie Tall Chief to become Maria Tallchieva. They believed this name would give her just the right touch of Russianized glamour.

But the young woman flatly refused. She had grown up a lot on the Canadian tour, and she was no longer the obedient little girl who would agree to do a fake Indian dance just to please her teacher. Though raised in Beverly Hills, far from Osage country, Betty Marie insisted on remaining recognizably Osage both onstage and off. She would not Russianize the proud Osage name of Tall Chief. Finally, she and the company officials compromised. She agreed to become Maria Tallchief, a name that would look slightly exotic on ballet programs but would not disguise her American Indian identity.

Maria worked very hard learning her roles in the classes she took as part of her work with the

Ballet Russe. On the side she also continued her
classes at Balanchine's School of American Ballet. Her commitment to her career was complete,
and as she aspired to becoming a *prima ballerina*,
she devoted extra time to learning all the roles
in the Ballet Russe's repertoire. She was soon
prepared to take over any solo part when the need
arose. That winter, the Ballet Russe put on *Rodeo*,
Agnes de Mille's lively ballet about the American
West set to the music of Aaron Copeland. Many
of the European dancers in the company were
scornful of this rip-roaring production. How
could a ballet have cowboys sashaying around
the stage swinging their lariats? Where was the
grace and dignity of "real" ballet? But Maria,
born in Oklahoma, thought *Rodeo* was a wonderful American ballet. She hung around in the
wings during rehearsal, admiring de Mille's direction. Noticing her interest, de Mille wrote a
tiny part into the ballet just for her. When the
Ballet Russe production of *Rodeo* opened on January 16, 1943, Maria flashed on stage for a few
moments as a flirty western belle. She swished
her long skirts and made eyes at the male lead,
the Champion Roper, a gawky cowboy who eagerly chased after her.

Maria enjoyed dancing in *Rodeo*. But during
that first year as a professional dancer in New
York, it seemed as if the one role she wanted most
was one she was not destined to win. The Ballet
Russe had announced that Madame Nijinska's
ballet choreographed to Chopin's Concerto in

E Flat would be among their upcoming offerings for the 1942–43 season. Madame herself was coming to New York to supervise the production. If only she could dance perfectly in that ballet, Maria thought, it would make up for the shame of her fall in the Hollywood Bowl, a shame she still felt keenly. But she was too inexperienced to be given such a big part here in New York. Three of the company's featured ballerinas were given the roles once danced by Maria, Marjorie, and Cyd Charisse.

Nonetheless, Tallchief attended the rehearsals as often as possible, studying the dancers' movements intently. Madame Nijinska had altered many of the steps since the piece had premiered that night in the Hollywood Bowl, and now Maria carefully memorized all the changes. If a chance came to substitute for someone, she wanted to be ready. Suddenly, on Christmas Day, Sergei Denham told Maria that on the following day she might have to take the place of Nathalie Krassnovska, one of the three principal dancers in *Concerto*.

On the day of the performance, coached by older dancers, Tallchief practiced to Chopin for hours and hours, breathing carefully to remain calm. She *knew* she could do it, even if the role she'd be dancing was the one Cyd had danced back at the Hollywood Bowl. Always, she had paid attention to everyone's part as well as her own. She remembered Cyd's steps from a few years ago, and she now had memorized the changes Madame Nijinska had made in the choreography. That evening, Helen Kramer and Ruthie Rickman, her closest friends in the corps, helped Tallchief to dress. They were surprised at how focused she seemed, not nervous exactly, just very intent and ready to do what she most wanted to do. Within minutes of curtain time, as Maria waited in the wings to make her entrance, Denham himself suddenly appeared and ordered her to change out of her costume. He said that Aleksandra Danilova, the prima ballerina of the ballet, felt Maria was simply not ready yet. One of the more experienced dancers would fill in for Krassnovska after all.

Somehow, Tallchief found herself back in her ordinary clothes, standing in the holiday streets of New York. All the stores shone with gold and silver, holly and ivy, and carols about joy and hope rang through crisp December air. She walked numbly back to her hotel room, past windows bright with Christmas trees and menorah candles. Soon she would appear in *Rodeo*, but nothing that night mattered so much as the last-minute crushing of her dream to right an old mistake by dancing a perfect *Concerto*.

As soon as people heard what had happened to Tallchief, excited rumors swirled around the Russian Tea Room and the rehearsal stages of New York. Everyone knew that Nathalie Krassnovska was not getting along with Denham and the Ballet Russe. Some people said that by threatening to replace her with a humble member of the corps

de ballet, Denham was saying to Krassnovska
that she was no better than an inexperienced
newcomer. Others guessed that Denham had
really wanted Maria to fill in, but Aleksandra
Danilova thought Maria Tallchief was such a brilliant young dancer that she was secretly afraid
to appear on the same stage with her. Danilova
herself took Maria aside and insisted that she simply thought Maria was not quite ready for such
a big New York role, and it would have been hard
for both the company and Maria's career if she
had not danced well.

Tallchief did not really know what to make of
all the politics and gossip. She just knew she felt
as though she wasn't getting very far, and she
was feeling lonely and ill. All that late winter and
spring of 1943, she had a terrible cough that
wouldn't go away, and she was losing weight. She
kept dancing the small parts given to her, though
her mother was urging her to come back to Los
Angeles, where Marjorie was happily dating Maria's old boy friend Dave and dancing for the Los
Angeles Light Opera Company. But Tallchief
stubbornly hung on. She wouldn't settle for anything less than a real ballet company, hard as her
life seemed right now. Finally, on the first day of
May, 1943, while the company was on tour in
Philadelphia, her chance came again. Krassnovska hurt her foot and could not dance *en pointe*,
and Tallchief was told to prepare for the role. Ill
as she was, she was fearful that this time she
might be too dizzy and weak to dance the role.

But as she waited in the wings, she felt suddenly well and strong. She leaped onto the stage at her cue and danced, and when the last bars of the Chopin sounded, the applause and bravos thundered over her. The star, Aleksandra Danilova, stood aside to let Maria take a bow on her own. Denham told her the role was hers until Krassnovska's foot could heal, though Krassnovska's name, not Maria's, remained on the program. Maria didn't care. Getting to dance the part was all that mattered.

The Ballet Russe, ever on the alert for opportunities to publicize their exotic glamour, gave out press releases highlighting the new young soloist in the Nijinska ballet as "the beautiful dancing Osage." Tallchief wasn't happy with this. She was distressed to see her nationality exploited for publicity purposes. It seemed to her to be very undignified. She was repeatedly upset by journalists' requests for stories about growing up "Indian," and she couldn't come up with any of the sort they wanted to hear. Although she was certainly Osage, she and Marjorie had not worn buckskins and moccasins or learned traditional Osage dances. They did not even speak the Osage language at home. Her father didn't hunt with bow and arrow; he managed his investments and played golf in Beverly Hills! But this did not mean that Maria and Marjorie were non-Indian. Indeed, their experience was more common among Native peoples during the era of the Great Depression and the Second World War than at any other time in this century. Encouraged and compelled by the government, it was a period when more and more Native people were beginning to adopt white ways — to live off the reservations, to attend white schools, to speak, read, and write only English, to dress in Anglo-American styles. However they lived, the Tall Chiefs were of Osage blood, and they had Osage pride and Osage honesty. Tallchief would not make up stories about tepees and feather headdresses just to please reporters.

The wonderful ability Tallchief demonstrated as a soloist, and the publicity she had gained, brought her once again to the attention of George Balanchine. In 1944 he accepted the Ballet Russe's offer to become their choreographer and dance director. Tallchief became his student, and he her delighted mentor. He was very taken with the long-legged, olive-skinned, lustrously beautiful young dancer. To his eyes her facial structure, with its high cheekbones and almost slanted eyes, was strongly reminiscent of the beautiful ballerinas of his homeland, Russia. He was fascinated by her Native American heritage and began to learn all he could about Native people.

At the Ballet Russe, Balanchine delighted in choreographing ballets in which Tallchief danced more and more important roles. He was as impressed with her willingness to practice long hours and to follow his instructions diligently as he was by her talent, youth, and beauty. As a teacher, he was fiercely demanding. No dancer was to vary in the least from his instructions. It sounds as though dancing under Balanchine would be a confining, oppressive task, but Maria Tallchief, like many of Balanchine's other ballerinas, has always insisted that it was not. With him as a teacher, she felt instead very creative and challenged to follow his directions perfectly. Sometimes, when he demonstrated for her just how a certain movement should look, she would sigh and think that she herself could never make that movement look so beautiful. But he inspired her to work harder than she ever had in her life, and she knew her dancing was gaining in depth. An added happiness in that year of 1944 was that Marjorie Tallchief came to New York to dance with the Ballet Russe's rival company, the exciting new Ballet Theatre. Maria loved having her sister close by. Still, she was a little dismayed to see how Marjorie was instantly given the sorts of roles that she herself had had to wait so patiently for in the more conservative — some said stodgier — Ballet Russe.

Balanchine was waking up the Ballet Russe, demanding the absolute best from his dancers. The first big part he gave Maria was in *Ballet Imperial*, danced to the music of Tchaikovsky's Piano Concerto Number 2 in G, a piece she knew well from the days of piano practice. Loving the music, she was sure she could do well in the part. Perhaps she overpracticed, or was nervous about her first major role for the master. For whatever reason, she was not brilliant in the role, and the papers paid no attention to her performance. Instead, they praised another young Balanchine dancer, Mary Ellen Moylan. Tallchief was crushed, but Balanchine did not lose faith in her. Right away, he gave her a part in *Les Sylphides*, a one-act ballet where graceful sylphs dance in the moonlight to the music of Chopin. This time, everyone noticed Maria. One reviewer wrote, "The Ballet Russe's Tallchief danced with such rapture we worry only that she will fail to show us the same sublimity again." That made Maria a little nervous, but Balanchine just laughed. He had only begun to work with Tallchief, and he knew that many more triumphs lay ahead of them.

Tallchief, under Balanchine's direction, received rave reviews again for her lead performances in *Danses Concertantes* in 1944 and in *La Somnambula*, known in English as *Night Shadow*, in 1946. That same year she danced in her most elaborate and difficult part yet in a Balanchine production. The ballet was *Le Baiser de la Fée*, or *The Kiss of the Fairy*, based on a story by the Danish folklorist Hans Christian Andersen and set to the music of the modern composer Igor Stravinsky. Maria was to play the Ice Fairy who finds a baby boy lost in a storm. The Ice Fairy kisses the freezing child, and though the kiss revives him, it binds him to her forever. Peasants bring him up, and when he is a man he is betrothed to a pretty village girl. While he is celebrating his coming wedding at a dance at an old mill, the Ice Fairy enters disguised as a wild Gypsy fortune-teller. She leads him away from the crowd and tempts him to make love to her, then sends him back to his bride-to-be. After the wedding, as the bride and groom share their first dance as a married couple, a mysterious second bride appears dressed in black. It is the Ice Fairy, once again in disguise, who claims the young man and carries him off forever to her frozen realm. The tricky part of the role is that the dancer must appear not only as the Ice Fairy herself, but also in her disguises as the Gypsy woman and the mysterious dark bride, and she must be able to convey to the audience that she is the Ice Fairy all along.

Marie Tallchief was spectacular in this triple role. One young reviewer named Robert Garis wrote, "The Gypsy moves in the quiet of evil, circles throbbingly about the bridegroom, hushes the whole stage with the curious lift of her arms and the sway of her body. . . . The young man has come, under some evil compulsion, into another world, a tight breathless world, which closes in a circle about him, in the Gypsy's movements, until she pounces on his hand." A half century later, Garis still remembers how "riveting" Maria was in the performance. It proved that she was more than a fine technician, that she could do more than dance the pretty roles of graceful sylph or spirited cancan dancer. She could convey the power of evil just through movement. She was a great dramatic dancer.

The Tallchief-Balanchine collaboration was
working very well indeed. As she danced the roles
he designed for her, his work gained wider attention. By now, Balanchine had been divorced by
his third wife, the ballerina Vera Zorina. Tallchief
was in awe of Balanchine, but she thought he
often seemed sad, and she felt sorry for his pain.
They began spending more time together outside
of rehearsals. In quiet moments, they shared their
love of music. Balanchine knew well that not very
many dancers truly understand the music they
perform to, but Maria had long training as a pi-
anist, and she had suffered much in her teens
trying to decide whether she most wanted to be
a musician or a dancer. Together the two could
often be found at the Russian Tea Room or the
Sixth Avenue Delicatessen excitedly talking over
a score spread out on the table. They discovered
they enjoyed playing four-handed duets on the
piano together. And always, they worked together
as teacher and pupil, refining Tallchief's skills.

That July of 1946, Ballanchine suddenly announced he was leaving the Ballet Russe to form
a new company, Ballet Society, with his old
friend Lincoln Kirstein. At nearly the same time,
much to the surprise of the 21-year-old Maria, the
42-year-old Balanchine asked her to marry him.
Though she thought he was wonderful, and listened intently to his every word, it had somehow
never occurred to her that he loved her. Despite
her surprise, she accepted his offer. How could
she say no to the man whose every direction she

had come to obey? Maria Tallchief and George
Balanchine were married August 16, 1946.

Thinking back on it all in 1989, Tallchief
mused, "When we were married it was almost
really like I was the material he wanted to use."
Balanchine was starting a new company, and a
wife who was a premiere dancer could eventually
be one of its featured dancers. Balanchine was
building his own career as Tallchief was building
hers, though at a much more complex level. He
aspired to head a major *avant-garde* dance company that could compete with top dance companies such as the Ballet Theater and the Ballet
Russe, whose reputation had lured him away
from his own School of American Ballet two years
before. He had a strong vision of a new kind of
ballet theater, one in which the outer limits of
ballet could be explored. The Ballet Society he
founded with Kirstein did not seek a large popular audience who wanted to see again and again
only the old romantic ballets like *Swan Lake* and
The Nutcracker. Instead, the Ballet Society was
designed to attract a small group of artists and
intellectuals who were eager to see the newest in
ballet. At the Ballet Society, people couldn't just
decide at the last minute that they'd like to catch
a ballet on Friday night; instead, they had to sub-
scribe ahead of time for season tickets.

After Tallchief married Balanchine, many in
the dance world guessed that she would immediately break her contract with the Ballet Russe
to join her husband's company. But both of Ma-

ria's parents had taught her never to go back on her word. She served out the year left of her contract, even though everyone in the company knew she would soon be leaving, and that meant she probably would not get many good roles. In fact, the company realized that she was such a big attraction that she got to dance a great deal in that year.

Being married to George Balanchine was not just a long round of being told what to do. Years after their marriage, Tallchief spoke of how generous Balanchine had been about doing housework and cooking meals after they came home together from exhausting rehearsals. Though Balanchine over his lifetime would have five ballerina wives, all of them praised him as a teacher even after their marriages to him were over, affectionately calling him "Mr. B." and continuing to attend his classes. The ballerina Felia Doubrovska remembered walking into a room at Balanchine's School of American Ballet and seeing all of Balanchine's wives, including Tallchief, quietly waiting together for class to begin.

In the spring of 1947, Balanchine went to France to guest-direct the Paris Opera for a season. In May, when Tallchief also joined the company as a guest artist, she became the first American dancer to perform with that company in 108 years. The Parisian audiences applauded her wildly when she danced the role of the Ice Fairy before them. French reviewers were intrigued with her Native American background, and like the American press they were eager to invent a romantic wild Indian childhood for her. She got her great elegance and dignity, they claimed, from being an "Indian princess," a title that Europeans found particularly appealing. Tallchief knew well that Native American tribes did not have royal families the way European nations did, and the phony title upset her.

Ironically, other French critics and reviewers were unwilling to admit that an American of any heritage was up to performing on the stage of the Paris Opera. No mere American could dance as elegantly as Maria Tallchief, they insisted. They started the rumor that she was secretly Russian and French, and they claimed she had changed her Russian name to one that would sound romantically Native American! Marjorie Tallchief was also living in France now. With her new husband, the dancer George Skibine, she had joined a company in the south of France. Together, the sisters shook their heads at the way the press could turn the truth inside out so thoughtlessly.

When she returned to the States, Tallchief joined her husband's Ballet Society, which soon changed its name to the New York City Ballet. Many of her fans were astonished that she would give up her brilliant career with the Ballet Russe to go with a tiny, experimental company. But Maria Tallchief was now channeling all her energy into becoming her husband's lead dancer. He was simply the most brilliant choreographer and teacher of his time, and wherever Balanchine was, that was where the most exciting things in dance were happening. "I was in the right place and I knew it," she has said, recalling her decision.

Soon enough Tallchief was the *prima ballerina* of the New York City Ballet Company, and her husband created roles for her that left the dance world stunned with her great versatility and excellence. Her performances in three postwar productions, *The Four Temperaments*, produced in 1946, *Symphonie Concertante*, produced in 1947, and *Orpheus*, produced in 1948, drew rave reviews from dance critics who wrote for major papers.

In 1949, Balanchine decided to create his own production of *The Firebird* to showcase his wife. *The Firebird* is based on an old Russian folktale. Prince Ivan strays from his hunting party and finds himself in a clearing in a mysterious forest where he captures the dazzling Firebird. Begging him to let her go, the Firebird gives Ivan a single feather he can use to summon her if he is ever in danger. Sure enough, he soon calls on her to help him defeat a wicked sorcerer and rescue a princess.

Balanchine scrapped all Mikhail Fokine's 1910 choreography of the ballet and designed his own around Tallchief's special strengths. From another company, he bought the darkly mysterious forest backdrops and the costumes designed by artist Marc Chagall for an earlier production. He supervised even the smallest detail of this ballet.

Balanchine designed the role in four days, but it took Tallchief weeks to master it. Balanchine had a penchant for inventing fast, intricate routines that were far more demanding than more traditional modes. For the role of the Firebird, Maria would need to seem as if she were truly a winged creature. She must be at once beautiful and unearthly, full of magical power as she danced to the swooping dramatic modern music of Igor Stravinsky.

Balanchine's *The Firebird* premiered on November 27, 1949. Tallchief's performance stunned the audience. Fifty years later, critic Robert Garis recalls, "I have a treasury of memories of her Firebird: the silky sinuosity of her beautiful legs and knees in the first *pas de deux*, when she has been caught by the Prince and is stretching voluptuously under his care, the power and speed of her pirouettes as she flashes in bearing a sword to help him fight the Katschei." Many think that the moment when Tallchief's golden-red Firebird first soared across the stage in a fierce blaze of energy was the moment when New York became the world center of ballet. Maria Tallchief was now established as a *prima ballerina* of international stature.

But life with Balanchine was getting very difficult, and Tallchief was growing exhausted trying to please him. He was an extremely demanding taskmaster, creating dance routines that were more and more complicated and insisting they be danced with greater and greater speed. As *prima ballerina* and Balanchine's wife, Maria Tallchief was expected to perform these extremely challenging routines flawlessly because it was she who set the example for the entire company. Her performance began to suffer under the pressure, and she received ever more disappointing reviews. The critics were not at all impressed with her performance in two new ballets that she danced in 1950. In *The Prodigal Son*, she portrayed a seductive siren, and in *Jones Beach*, a saucy teenage beach bunny. Her cool proud elegance was simply not suited for either role. To the reviewers and her audiences, she seemed to be losing the vitality that had caused her to catapult to international fame.

Even more discouraging to Tallchief was the way Balanchine was starting to give more and more of his time and attention to newer, younger dancers instead of to her. She was barely 25, but already her husband seemed to find her too old to be really exciting to him. At her request, their marriage was annulled in 1951. She put forth as her main reason for annulment Balanchine's refusal to have children. He did not even like his dancers to get married, unless they married him, and he thought having babies ruined a dancer's figure and took her mind away from dance. Tallchief, who came from a happy home, found herself thinking more and more about having a real family.

Although they were no longer married, Balanchine and Tallchief continued their professional association. With the strain of the marriage in the past, her career picked up as the New York City Ballet grew in prominence in ballet circles. In quick succession in 1952 she danced *Serenade* and *Scotch Symphony*, new roles Balanchine created for her, and in 1951 and 1954 she danced roles she had thought as a teenager she would never dance: the role of Odette in *Swan Lake* and the role of the Sugarplum Fairy in *The Nutcracker*. Once, she had thought no one would ever tolerate a dark-haired, dark-skinned woman as the gleaming swan-princess or the shimmering fairy. Now she danced both roles easily. In the years since her breakup with Balanchine, she had developed an authority and presence that came with maturity. She was no longer just the creation of her choreographer husband; she was her own strong woman.

In 1953 Tallchief received special tribute from her native state of Oklahoma, when the governor declared June 29 Maria Tallchief Day. At the same time, the Osage Tribal Council honored her in a ceremony they staged at Fairfax, her childhood home, where Alexander and Ruth Tall Chief had returned to live. For the occasion, the Council dressed Maria Tallchief in traditional Osage garments and placed a crown of exquisite beadwork done in traditional Osage design on her shining black hair. Memories of her early years attending ceremonies with Eliza Tall Chief washed over her as tribal members danced Osage dances, made speeches, and sang Osage songs. They served

wonderful Indian foods like corn soup, beef stew,
fry bread, and persimmon cakes.

The high point of the celebration for Maria
came in her father's own Tall Chief Theater,
where she was given an Osage honor name. It had
been carefully chosen by her grandmother Eliza.
The name was supposed to say something important about Maria. It would announce to the
Osage world what kind of person her granddaughter had grown up to be. Tallchief's new
name, Wa-Xthe-Tohnba, means Woman of Two
Standards, or Woman of Two Worlds. The name
told people that Maria and her achievements belonged to two worlds, the Osage and the white.
When she received her name everyone cheered
and applauded. Maria Tallchief had come home.
No honor ever would mean more to her.

In 1955 Maria Tallchief once again toured Europe. The Ballet Russe wanted her to rejoin their
company and head a European tour they were
planning. They felt they needed her international
reputation to help them make the tour a rousing
success. The Ballet Russe had wanted her participation on their European tour so urgently that
they paid her handsomely. With her salary ru-
mored to be $2,000 a week — the equivalent of
$10,000 or more in the 1990s — the October 11,
1954, issue of *Newsweek* reported her to be the
highest-paid ballerina in the world. As the Ballet
Russe foresaw, Tallchief was a top draw at the
box office. She was acknowledged to be the only
living American dancer who could match or best

the great ballerinas of Europe and Russia.

Despite her lengthy participation in the tour, she was injured often that season. Her expectations as a dancer were often hard to live up to as well, so although the money was excellent, other considerations weighed heavily on her. She left the Ballet Russe and went home to New York. There she rejoined the New York City Ballet. She was to stay with Balanchine's company as its most prominent dancer until she retired.

Tallchief had made a brief marriage to the handsome charter pilot Elmourza Natirboff in the early 1950s. That ended when Natirboff insisted she choose between him and her career. Maria Tallchief had been deeply shaken by the failure of her second marriage. Perhaps love and family were just not her destiny. But in 1956, at the age of 31, Tallchief made a third marriage to handsome, genial Henry "Buzz" Paschen, Jr., a man not unlike her own father. She moved to Chicago, where her husband was an executive in a construction company. Paschen did not insist that his wife leave ballet behind for him. He understood that her decisions must be her own.

For several years Tallchief continued her work with the New York City Ballet, regularly making the long commute from Chicago to New York. By the time their daughter Elisa Maria was born in 1959, the journey was becoming increasingly difficult. In 1965 Maria Tallchief retired, desiring to be free of the onerous commute. For nearly thirty-five years, dance had been the center of her life.

Now she planned to devote her energy to her family and her life in Chicago.

But for all her devotion to her family, Maria Tallchief did not just disappear from public life. Her naming ceremony had sharpened her interest in her own Osage heritage. In 1967 an American Indian organization, the Council of Fire, awarded her their Indian Achievement award and invited her to serve as a member of the council. She accepted their offer and traveled to address different American Indian groups and university audiences about Native Americans and the arts.

Tallchief has maintained her involvement in the dance world as well. Although she had hung up her dance slippers permanently and would never again appear as a dancer, she said yes when the newly developed Lyric Opera Ballet in Chicago asked her if she would coach their players how to enter and exit the stage gracefully. That simple task reawakened her interest in the ballet and led to the formation of her own company. By the mid 1970s, her Ballet School of the Lyric Opera had its own dance troupe and was touring the Midwest. In 1980, Tallchief ended her involvement with the Lyric Opera, and, encouraged by an aging Balanchine, she and her sister Marjorie formed the Chicago City Ballet, affiliated with Balanchine's School of American Ballet.

During the years that Maria Tallchief was mostly dancing and working in New York and touring Europe occasionally. Marjorie Tallchief had also enjoyed a distinguished career in ballet, mainly with European companies. Now middle-aged, the sisters put their considerable expertise to work as teachers and directors. George Balanchine's methods were so exacting that many companies were redesigning Balanchine's routines, eliminating difficult steps to make the role more easily danced. Maria Tallchief scorned such shortcuts and encouraged her young dancers to learn the proper Balanchine technique.

Like many arts organizations in the eighties and nineties, the Chicago City Ballet closed down by 1989 for lack of funding. Despite her forced departure from the teaching and directing side of ballet, Maria Tallchief goes on making her unique contributions to her beloved dance. Since Balanchine's death in 1983, she remains one of the world's leading authorities on the pure Balanchine technique. She has been a major model for Native American youth and an important source of information about Native Americans as well as the dance, for all Americans. Her beauty, talent, dedication, and achievement have combined to make her one of the most loved and renowned American Indian women of the century. Maria Tallchief continues to be Woman of Two Worlds, Wa-Xthe-Tohnba.

6
Senator Ben Nighthorse Campbell

The theme of the Tournament of Roses Parade for New Year's Day of 1992 was "Voyages of Discovery," in commemoration of the five-hundredth anniversary of a sailor named Cristóbal Colón — Christopher Columbus, as he is called in English — stepping ashore on an island in the Caribbean. That quincentennial year, Congressman Ben Nighthorse Campbell of Colorado, a descendant of Cheyenne Native Americans and Portuguese-Americans, was the co-grand marshal of the parade. The congressman was resplendent in traditional buckskins trimmed with handsomely designed turquoise, red, white, and deep yellow beadwork. Riding astride his beloved black-and-white paint horse, Black Warbonnet, the Cheyenne congressman wore beaded buckskin gloves and carried the beautiful ornamental lance he had made himself.

A long trailer of beaded leather streamed from either side of his eagle feather headdress. Each trailer bore thirty-six golden eagle feathers, representing the congressman's seventy-two victories in international judo competitions as a young man.

Congressman Campbell shared the honor of being grand marshal with Cristóbal Colón, the Duke of Veragua, Spain, a direct decendant of the original Cristóbal Colón. Though both were grand marshals, Campbell rode horseback through Pasadena at the very head of the parade, some distance ahead of the open carriage bearing Colón and his family. Campbell led the way to symbolize that Native Americans were here in the Western Hemisphere long before Europeans.

A little over a year later in Washington, D.C., Ben Nighthorse Campbell, now the junior senator from Colorado, would once again dress in his traditional Cheyenne outfit and ride Black Warbonnet in an important parade to mark the inauguration of President Bill Clinton. For many observers, the most significant thing about both parades was Campbell's very presence. When they first planned their celebration, none of the Tournament of Roses officials had thought to pay tribute to the Native Americans who were here long before Columbus, or to acknowledge that great harm came to Native Americans because of Columbus. But in the Clinton inaugural parade in January of 1993, Ben Nighthorse Campbell rode down Pennsylvania Avenue as one of the few

Native American senators in United States history, and the only one ever to identify himself proudly as an American Indian.

The path Ben Nighthorse Campbell took from his birth to the United States Congress was long and difficult. He was the son of an alcoholic and sometimes abusive father and a mother who was brave and loving, but sometimes too ill with tuberculosis to care for Ben and his sister. His courage, sociability, and creativity turned Campbell away from what could easily have been an early death from alcohol, drug addiction, or suicide. With the help of his mother and certain special teachers who came his way, the young man reached out toward a life in which he could provide leadership, vision, and service to many groups in the American community who are often ignored, particularly those whose childhoods were as difficult as his.

Campbell worked very hard to develop many of his most valuable character traits, but he may have inherited them as well. One remarkable ancestor was his father's grandfather, a Southern Cheyenne named Black Horse, who spent his young manhood fighting for his people's survival during the final, devastating years of the American war against Native Americans.

On June 25, 1876, Black Horse was among the thousands of Sioux, Arapaho, and Cheyenne Indians who were encamped with Sitting Bull along the Greasy Grass, the meandering river white Americans called the Little Big Horn. A few days before, they had fought a battle with General Crook's soldiers and successfully turned them back. Now they were at rest, digging wild turnips and letting their horses graze on the lush grass of early summer. Some hunted antelope on the rolling plain or swam and splashed in the cool river in the shade of cottonwoods. They were steadily fighting off the U.S. Army, but on this day it seems that no one expected a battle. Then people began to shout and point to the clouds of dust rising in the distance. Soldiers, bluecoats! How could one detachment of cavalry think of charging this gathering of so many warriors?

Under the heedless leadership of General George Armstrong Custer, the United States Seventh Cavalry blundered into the huge, very surprised Indian encampment. No one knows the numbers exactly, but at the Little Big Horn there were probably about 210 U.S. soldiers under Custer attempting to attack a village of almost 2,000 fighting men. The Indians scrambled to get the women, children, and elderly out of the way and snatched up bows, arrows, and lances. Within less than half an hour, the Seventh Cavalry was wiped out. In the eerie silence that followed, a single army horse stood shivering on the battlefield.

Sitting Bull and his combined armies had won the battle, but their swift unexpected victory that June afternoon was to prove costly for all Indian people. News of Custer's defeat reached people back East early in July of 1876, just as the United

States was proudly celebrating its first hundred years since the signing of the Declaration of Independence. Many white people were furious. They called for harsher military action against the Indians of the plains. Within fifteen years, all Indians in the United States had been forced to live on reservations.

Black Horse continued to fight to keep his people from being sent to reservations in Indian Territory, in what is now Oklahoma. In 1879, the Northern Cheyenne were at last granted permission to settle in Montana, amid the rolling northern hills they loved.

It wasn't until he was a grown man of thirty-five that Ben Nighthorse Campbell learned the story of this brave great-grandfather or began to piece together the full story of his Cheyenne heritage. His own father, Albert Valdez Campbell, the grandson of Black Horse, mostly chose to renounce his own Indian identity, and Ben Campbell grew up far removed from the supportive Native family and community he would discover later in life. Albert Campbell was not one to talk very much about the past. He was born in Pagosa Springs, Colorado about 1901. He would sometimes admit he was part Cheyenne Indian and he said that when his mother died he ran away and lived for a while in Montana on the Lame Deer Reservation with relatives named Black Horse. But he told his children not to talk about being Indian. That was something it was just better to forget. For the most part, Albert Campbell's early life was a mystery to his own wife and children.

Documented knowledge of him starts with his army records. At the age of 18, Albert Valdez Campbell enlisted in the U.S. Army in Sheridan, Wyoming and served overseas for three years in China. He was honorably discharged in August of 1922. His discharge papers describe him as a man of good character, but he was already a very heavy drinker. Albert soon found his way to California, where he was employed as an orderly at the Weimar Joint Tubercular Sanitorium in the wooded foothills of the Sierra Nevada mountains east of Sacramento.

At Weimar Sanitorium, Albert Campbell met Mary Vierra, born in 1898 in the Azores Islands off the coast of Portugal. By the time she was 19, Mary was a tuberculosis patient at Weimar. For twenty-two years she would mostly live in and around the sanitorium, sometimes as a maid or an orderly, sometimes as a patient herself whenever her illness worsened. Mary Vierra and Albert Campbell were married in August, 1929 after a few years of courtship. Their daughter Alberta was born on her father's birthday, July 12, 1930, and their son Ben on April 13, 1933. Both children were baptized in their parents' Roman Catholic faith.

Mary Vierra Campbell was as resourceful and courageous as any warrior. She found ways to feed, clothe, and educate Alberta and Ben despite illness, poverty, and marriage to an alcoholic husband who was often absent from home. Sometimes Mrs. Campbell was too ill to take care of Ben and his big sister Alberta, though with advice and help from Catholic charities and the directors of the sanitorium, she managed to keep the family intact during their early years. Sometimes the children lived with her in the sanitorium while she was hospitalized. In 1939, Albert was jailed for drunkenness and failure to support his children, and Mary was again very ill with tuberculosis. This time, she was forced to leave Alberta and Ben at St. Patrick's Home, an orphanage in Sacramento. The orphanage had separate quarters for boys and girls, and the children were mostly separated from one another. Being apart from her mother and brother at such an early age was harder on Alberta than on her more outgoing younger brother. She and Ben never regained the close companionship they had enjoyed before being sent to St. Patrick's.

The family was reunited in the 1940s, but their life remained difficult. Albert was still drinking heavily, and all too often Alberta and Ben were sent out to find their father. They would venture into Sacramento's skid row to look for him, turning over the bodies of unconscious drunken men until they saw their father's face. Things weren't good when Albert was home, either. On several occasions Ben's father struck his mother while the children were watching. At one point when things got very bad, the Campbells separated.

Later, because she was a strong Catholic and deeply committed to the sanctity of marriage, Mary took Albert back.

In spite of poor health and her problems with her husband, Mrs. Campbell opened a small market and diner in her cabin while her children were still young. With the help of her brother Frank and eventually Albert, who began at last to cut back on his drinking, Mrs. Campbell's little business actually began to bring in a bit of money. Eventually, a new highway was routed right past their place, and then the Campbell business really began to thrive.

From the time Ben was 12 or so, he earned money doing odd jobs. Living in an area where farming was a major source of income, young Ben picked fruit and worked at the pack sheds. In high school, Ben and his part-Sioux friend Noel Burgan would hop a local freight train and ride atop the boxcars to Truckee, a logging town farther up in the Sierras. Burgan, now a horse wrangler in Nevada, still remembers the danger and beauty of the first of those stolen rides:

You have never seen a moonrise until you have watched it from the top of a boxcar overlooking Donner Lake. As the moon came up, it lit the tops of the pine trees and made the tracks behind us look like two ribbons of quicksilver. God meant for us to see it, and seeing it the first time is something that comes around only once in life. Ben and I took many freight rides together, but that first one was the best.

Around Truckee the boys worked with loggers, who helped them to find summer jobs in the saw-mills. During the holidays they would cut trees for a local Christmas tree lot.

Ben was always conscious of his Indian blood and tried hard to find ways to express his Indian identity. With two other boys, Lowell Heimbach and Cyril Daniels, he formed a club, the Black Knights. Ben made them all bows and arrows and beaded quivers for the arrows. Cyril Daniels says the bows Ben made were "no toys," but real weapons able to bring down a deer.

Once, the Black Knights ran away from home and lived in the woods not far from their parents' houses for about a week. Ben kept a diary of their adventures. The diary shows a good sense of narrative and drama, and gives the reader some idea of the boy's closeness to the natural world:

Found the camp safe on our return and then had a very large breakfast. After that we washed dishes and started for the American River. On the way down we saw a water snake, two hawks, numerous frogs and fish. In one place we found one of the most buetiful [sic] water falls we had ever seen, and a cave not far from it . . .

Despite his dislike of school, the fact that Ben kept a journal of their adventure shows that there was something different about this frequent runaway and eventual dropout. In the woods and fields, and in the quiet places of his own thoughts, Ben found strength.

Growing up in a family in such turmoil seemed to be too much for sensitive, shy Alberta, who got pregnant and ran away to marry before graduating from high school. Marriage and the birth of a son did not bring her security. The early hardships of her life seem to have permanently marked her, and there was little chance of someone like Alberta getting counseling in those days. As she drifted through life, she would send wistful greeting cards to her parents, saying she loved them, regretting she had no money to buy them presents. She remained troubled until she died in her early forties from a combination of alcohol and sleeping pills. Her brother Ben thinks her death was not accidental. She had attempted to kill herself several times before.

Unlike Alberta, Ben was a fighter and a survivor. However, he too wanted to be free of school and home. Ben took the route of many young men, including his father, and joined the armed forces. It was probably a timely decision, for Ben was hanging out with a rough crowd and beginning to get into trouble for "borrowing" cars and stealing gasoline. He even did a little time in jail. The Air Force would give him a structured, purposeful life.

While he was in the service he earned his general equivalency diploma. The GED certified that though he had dropped out, he had studied enough on his own to pass tests in all the required high school subjects. But Ben Campbell did not officially receive a high school diploma until he was a United States congressman. When he asked if he might march in the graduation procession with the class of 1991 at his old high school, they agreed, provided he would be their commencement speaker.

In the Air Force, Campbell asked to be assigned to the Air Police because he knew part of the training involved judo, which had become one of his favorite sports. He had discovered judo in high school when he got into a scuffle with a young Japanese-American co-worker at a local fruit packaging plant. Campbell threw a punch at the much smaller boy and somehow, without knowing what happened, he found himself flat on his back. The two boys soon became friends, and Campbell set out to learn all he could about judo.

At the time of his Air Force enlistment, the Korean War was on and Campbell hoped to be sent to some base in Asia, where he might learn more about martial arts. By that time, he was beginning to see that judo wasn't just a matter of finding a more efficient method of beating up other boys. Campbell had begun to see in judo the ideals of physical and spiritual discipline. He began to understand the connections between his mind and his body, and to appreciate how single-

minded concentration on a task could leave him
feeling clean and clear and energized. In 1952,
just as he had hoped, he was stationed in Pusan,
Korea. Every spare minute when he was off-duty,
he studied with the judo master Dr. Chang Han
Ju and his brother Chang Han Sin, finally earning
a diploma and a brown belt in the sport.

After he was discharged, Ben Campbell attended college, choosing California's San José
State University, which had a reputation for its
fine judo program. His coach and teammates describe him as a perfectionist who worked hard
and demonstrated enormous discipline, concentration, and devotion to his sport.

He graduated from San José State in 1958 but
stayed on to get a master's degree in physical
education and to continue refining his technique.
His dream was to represent the United States at
the 1964 Olympics in Tokyo. During that time,
he supported himself by teaching physical education in the San José school system.

In order to pursue his goal, he moved to Japan
in the early 1960s, where he enrolled at Meiji
University in Tokyo. That made it possible for
him to train with some of the greatest judo champions in the world. The judo coaches at Meiji
University were hard taskmasters. They believed
that success at judo required developing the skill
of persistence. Their students learned not to give
up, no matter what. That was a skill that Campbell's great-grandfather, Black Horse, and his
mother, Mary, had both developed, and Campbell

found a challenging modern way to follow their path. It would take him as far as their persistence had taken them, though in a more public direction.

In 1964, Campbell was in the parade of champions that kicks off every Olympics. By then he had become the first American to complete the demanding Meiji judo program and had subsequently earned a seventh-degree black belt in the sport. As Campbell vividly remembers, "The training was absolutely brutal. My nose was broken a couple of times, I lost two teeth, and I guess I broke or dislocated virtually every finger and toe I've got and suffered any number of bruises, contusions, and swollen ears." Campbell eked out a living by teaching English and taking bit parts playing in Japanese movies. In 1963 he bested the captain of the Meiji team to win a gold medal at the Pan-American games.

Campbell was all set to acquit himself with valor at the Tokyo games, but he suffered an injury to his knee during the pre-Olympic training. There wasn't enough time before the Olympics to let the knee heal properly. His U.S. teammates worried for him. The four had become very closely bonded. The 1964 U.S. judo team was made up of Ben Campbell, the descendant of Portuguese and Cherokees; George Harris, a towering African-American serving in the Air Force; Paul Maruyama, a Japanese-American who'd grown up in California; and Jimmie Bregman, a Jew from Virginia who'd discovered the sport as therapy for his childhood asthma. Of course all had been chosen for their athletic ability, but it seemed to the team themselves that they symbolized the diversity of the United States. They all remember to this day the German newsman sent to photograph them who looked at the grinning young men in puzzlement and asked, *"Ja, gut* [Yes, okay], but where are the Americans?"

Ben Campbell was a contestant despite the injury and faced the formidable Klaus Glahn of Germany in the second bout. During the competition his bad knee gave out, forcing him to forfeit the match. As he lay on the mat, knowing he was out of the competition, he wept, and his Japanese and American supporters in the stands wept with him. Phil Porter, one of Campbell's friends from the States, sat ringside with several Japanese friends as he covered the games for a judo magazine. He recalls, "Oh, God, there we were, with tears streaming down our faces, just gritting our teeth, knowing that a great career had come to an end."

Campbell would say later that he could not have won the gold against Klaus Glahn, whose height gave him a much greater reach than Campbell's. Still, he remains sure that he could have won a silver had he not been injured before the competition. Given his indomitable tenacity, he's probably right.

In spite of his pain, Campbell represented the United States in the closing ceremonies, carrying the United States flag from the arena. He recalls now, "My knee hurt like hell, but I was not about to let someone else carry that flag." This procession would not be Ben Campbell's last parade, though the young athlete didn't know it at the time. Later, as a United States senator, he would credit his judo years with developing his inner strength and will to succeed.

Campbell's judo career didn't end in Tokyo. When he returned to California to resume teaching, he was determined to make judo a major sport in the United States. He landed a teaching position in physical education for the San Juan Unified School District, located near Sacramento, California. That enabled him to pursue his new goal. He taught judo for eight more years, making Sacramento the nation's leading judo center. During that time, he published a book entitled *Championship Judo: Drill Training* in which he outlined his innovative training methods that gave Sacramento its leading edge in the sport. He also established a summer judo camp in Squaw Valley, California, and a number of his students gained junior- and senior-collegiate judo gold medals. He formally ended his judo career in 1972, bestowing upon the nation three members of the Munich U.S. Olympic judo team, who had all trained with him.

During the mid-1960s, while he was working to see judo established as part of the state's public school curriculum, Campbell began dating Linda Price, a young American woman of Scandinavian descent. Linda taught physical education in the

Sacramento school system and dealt blackjack at Lake Tahoe in the summers. In some ways Ben Campbell and this fresh-faced blonde Coloradan couldn't have come from more different backgrounds. Linda came from a close-knit family of ranchers and had grown up feeling totally loved and secure. At 23, she was fresh out of college, while 34-year-old Ben Campell had survived a rugged childhood, traveled around the world, and already gone through two brief and thoughtless marriages. But both loved animals, the outdoors, and working with children. Ben touched Linda by confiding to her that she scared him. When she expressed surprise, he explained that all his life he had carefully built a wall around himself to keep from getting hurt. Now, he told her, she was getting through that wall, and that was frightening for him.

Linda Price must not have scared Ben Campbell too badly. They were married on July 23, 1966. The wedding chapel in Reno, Nevada was so sleazy that they worried about whether the ceremony was even legal, but their marriage has strongly endured. They have a son, Colin, and a daughter, Shanan, now in their twenties.

While teaching judo and industrial arts during the 1960s, Campbell took on some volunteer work with the newly established Mounted Sheriff's Division in Sacramento, helping to patrol on horseback the extensive trails along the American River. His interest in police work led him to return to college to study police science. At the same time he began breeding and raising horses. As a horseman, he was driven by the same spirit to achieve and excel that had driven his forebears and fueled his championship judo career. Perhaps he was seeking something close to his heart to replace his beloved judo.

Campbell's health began to suffer from his overwhelming schedule. When his doctor ordered him to ease up, he resigned from the Mounted Sheriff's Division. But soon he was restless. He had become accustomed to sleeping four hours or less a night, and he felt that he had too much spare time, so he got involved in counseling American Indians in prisons in Folsom and Vacaville. He also counseled at the Indian halfway house in Sacramento, eventually serving as chairman of the board.

In 1970, at the suggestion of a school principal, he began to teach Indian jewelry-making as one of his classes in industrial arts, especially targeting unemployed Native Americans in the adult education program. As a boy Ben had loved whittling figures out of soft wood and designing beadwork for the quivers and Indian-style clothing he had fashioned for the Black Knights. Once in a while, he had even watched his father Albert make jewelry, a skill he claimed to have picked up from a Navajo friend. Albert Campbell had no money for costly supplies like metals and gemstones, but he would pick up pieces of serpentine and soapstone, and hunt for animal bones and antlers. These materials were all free and carvable. For metal he would melt down coins, or salvage the copper from discarded wiring. Campbell believes his father sometimes traded pieces he'd crafted for food, but he never got to the point of selling his jewelry as a regular source of income.

Later, in college, Campbell had taken a few jewelry-making classes, but as often happened in his life, he didn't listen when his teachers tried to tell him he was truly gifted. Like most people, he had to be ready to hear a piece of advice before he was willing to take it. Yet his interest in stone and metal and the beauty that could be shaped from them seems never to have really deserted him. While he was in judo training in Japan before the Olympics, he had been fascinated to watch swordmakers at work fashioning patterned samurai blades by carefully layering metals of different types and colorations.

Back in California, Campbell loved teaching the jewelry-making classes and instinctively seemed to know how to help a student discover his or her own creativity. Many of his adult education students went on to become professional jewelers, some of whom have even won awards. The classes led their teacher himself into a career in jewelry design, production, and sales. He started a jewelry sales business named Nighthorse Studios to aid Native jewelers in marketing their products by providing them a space to show their work to potential buyers. In 1979 Campbell, along with several other Native American jewelers, was featured in a major article in *Arizona Highways* entitled "Contemporary Indian Jewelers." In time he was creating pieces that were displayed in galleries and museums across the country.

Campbell would never be the sort of jeweler who'd be content just to make the traditional-looking pieces of jewelry guaranteed to sell well. Back in Japan, the swordmakers' delicately layered patterns of different-colored metals had reminded him of something. It made him think of sandpaintings, the large ritual drawings that figure importantly in Navajo curing ceremonies. Sandpaintings are made on the earthen floor of a ceremonial place by a *haatathli*, a Navajo healer who patiently sprinkles layer upon layer of colored sand to form the elaborate finished painting. Campbell got the idea of trying to combine American Indian designs with the Japanese art of layering different kinds and colors of metal. "Over a period of months," Campbell recalls, "I taught myself how to use sterling silver, gold, brass, German silver, copper, and red brass as design elements for an all-metal jewelry form." This style, which Campbell named "Painted Mesa" after the infinitely shaded pink, gold, gray, red, and beige mesas of the Four Corners region, has been recognized as a landmark innovation in American Indian jewelry.

When Campbell began to make and sell Indian jewelry, he took Ben Nighthorse as his professional name. He had always known he was part

Cheyenne, and now he felt the need to choose a name that expressed his Indian heritage more surely than Ben Campbell. But just picking a name for himself was not enough. It was as if the designs forming beneath his hands were leading him back to a place he needed to go. Finally, he began to seek out the Cheyenne relatives his father had determined to leave behind years before Ben was born.

Some have credited Campbell's interest in his Native roots to his judo years. They have suggested that as his involvement in judo faded, he sought to maintain his involvement with the Eastern values and philosophy by turning to his Native spiritual heritage and family. The senator himself believes that his early affinity for judo and Eastern philosophy was a reflection of his inner sense of self. Perhaps his boyhood dedication to making bows and arrows and his later devotion to Eastern martial arts, values, and philosophy were both ways of filling the place inside himself he felt was still empty — his knowledge of his own roots. When he was ready, Ben Nighthorse Campbell began to try to find his Cheyenne family.

Going on the few things Albert Campbell had been able to tell him, Ben Campbell followed the trail to the Lame Deer Agency in Montana and then onward to Lame Deer Creek, where he contacted the Black Horse family and other relatives who lived there. The moment in the summer of 1966 when Campbell first walked through the cabin door of Alex and Mary Black Horse was very awkward for him. It is hard for anyone who has tried to track down lost relatives to knock on a door, and say to the stranger who opens it, *Excuse me, you don't know me, but I think we are relatives.* Campbell blurted out to Alex Black Horse, "My dad told me that in some way I'm related to you through your older half-sister." Alex Black Horse just watched the nervous stranger try to spew out the bits of his father's history he'd been able to put together. When Campbell stopped talking, the older man just smiled at him and said, "I'm glad you came. I needed another son." With those words, Alex Black Horse welcomed Ben Campbell home. It is impossible to prove Campbell's ancestry completely, but the Black Horse family, the Northern Cheyenne, and Campbell himself are content that he has found his way back to his family. In 1980, Alex Black Horse and his wife Mary Black Horse, who had already formally adopted Ben Nighthorse Campbell as their son, officially enrolled him in the Cheyenne Tribe.

In addition to jewelry, Campbell had been engaged in breeding and raising championship quarter horses. In the late 1970s, while he was in the Southwest on a business trip, he was approached by a delegation from the Southern Ute Reservation who recruited him to become their tribal horse trainer. He accepted and moved his family to Ignacio, Colorado, where they bought a ranch. That made it possible for Campbell to direct the tribe's horse-training program while he and his wife continued their own quarter horse business.

It was in Colorado that Ben Nighthorse Campbell, rancher, horse breeder and trainer, jeweler, and former judo champion, got involved in politics. It happened almost accidentally. Campbell left his ranch in Ignacio one day in May, 1980, planning to fly himself in his small plane to San Francisco to deliver some specially ordered jewelry he had just finished making. When he discovered that a storm would delay his flight, he decided to drive to nearby Durango and visit Al Brown, a friend from the police science program at San José State, who was in town to attend a Four Corners District Democratic Party meeting. Campbell himself was a registered Democrat strictly because his mother had been, but he had never been active in politics.

At the meeting, when Brown's name was put up for sheriff, Campbell took the opportunity to say a few words in his friend's favor. Brown won the nomination and went on to be elected sheriff. Then it came time to nominate someone to run for the Colorado State Legislature from the Fifty-ninth District, which includes the county on the western slope of the Rockies where the Campbells' Ignacio ranch is located. The Republicans already had a surefire candidate, a handsome, well-connected local man. The Democrats gathered at the Durango meeting were sure they couldn't win that race. They just needed a name to put on the ballot because they did not want the Republican candidate to run unopposed.

A number of men were asked to put their hats in the ring, but all of them made excuses. The truth was that no one wanted to spend the time and money necessary to wage a campaign that was sure to be a lost cause. Ben Campbell was a political innocent who had no idea what was involved in a political race, and when he was asked if he would accept the nomination, he tentatively agreed. But before he committed himself he asked the assembled Democrats three questions: How much time would it take? How much money would he need to spend? How much would he need to know about issues and strategies? The Colorado Democrats told him running for office wouldn't require much of his time and assured him they would provide him all the information and money he'd ever need. Campbell has since remarked, laughing, "They were wrong on all three counts."

People at the Durango meeting didn't realize they had just nominated a man who wouldn't ever give up, a man whose parents, grandparents, and great-grandparents had not known the meaning of the word "defeat." "Nobody expected me to win," Campbell muses. "Certainly I didn't know enough to have any expectations whatever. Can you imagine what those Democrats were thinking of me at the time? In those days, I wore my hair in a ponytail clear down to the middle of my back." But when one of the old political veterans remarked that he saw Campbell as having two chances at winning, namely "little and none," the election was won. Ben Nighthorse Campbell decided that he would work as hard to win the election as he had to win a spot on the United States Olympic judo team.

Campbell waged a powerful campaign, traveling the far-flung mountainous district for six months, talking to everyone he could engage in conversation, addressing every gathering he could get an invitation to, and exhausting himself financially and physically. The result of his untiring efforts was his election to the Colorado State Legislature in November of 1980, making him the second American Indian elected to that office in Colorado. Ben Nighthorse Campbell, the candidate with long hair, no political experience, and little or no chance of winning took about 57 percent of the vote and was re-elected three times.

Some of the legislation he worked on in those terms included the upgrading of the Sand Creek Massacre site, a place where, in 1864, one of the worst slaughters of Cheyenne people had occurred. Now the site was privately owned, and the property owner charged people admission to see the place where two hundred Cheyenne, mostly women and children, had died at the hands of a bloodthirsty, Indian-hating Colorado volunteer army. He managed to get a large commemorative sign placed on the highway adjoining the place where the doomed Cheyenne were encamped. Campbell also worked for improvement of in-state funding for Olympic athletes training in Colorado, land restoration of private property destroyed by pipeline companies, and support for the Animas-La Plata water project, which involved bringing fresh water to the Ute Mountain Reservation. The Animas-La Plata project was delayed for years by litigation, as local business interests attempted to prevent the project's construction.

While he served in the state legislature, Campbell was severely injured in a horseback riding incident. Since he'd been nominated for office, he hadn't had time to continue his work with his jewelry. He used the time he spent recuperating from the accident to craft a concho belt that earned him the Handy and Harmon Most Creative Metalsmith award in 1983 at the prestigious Gallup Intertribal Ceremonials.

In 1984 Representative Campbell decided not to run for another term in the state legislature because he wanted to spend more time with his family and his jewelry business. But two years later the Democratic Party persuaded him to run against the Republican candidate for the United States Congress. This time they counted on his win, though it was rare that American Indians had attained national public office. Ben Reifel, a Sioux from Rosebud Reservation in South Dakota, was the last Native congressman. Reifel left office at the end of the 1970 session. Including Reifel, some six Native men had served in the House and three had served as senators. One of

them, Senator Charles Curtis, a Kaw-Osage Indian from Oklahoma, was Vice President of the
United States during the Republican administration of Herbert Hoover.

Once again, as befit the name he chose for himself, Campbell was the "dark horse" candidate.
His campaign material described him as a
"semiorphan, high school dropout, Korean War
veteran, small businessman, Olympic athlete,
artist, truck driver, teacher, rancher, and admired state legislator," in hopes that his diverse
background would appeal to an equally diverse
electorate. In a hard-run campaign, Campbell
pulled slightly ahead of his popular opponent and
won a close victory with 52 percent of the vote.
In that way, Ben Nighthorse Campbell — almost
lost son of the Cheyenne people, child of a Portuguese immigrant mother, Olympic competitor,
jewelry maker, businessman, and all around son
of the West — went to Washington.

Campbell's career as United States congressman was as successful as all of his previous
endeavors had been. The local Denver paper
Westward voted him the Best Colorado Legislator
of 1987, because among the eight Colorado con-
gressmen, Campbell, in his very first term, held
the record for the highest percentage of bills
introduced and passed into law. To his great satisfaction at the time, the dispute over the Animas-
La Plata water project was settled in the United
States Congress after thirteen years. When he ran
for his next term, he was easily elected.

While serving as a congressman from Colorado, Campbell was selected as a member of the Colorado delegation to the Democratic National Convention held in Atlanta in 1988. He was joined there by fifty other Native American delegates from across the country, and together they formed the first Democratic American Indian Caucus. Campbell was selected to address the convention on behalf of American Indians, and, as he recalls, "while I was speaking all fifty of my Indian brothers and sisters stood before the podium wearing their Indian traditional dress to lend me moral support."

With Senator Daniel Inouye of Hawaii, Congressman Campbell worked on legislation to establish the Museum of the American Indian in Washington, D.C. President George Bush signed the bill granting space for the construction of the museum on the Capitol Mall.

Senator Campbell also waged a long struggle to get Congress to change the name of the Custer National Battlefield Monument to Little Bighorn National Battlefield Monument. Senator Campbell, like many other Indian people, felt that both the name and the exhibits at the site unjustly glorified Custer and did little to help visitors understand the story of the Native Americans at Little Big Horn. At the same time, he called for the construction of a memorial to the Native people who fought and died there to balance the already existing memorial to soldiers serving with the United States Cavalry and the grave markers

of individual U.S. soldiers scattered about the
site. Native people all over the country, along
with many other Americans who knew the true
history of that great battle, had supported the
proposed changes for a long time. The earliest
efforts to get some sort of marker on the battlefield that would celebrate American Indians go
back to 1925. The Little Big Horn was one of the
few battles in which Native defenders triumphed
over the invading American armies. It was perhaps because of that that numerous Americans
were passionately against any changes which
might draw attention away from the bravery of
Custer and his men. The fight was a bitter one,
but on December 10, 1991, President George Bush
signed the legislation officially making the monument the Little Bighorn National Monument
and authorizing a memorial to American Indians
who fought there. The pen the president used to
sign the bill, along with a note he wrote to Ben
Nighthorse Campbell and a copy of the bill, were
framed and placed on display at the battlefield's
visitor center.

Soon after his triumph in the matter of the
Little Bighorn National Monument, Congressman Campbell was once again embroiled in
controversy, this time around the selection of
Cristóbal Colón as the grand marshal of the upcoming 1992 Tournament of Roses Parade. When
pressure was brought to bear on the parade
committee by activists across the country, particularly those from Chicano, Latino, African-

American, and Native American communities, the committee made a slight change in its program. It refused to drop Colón as grand marshal, but it did belatedly ask several well-known Native people to ride in the parade. All indignantly refused — except Ben Nighthorse Campbell, who had never seen a fight he didn't enjoy. He set some important conditions on his acceptance. He would have to be named co-marshal of the event, riding ahead of the old voyager's descendant in the parade. He also demanded free air time to discuss current issues of concern to the American Indian community nationwide.

While this arrangement soothed some of the disgruntled groups on both sides, many remained distressed. Campbell realized that, but as a descendant of both Native Americans and European immigrant Americans, the congressman felt that inclusion was the better course. After all, exclusion had caused great pain to all too many Americans of a variety of ancestries, and the congressman believed this five hundredth anniversary was a perfect time to mark a profound change in that policy.

He said, "It is my hope that we can begin planting the seeds of harmony and understanding, of cooperation and mutual respect, and, above all, love and brotherhood, and have faith that those seeds will grow into the tree of life of which Black Elk once spoke, so that we may make a better life for all of God's children." With these words Congressman Campbell reiterated the profound vision Native speakers had articulated for over two hundred years. With his words, he asserted once more the ancient Native values that had made America the land of freedom and opportunity it has always been.

On the day of the parade, in spite of the controversy surrounding his decision, Congressman Ben Nighthorse Campbell rode Black Warbonnet at the head of the Tournament of Roses Parade. His splendid presence signaled to millions of viewers around the world that the Native spirit is as enduring as the values Native peoples have upheld since time immemorial.

On a cold January day in 1993, newly elected Senator Ben Nighthorse Campbell again donned his beautiful buckskins. Carrying the lance he had made, he rode Black Warbonnet down Pennsylvania Avenue, which is also known as the Avenue of Presidents. On this solemn occasion, he was not the only Indian taking part in the parade honoring the inauguration of Bill Clinton as president of the United States. Two dozen men and women representing Native nations from all over the United States rode with him. The six Cheyenne among them were especially proud to honor the first Cheyenne United States senator.

For the senator, the greatest joy of this parade was the presence of his Cheyenne mentor and spiritual advisor, Austin Two Moons, grandson of Chief Two Moons, who had fought alongside Black Horse in the Battle of the Little Bighorn. Despite the winter temperature, his age, and a bad leg, Mr. Two Moons refused the wheelchair provided for him and stood tall in his place along the parade route. He carried an American flag as well as an eagle-wing fan that had belonged to the great Sioux leader Red Cloud.

As he watched President and Mrs. Clinton, Vice President and Mrs. Gore, and Senator Campbell and his retinue pass, the Cheyenne spiritual leader waved both flag and fan. "You know, we have a right to this flag," he told Herman Viola, Campbell's official biographer, who was standing beside him. "When Custer came to drive us from our land, he carried it. My grandfather told me that at the Little Bighorn, Custer dropped the flag and the Cheyenne picked it up. We have kept it ever since. Now the flag unites all of us in this great country. Now we are all friends and we need to work for world peace."

Most recently, Senator Campbell has once again reminded the nation that, as he puts it, he "calls 'em like I see 'em." He has often supported causes that are identified as "liberal," like abortion rights and federal programs to aid the poor, but in other matters he has often voted with conservative colleagues. On March 2, 1995, the Republican-sponsored Balanced Budget Amendment to the Constitution failed by one vote to secure the necessary two-thirds majority. Campbell was one of the few Democrats to support the measure. The following day, March 3, he announced that he was defecting from the Democratic to the Republican party, with whom he had come to feel he had more in common. He made it clear, though, that he was not a politician to follow any one party line and that he would continue to support causes he believed in, even if most Republicans opposed them.

Now well into his first term as senator, Ben Nighthorse Campbell has distinguished himself in a number of ways, besides his dramatic announcement that he was switching parties. His face is often seen on late-night television encouraging young people who have dropped out of high school, like he did, to get their GEDs. In a great variety of ways, the first Cheyenne senator carries on his ancestors' fight for liberty, self-determination, and dignity. In his dedication, energy, and social commitment, he encourages every American to join him in that most important enterprise.

7
Wilma Pearl Mankiller

One day in 1970, a strong-featured young Cherokee housewife stood on the deck of a motor launch chugging across San Francisco Bay, looking back at the grim buildings and watchtowers that topped a rocky little knob of an island. Gulls, terns, and other seabirds swirled and cried in the sky overhead. Long ago, Spanish explorers venturing into the harbor had named the island for one of the species of birds who nested there — Isla de los Alcatraces, Island of the Pelicans. Nowadays, people called it Alcatraz, or just The Rock.

Many others besides the seabirds had found a use for the little island. The Spanish had placed cannon on Isla de los Alcatraces to guard the harbor, and in the nineteenth century the American army had built a military prison there. In 1933, the federal government took over Alcatraz from

the army and made it into a prison for the men
it considered its most dangerous convicts. The
prisoners of Alcatraz were treated very harshly.
They had no privileges, and no activities or visitors broke the long monotony of their days. It
was almost impossible to escape from Alcatraz,
and most of those who tried ended up drowning
in the cold gray waters of the bay. In 1963 At-
torney General Robert Kennedy ordered the closing of the prison, and soon the island was deserted
except for a caretaker.

Strangely enough, despite Alcatraz's bleak history, Wilma Pearl Mankiller Olaya, the young
woman looking thoughtfully back across the
boat's wake toward the island, had come to think
of it as a place of hope. In November of 1969, a
group of American Indians from many different
tribes evicted the caretaker and occupied the island. Eventually, over one hundred Native people
came to live on Alcatraz. They got the prison's
electricity and plumbing working, opened a com-
munal kitchen, and started a school and a health
clinic. They created a whole community of protest there, calling themselves Indians of All
Tribes. Alcatraz, they said, symbolized all the
lands across the United States that had been
taken from Indian people. Now these protesters
were demanding that tribes be given back their
lands or else that the government pay fairly for
the land it had stolen. They were also taking ad-
vantage of the news coverage to point out other
injustices Indians had suffered.

Mankiller felt very strongly about those issues, as did all her family. Four of her brothers and sisters, together with their children, her nieces and nephews, were among the occupiers. Though she visited them often on the island, as she had today, Mankiller herself thought she could do more good on the mainland, where she worked to raise money to keep the Alcatraz community going and to keep making non-Indians aware of Indian problems and grievances.

Wilma Mankiller knew that her own Cherokee people had experienced a long history of betrayal by the United States government. During the bitter winter of 1838–1839, they were made to leave their original homelands in Appalachia and force-marched to Indian Territory in what is now the state of Oklahoma. Many died of cold, disease, and malnutrition on that brutal march, called by the Cherokee "The Trail Where They Cried" or the Trail of Tears.

Once in Oklahoma, the Cherokee who survived did very well, but they were not allowed to keep the land set aside for them there for long. The government did not like the fact that the Cherokee, like most Indian people, preferred to own their land communally. It wanted Indians to live like whites, with each family privately owning land. Only private ownership, the government said, spurred people on to work hard. By the beginning years of the twentieth century, the government had forced the so-called "allotment system" on the Cherokee, giving each Native family its own parcel of land. Then the government took the large amount of land that was left over and made it available to white settlers.

During her time of growing up and her early marriage and young motherhood, Wilma Mankiller had not been especially concerned with Cherokee history. Now, through the occupation of Alcatraz, she had come to feel deeply her connection to the cause of seeking justice, not just for the Cherokee but for all Native people. No wonder the knobby little island growing smaller in the distance seemed like a place of hope and vision to her. The spirit of Alcatraz would live on in her heart long after the protesters were removed from the island. In time that spirit would lead her back to Oklahoma, the land of her birth, where she would one day serve three terms as Principal Chief of the Cherokee Nation, the first woman elected to that office.

Wilma Pearl Mankiller was born November 18, 1945, in Tahlequah, Oklahoma, the capital of the Cherokee Nation. She was the sixth of eleven children born to Charles Mankiller, a full-blood Cherokee, and Clara Sitton Mankiller, of mixed Dutch and Irish descent. Though she herself was not Cherokee, Clara Mankiller loved her husband dearly, and she fully accepted his people and culture, learning to speak some Cherokee and wanting her children to be raised in their Native heritage. As her daughter Wilma says of her, "She sometimes forgets she is white."

The family name Mankiller, in Cherokee

asgaya-dihi, is very common among Cherokee people, but outside of Cherokee country, Wilma Mankiller has had to endure a lot of ignorant and insensitive teasing about her name. The name Mankiller does not signify that one of the family's ancestors was a murderer. In the old days, *asgaya-dihi* was a rank or a title, like major or captain. It designated an official within a Cherokee community who commanded the warriors who defended Cherokee land and people in time of need. In the past each Cherokee town had its *asgaya-dihi*. Others say the title could sometimes refer to a person who was skillful at spiritual warfare, at turning evil back on someone who had done harm.

About five generations back, the Cherokee began to adopt white people's practice of passing down last names from parents to children. Just as it is likely that a white person named Smith had a distant ancestor who worked at a forge, it is likely that one of Wilma's Cherokee ancestors five generations back held the office of *asgaya-dihi*.

Wilma enjoyed a warm and loving family life. The Mankillers were close, despite being what she calls "dirt poor." On their holdings at Mankiller Flats, her hardworking father grew vegetables for the family to eat and raised crops of strawberries and peanuts to sell. He also worked seasonally on big farms in Colorado. She and her brothers and sisters walked the three miles back and forth to their one-room schoolhouse, where the Mankiller

children often started the school year barefoot.
School opened in August, and the family had to
wait for Charlie Mankiller to get back with his
pay from the autumn harvest in Colorado to buy
new shoes. There was no money for store-bought
clothes except for shoes and winter coats, and so
Wilma usually wore handmade dresses and un-
derclothes that her mother and sisters sewed out
of cotton flour sacking printed in floral designs.
One terrible day her schoolmates glimpsed her
flour-sack underpants and made fun of them.
It was the first time she understood that her
family's poverty somehow made her different.

Wilma remembers her father's storytelling
and visits between relatives and friends as the
family's primary entertainment. Charlie Mankiller told wonderful stories, both traditional
Cherokee tales and stories about things that he
had experienced. Once when the family was driving around on back roads in their old Ford late
at night, a low-hanging tree branch brushed their
windshield like long fingers raking across the
glass. Charlie told the children how the same
thing had once happened to him, only that time
the eerie branch had left long streaks of blood on
his windshield. The children were terrified! Charlie said the blood was probably just from an owl
who had been shot in the tree, but that scared
them still more, for owls are frightening bad-
omen birds for most traditional Cherokees.

Maggie Gourd, Wilma's great-aunt, was another wonderful source of stories. She loved to

recall the deeds of the many outlaws like Pretty
Boy Floyd and Cherokee Bill who had roamed
Oklahoma Territory and maybe hidden their
stolen loot nearby. Aunt Maggie cautioned the
Mankiller children about the mysterious *Yunwi
Tsunsdi*, the Little People. They look like Cherokee, but they are very short and good at hiding
if they don't want to be seen. It is said they will
steal a Cherokee child and raise it as their own
if the baby's natural parents do not watch over
it carefully.

Visiting back and forth with family was always
an exciting experience for the Mankiller children.
While the grown-ups talked and prepared food,
Wilma and her cousins would race wildly around,
playing hide-and-seek or tag. Toward dusk, they
would go about collecting lightning bugs in a mason jar with holes punched in the cover so they
could watch the mysterious creatures flash on
and off, off and on in the humid Oklahoma
darkness. Afterward, the children would always
release them to fly free into the night. As the
grown-ups laughed and visited and played endless hands of cards far into the early morning,
the cousins were bedded down to snuggle on
quilts on the floor. The reassuring murmur of
their parents' voices speaking both Cherokee and
English was the background music that accompanied these children into sleep.

Though Wilma grew up surrounded by loving
family and friends, and though her own mother
was white, as a little girl she would run to hide

if she saw a strange white person coming. Adair County, where Mankiller Flats is located, is the home of the largest population of Native Americans in a single county in the United States, so it is no wonder Wilma was shy around non-Indian people. Besides, she had already had some uncomfortable experiences with gushing white women who tried to give the family clothes and other things. Even as a little girl, Wilma did not like people who condescended to her.

When she was not going to school, Wilma joined the other members of her family doing farm chores and exploring the countryside. She was a sturdy child who loved playing outdoors, especially in her favorite season, springtime, when the redbud and dogwood trees around the family home on Mankiller Flats were in lacy bloom. The Cherokee name Wilma's father gave her is *a-ji-luhgse*, "flower," a fine name to give a little girl who loved to examine closely the petals of the small purple and yellow wildflowers that grew near her home.

Besides roaming the fields and woods, Wilma's other favorite way to spend time was reading. She says now that "this love of reading came from the traditional Cherokee passion for telling and listening to stories." The Cherokee Nation developed 98 percent literacy in the years after they were removed from their southeastern mountains to Oklahoma. It is a record not yet met by any modern nation except Japan, and far above the literacy rate in the present day United States. In the years before the Cherokee were forced from their Appalachian homelands, a leader named Sequoya developed a system of writing called a syllabary. The Cherokee used it to record legal documents and Cherokee history, recipes, stories, poems, and all the articles published in their national newspaper, the *Cherokee Phoenix*. Wilma's childhood love of printed words was indeed characteristic of the whole Cherokee tribe.

In the fall of 1956, when she was 11, Wilma's family moved to California in hopes of making a better living under the provisions of the government's new Relocation Act. It had suddenly become the United States' policy to "get the government out of the Indian business," as President Dwight D. Eisenhower phrased it. Now the government wanted to begin to terminate all treaty and policy responsibilities toward Native Nations. One way to make that easier was to persuade Indian people to stop living together in Native communities on reservations. The government began telling Indian families on reservations that it would help them move to cities, where more jobs and better schools would improve life for them. The government's real hope was that American Indian people would soon forget their Native identities and melt into the urban population, so that soon there would be no more need of reservations and no more need for the government to spend time and money on Indian tribes.

The Mankiller family was very uncertain about

going to live in a distant city. Wilma and her sisters and brothers would eavesdrop anxiously as the adults discussed the pros and cons of relocation. Finally a Bureau of Indian Affairs agent somehow convinced Charlie Mankiller that moving to a city was for the best, and the family moved to San Francisco. At first they stayed in a low-rent hotel in the Tenderloin, a crowded district in the downtown area populated mostly by poor people and filled with crime. The family was bewildered by the sights and sounds of city life. Even menus in restaurants confused them. They were used to the biscuit-and-gravy country breakfasts of their home, not to the eggs, bacon, and pancakes offered in San Francisco diners. One afternoon as Wilma and her brother stood in the hallway of their hotel, they watched part of the wall slide open, revealing a box. People walked right into the tiny space, and then the doors slid shut. When the doors slid open again, different people walked out of the box. The frightened children vowed never to go near the fearful elevator.

Soon Wilma's father and her oldest brother Don found work in a local rope factory, and the Mankillers moved into a low-cost flat located in the Portrero Hill district. The flat was small for a big family which now included a new baby, James Ray. Even with their own apartment, Wilma still didn't like living in the city. She was homesick for Mankiller Flats. School was particularly difficult for her. In the fifth grade she found that her classmates were more advanced in both math and language skills, although she could hold her own in reading. But her classmates' cruelty pierced her. They made fun of her name and of the way she dressed and talked, teaching her just how far from urban America her home and the Cherokee Nation were. Wilma and one of her sisters used to stay up late at night reading out loud to each other so they could learn to talk with a West Coast accent instead of the Oklahoma drawl they grew up using.

The family moved to Daly City, just south of San Francisco, as their finances improved. Their new home provided more space, and Wilma's father began regularly to visit the San Francisco Indian Center where he and the family could meet other Native Americans. At first, Charlie was just looking for a friendly poker game. He was a sharp player, and his poker winnings helped to add to the family income. But soon the Mankillers were drawn into other activities as well, like dances and powwows. Wilma found a haven at the center, but she still didn't like living in Northern California. Now 12, she had lived in three different places around the Bay area, changing schools and neighborhoods each time, and she had grown very insecure and confused. As a result she began to run away from home, heading each time straight to her mother's mother, Grandma Pearl Sitton, who lived in the nearby town of Riverbank, California.

Grandma Sitton was a tiny woman, full of life

and energy, a woman who held strong opinions about everything. She enjoyed working in her vegetable garden and raising chickens and tending her dairy cows. She would marry three husbands over her lifetime, the last when she was in her eighties, and she outlived them all. Wilma loved this spirited grandmother. By the time she was in the eighth grade, Wilma's parents agreed to let her live with her Sitton relatives on their dairy ranch for a year.

At first Wilma had some trouble adjusting to still another change in residence and school, as well as to her new family. Getting used to four new cousins was difficult, especially since she was feeling very self-conscious and anxious. One day her cousin Teddie wouldn't stop his teasing, making fun of her and pulling her hair, until Wilma lost her temper. She finally whirled around and punched Teddie in the jaw, sending him to the ground. Of course the Sittons were upset over her unruly behavior, and there was some talk about sending Wilma back to Daly City. Soon, though, she began to adjust to her new circumstances, and under the firm guidance and love of her grandma, she began to gain some self-confidence. She still had no love of school, but she did much better in Riverbank. She took readily to farm life, helping with chores such as milking the cows and cleaning the barn. In her spare time she explored the surrounding countryside. The year shaped her character and gave her strength.

After the year at her grandmother's, Wilma returned to her family. By now the Mankillers had moved from Daly City, south of San Francisco, to Hunter's Point, a neighborhood on a spit of land jutting into the bay in the southeast section of San Francisco. Wilma's father was working as a longshoreman at the nearby docks. Hunter's Point was home mostly to African-Americans, though there were some Samoans and a few Asian-American and Native American families. Like the Mankillers, the other Native Americans of Hunter's Point had been urged to move to the city as part of the Bureau of Indian Affairs relocation program.

Hunter's Point was a rough neighborhood wracked by gang warfare, but Mankiller says she will always be grateful for her years there. At Hunter's Point she learned to appreciate inner-city problems, but she also learned of the strength and resilience of the people who lived there, especially of the women who held families together.

With the move back to her family, the American Indian Center of San Francisco became even more important in Wilma's life. The Center was located amid the flophouses and seedy bars of the Mission District, a notoriously tough part of town. But for Wilma, the second floor of the shabby frame building on Sixteenth Street meant safety among people like herself who accepted her. The Center became her second home. After school she went there to socialize with other Native teenagers like her who had come to the city under the relocation program and were feeling isolated in this alien land in which they found themselves. "We would jump on a city bus and head for the Indian Center the way some kids today flock to shopping malls," she remembers.

The Center sponsored dinners, dances, outings, intertribal powwows, and bingo games for the recently urbanized Native families, but it was not just a place for recreation. Native people met there to talk about important issues that affected them both in San Francisco and all around Indian Country. Many different Native nations were now represented in the new population of urban Indians, thanks to the government's relentless drive to relocate Indians. Unknowingly, the government really was helping to draw Native Americans together politically. Over the years the discussions taking place in urban Indian Centers around the country helped Native nations think about the changes they would like to see and plan how to bring them about. Over time intertribal groups of Native people were able to approach the white government at local, state, and national levels with petitions, proposed legislation, and, with growing frequency during the sixties and seventies, a variety of lawsuits. Wilma's father Charlie Mankiller was one of the people drawn more and more into political activity. He quit his job as a longshoreman and became a union organizer. He led the fight to establish a free health clinic for American Indians living in the Bay area.

These activities, especially her father's model of Native leadership, had a powerful effect on the young woman who would eventually become an able political leader in her own right. Above all, Charlie Mankiller taught his daughter the importance of persistence, of working tirelessly to make certain projects get completed. "Once I set my mind to do something, I never give up," she has said. "I was raised in a household where no one ever said to me, 'You can't do this because you're a woman, Indian, or poor.'"

Wilma graduated in 1963, just feeling grateful to be done with high school. Nothing there had touched her deeply except her sense of alienation. She moved in with her older sister Frances and took a clerical job with a finance company. During this period she began to develop her sense of personal freedom and responsibility. Hers was no glamorous life, but she was living on her own and holding down a job, and that did much to boost her self-confidence. For Wilma, college was not a real option. All around her the people she knew best began to work right away for a living when they left high school, and she followed their example. No teacher had taken the time to encourage her.

Mankiller had had a few boyfriends through high school, but none were very serious. Now, at seventeen, she began to date a young man from Ecuador, a handsome, soccer-playing college student with the aristocratic name of Hector Hugo Olaya de Bardi. Sophisticated Hugo introduced the pretty teenager with the flashing hazel eyes to a San Francisco she had never known, a world

of restaurants and nightclubs. It wasn't only friv-
olous fun Mankiller discovered there. In the clubs
and bookstores and cafes of 1960s San Francisco,
poets of the Beat generation and folk singers like
Joan Baez and Bob Dylan were communicating
all kinds of ideas in their poems and songs. It was
Hugo who first brought her to some of the places
where she would begin to learn about the civil
rights movement and, later, the antiwar movement of the Vietnam era.

That first summer after high school, Wilma met
Hugo almost every night to explore the city. Soon,
Hugo was anxiously pressing the young woman
to marry him. At first she was not enthusiastic,
but she had to admit that a life of working at the
finance company seemed boring. She suddenly
decided that marrying Hugo just might solve all
her problems. Five days before her eighteenth
birthday, she and Hugo married in Reno, Nevada.

The young couple honeymooned in Chicago,
where, on November 22, they learned of the assassination of John F. Kennedy in Dallas. They
spent the last days of their honeymoon glued
to a TV set, watching over and over the images
of a limousine under fire, a young widow in a
pink suit stained with blood, a parade of people
dressed in mourning, a riderless horse. The sense-
lessness of the President's death deeply impressed
Mankiller. She had not yet become very political
herself, but she had greatly admired Kennedy for
his fresh energy and his stand on civil rights. In
a sense, she says, his assassination symbolized

her own personal feeling of sadness and anger at growing up and losing her innocence. In that respect, Wilma Mankiller was clearly a typical member of her generation of Americans, the baby boomers born in the wake of World War II.

When they returned to San Francisco, Wilma and Hugo struggled to make a home. Hugo was a student at San Francisco State University, and they moved in with his cousins, sharing a house in the Mission District. Wilma kept her job at the finance company, and Hugo took on a night job with Pan American Airlines to make ends meet. When Wilma suddenly became seriously ill a few months after they returned, she was rushed to the hospital where the doctors diagnosed a kidney infection as well as a pregnancy. The kidney problem was nothing they couldn't clear up, they assured her — it would just take a few antibiotics. The drugs worked this time, but in truth Wilma's kidney problems would eventually threaten her life.

Mankiller's first pregnancy was difficult, with many complications, and her condition forced her to quit her job at the finance company. She was ill throughout her pregnancy and stayed bedridden for most of it. On August 11, 1964, Felicia was born. Almost two years later, Wilma and Hugo had another daughter, named Gina. Her second pregnancy went easily.

By now Wilma and Hugo had been married almost three years. They had two little girls and were renting a pleasant house of their own in a good neighborhood of San Francisco. But the marriage was beginning to show strains. Mankiller felt hemmed in by her role as a traditional middle-class housewife. Cooking, cleaning, shopping, and caring for her daughters somehow did not fulfill her. She wanted more, though she was not at all sure what that "more" might be. She felt better when she could spend time at her parents' home, talking, playing cards, and eating with the other Native Americans who were always dropping in there. Hugo was also feeling restless and restrained by work and fatherhood, but he wasn't satisfied by quiet evenings with the Mankiller family and friends. He preferred nights on the town, hanging out in nightclubs and at parties. Mankiller was only twenty-one, but more and more she was becoming aware of the differences between her background and values and Hugo's.

In 1969 events in the United States were signaling great changes in every area of public life. The "hippie" movement, the nationwide protests against the war in Vietnam, and especially the civil rights movement were like wake-up calls to America. The civil rights movement, instituted by African Americans in the southeastern United States and quickly taken up by Americans from coast to coast, speeded up these changes.

Mankiller was coming of age during the turbulence of the sixties. She was politically aware from her high school years, partly because of the injustices she had personally suffered in grade

school and because of her father's involvement at
the San Francisco Indian Center and in the union,
though she had yet to become active in any cause.

In September of 1966 there was rioting in
Mankiller's old neighborhood of Hunter's Point.
The trouble began when some police officers shot
an African-American teenager they suspected of
car theft. This riot did not erupt into large-scale
violence, but the incident called attention to how
unfairly police could treat people of color. Mankiller began attending rallies sponsored by the
new Black Panther movement, and she was
amazed. "I had never before seen any minority
stand up to police, judges, and other white people," she recalls. She identified strongly with the
Black Panthers because they stood for self-help,
and because these tough street-fighters took special responsibility for African-American children.
Groups of Panthers were out on the streets making sure children had breakfast before they went
to school, providing cultural education for them,
and teaching each child the slogan "Black Is
Beautiful."

Mankiller was familiar with the plight of farmworkers because her father and brother had held
migrant crop-harvesting jobs during her childhood back in Mankiller Flats. Now she also began
attending rallies and fund-raisers sponsored by
Cesar Chavez's National Farm Workers Association.

By the late 1960s these different movements
were affecting her deeply, even if she herself was
not yet very politically active. "Everything that

was happening in the world at that time — Vietnam, peace demonstrations, the civil rights movement, and the seeds of the Native rights movement — had a lasting influence on me. I began to question so many things in my life, including, once again, my marriage," she says of that time. Her activities, new friendships, and reflections led her to return to school and pursue a college education. She had always hated school and been a rather mediocre student, but now she realized that education could be the way into a more meaningful life for her. She enrolled in classes at Skyline Junior College near San Francisco, taking just a class or two at a time in subjects she knew she enjoyed, like literature. She did well and soon transferred to San Francisco State University. Increasingly she became involved with school and the local community, especially the American Indian Center.

There, plans were afoot to occupy Alcatraz. Back in 1964, shortly after Robert Kennedy had closed the prison, a group of five Sioux political activists had already occupied the island for a day, claiming it for American Indians. Ever since, Alcatraz had been symbolically associated with land claims in the hearts and minds of American Indian people. Now in September of 1969 the city of San Francisco was on the verge of selling the island to Texas oil millionaire Lamar Hunt, who had plans to develop it into a sort of theme park and shopping mall for tourists. American Indian groups had been secretly planning to reoccupy the island not just for a day, but for an ongoing protest in which Native Americans would actually take up residence on Alcatraz. They had scheduled the takeover for the summer of 1970, but as the city's deal with Hunt went forward, they realized that, cold weather or not, they would have to act right away. The first boatload of protesters arrived on the island on November 9. They claimed the island under the terms of the Fort Laramie treaty of 1868, which stated that Indians could file for homesteads on unused federal lands. If the government wouldn't agree, they said, then they would buy Alcatraz outright, fair and square. They unfurled bolts of red cloth and displayed handfuls of glass beads worth about twenty-four dollars — the amount Peter Minuet was said to have paid the Wappinger tribes of New York for the island of Manhattan. The siege of Alcatraz was on, and the protestors would hold out for nineteen long months, until June of 1971.

By taking over Alcatraz and encamping there, they hoped that the public's attention would be drawn to the "Trail of Broken Treaties," the many legal agreements with Indian people the United States government had never bothered to uphold. They were charging the government of the United States with breaking its own laws in hundreds of instances.

Wilma Mankiller, in the meantime, was still trying to be a wife to a very traditional husband and care for her daughters. She did not go to live on Alcatraz, but she thoroughly involved herself in the protest by raising money to support those who were living there, many for the entire nineteen months of the siege. She identifies Alcatraz as the political turning point of her life.

During the occupation of Alcatraz, two other events occurred that would be important in the course of Wilma Mankiller's life. One was of a public nature. In 1970, the U.S. Congress passed a law enabling the Cherokee Nation in Oklahoma to elect their own tribal officers. Since 1917, all tribal officers of any importance had been appointed by the federal government, and naturally the government never appointed people who would fight government policies. Now the Cherokee were to be allowed to govern their own affairs. Every four years they were to elect a Principal Chief, a Deputy Principal Chief, and a fifteen-member tribal council to enact legislation concerning members of the Cherokee Nation. Wilma Mankiller, the young urban Cherokee trying to fit her family, her college classes, and her politics into her busy life, had no idea that within fourteen years she would be Deputy Principal Chief of the Cherokee.

The other transforming event for Wilma was the premature death of her father in February of 1971. Charlie Mankiller died of a kidney disease at 56, just one year too old to qualify for a kidney transplant in those years when the operation was still experimental. The death of this proud vital man was very slow and painful. "My father's death tore through me like a lightning bolt,"

Wilma remembers. Though he had given in to relocation and had worked for Native and labor causes in California for years, the Mankiller family knew it was right to bury Charlie Mankiller back in Oklahoma where he was born, among the Cherokee Nation. Even in her grief as she followed her father's body to his grave in Oklahoma earth, his daughter Wilma Pearl knew that at last she, too, had come home. All around her, she could hear Cherokee voices speaking, remembering stories about her father, speaking his name. Even the barren February hills and the bare trees of Oklahoma seemed beautiful and protecting to her. This sad visit home made it clear that her path would lead her back to Oklahoma some day soon.

Back at San Francisco State, Mankiller continued working on her college degree and kept herself involved in American Indian issues. While she was still an undergraduate she began working as the director of the Native American Youth Center in East Oakland. Young people went there after school to do their homework, listen to tapes of American Indian performers, and go on field trips. Alcatraz had taught Mankiller how to organize and raise money, and now she rapidly learned administrative skills through her position. She learned to write grants, and how to inspire others. When she desperately needed to get some remodeling done at the Center, she walked into a nearby bar called Chicken's Place where many Indian people hung out and asked for help, and people immediately volunteered.

Hugo did not approve of any of Wilma's activities with the Indian community. He wanted her to stay home, and he did not even want her to drive around the city by herself. Despite his disapproval, she marched out and bought a small car for herself. With her daughters, she now had a way to travel to Indian gatherings all up and down the California coast. The family went to powwows and ceremonies. They took part in the ritual gathering of seaweed with the Pomo people, and Mankiller spent much volunteer time helping the Pit River tribe fight to keep their ancestral lands from the Pacific Gas and Electric Company. In the course of their travels, she met many different elders, medicine people, and militant leaders who all taught her many things. She says today that these people were her best teachers.

The strain on her marriage finally became so great that she and Hugo were divorced in 1976. Soon, Wilma, her daughters, their dog, and their guinea pig were in a U-Haul truck headed back to Mankiller Flats in Oklahoma, where her mother was already living. She had no money, no house, and no job when she pulled up to her mother's tiny house, but Mankiller was certain she'd done the right thing. In time, she found work developing programs for the Cherokee tribe. Once people discovered how good she had gotten at writing grant proposals back in California, she was in a lot of demand. The year 1977 was an exciting time to start working for the tribe, because the Cherokee Nation voters had just ratified their new constitution. It seemed that the most devastating centuries of American Indian history were at an end, and that Native nations like the Cherokee could at last focus their attention on their own communities and sovereignty.

Gradually, most of Clara and Charlie Mankiller's children began moving home, and Mankiller and her children were surrounded with family. Mankiller felt proudest one day when she walked into the courthouse in Stillwell and overheard the old Cherokee men gossiping outside remark, "There goes John Mankiller's granddaughter." She knew she had found her place among her people after a long absence.

Wilma Mankiller built a home in Mankiller Flats and returned to her college education. She enrolled in the Community Planning program offered at the University of Arkansas at Fayetteville. Everything was going well for her until November 9, 1979, a day she now believes she was warned about.

Mankiller had never quite lost her old uneasiness about owls. Suddenly, on the night of November 7, as she and friends sat around talking about old-time Cherokee medicine, their talk was interrupted by the calls of owls. When she opened the door, she saw that not one, but many owls were perched in the trees around her house, their eerie cries echoing across Mankiller Flats. The very next day, on November 8, her car was hit head-on by a car going in the opposite direction. The other driver, a woman who was one of Mankiller's closest friends, was killed, and Mankiller herself nearly died. She was hospitalized for many months and underwent 17 operations. Her legs had been shattered, her ribs broken, and her face smashed. Recovering took a great deal of courage. She says now that what she gained from this terrible experience was losing all her fear of death. Now she thinks of death as "walking into spirit country."

After being released from the hospital, Mankiller soon discovered that she still didn't feel right. She often stumbled and dropped things. At first the doctors found nothing wrong, and Mankiller despaired. Then, watching a Jerry Lewis telethon for Muscular Dystrophy Association, she suddenly realized she must have some form of that disease. Finally she was diagnosed with myasthenia gravis, a disease that causes muscular weakness of many sorts. She returned to the hospital and underwent intensive drug therapy and more surgery. Meantime, she also turned to traditional Cherokee medicine people, who heal, as Mankiller has said, "from the inside out." Through them she learned how much attitude has to do with illness and healing.

It was nearly two years before she returned to

work full-time. Though she kept working at writing grants to raise money for tribal programs, she also turned her energies to help Cherokee people help themselves. That way, she believed, they could lessen and perhaps even end their dependency on the federal government and take control of their own economy. Mankiller was soon busy teaching people how to build their own houses and start businesses. She became best known for the Bell Community Project. She showed the little community of Bell, Oklahoma how to raise money to pipe running water into their town. Working together, community volunteers installed the water systems and repaired dilapidated housing.

The Bell Community Project brought Mankiller another gift besides the gladness of seeing a community revitalize itself. Her co-organizer on the project was a man named Charlie Soap, a bilingual Cherokee who was very good at getting things done despite bureaucratic red tape. A tall, handsome man, he was a gifted Plains-style dancer and storyteller who had a great deal of traditional Cherokee knowledge. In 1986 Charlie Soap and Wilma Mankiller married, after working together and being friends for years.

Enterprising work like Wilma Mankiller's Bell Project didn't go unnoticed long. Soon enough the Cherokee Principal Chief Ross Swimmer encouraged her in a number of ways, increasing her responsibilities. By 1979 Mankiller was tribal planner and program development specialist for the Cherokee Nation. Then in 1983 Chief Swimmer asked Mankiller to run as his deputy chief. Chief Swimmer was elected to his third term, Wilma to her first, as the first woman deputy chief of the Cherokee. Halfway through their term of office, Ronald Reagan named Chief Swimmer Commissioner of Indian Affairs, and Swimmer resigned from his tribal duties. On December 15, 1985, Wilma Mankiller became the first woman to serve as principal chief of the modern Cherokee Nation.

Wilma Mankiller continued to serve as the principal chief of the Cherokee, winning election in her own right in 1987. It was not an easy campaign, and she faced some rough going from opponents who tried to make an issue of her being a woman. They also tried to capitalize on her earlier injuries and illnesses, suggesting that she was not in good enough health to serve the nation very well.

But the voters had seen what the determined woman from Mankiller Flats could accomplish. As Cherokee, they had a long history of strong women leaders, a practice that changed only under the force of American law. In the end, the voters elected her over three male opponents with 56 percent of the vote. In that same year, Mankiller was named Woman of the Year by *Ms.* magazine.

By autumn of 1989, Mankiller began experi-

encing severe kidney problems of the sort that
had caused her father's death. A transplant was
needed, and despite his own fear of surgery and
hospitals, her brother Don agreed to donate one
of his kidneys. The surgery took place in June of
1990, and Mankiller was back at her desk by August, once more made aware of how precious life
is and determined to work hard for her people.
In 1991 she was reelected to the highest office in
the Cherokee Nation.

Her popularity stems from the effective administration she runs and the national visibility the
Cherokee have attained under her leadership. In
earlier days, Cherokee leaders, usually women,
were responsible for the welfare of the people. In
many ways, Wilma Mankiller carries the old tradition into the twentieth century. She has worked
tirelessly for strong economic development,
bringing jobs into Cherokee lands so her people
can remain home and make a living.

Her good work reaches beyond the Cherokee
tribe. In 1992 she was selected by President-elect
Bill Clinton to represent Native American nations
at a national economic summit held in Little
Rock, Arkansas. In April of 1994 she helped the
White House organize a conference between the
highest officials of the country, including the president and the vice president, and every head of
state among the Native nations whose lands are
technically within the borders of the United
States. At the conference Chief Mankiller introduced each Native speaker and the particular

topic of concern to the Native peoples under each head of state's leadership.

When Wilma Mankiller decided not to stand for reelection in the summer of 1995, initially she said she planned to "just rest for awhile." Typically, that plan did not last long, and soon she was exploring a way to share her expertise with others. In January of 1996, she began a nine-week appointment at Dartmouth College in Hanover, New Hampshire, as a scholar-in-residence. There she taught seminars in women's studies, Native American studies, and law. "I felt it was time for a change for me and for the tribe, and part of the change is to spend time reflecting on the past twenty-five years," Mankiller said as she began the term. She is uncertain what lies beyond her venture into teaching, but she invokes what the Iroquois people say about decision-making — the person doing the deciding should think about the seven generations in front of them and about the seven generations in back of them. Whatever Wilma Pearl Mankiller chooses to do, that decision will be made in the light of her sense of Cherokee history and her hope in the Cherokee future.

8
Michael Naranjo

Michael Naranjo is an award-winning sculptor from Santa Clara Pueblo. He shapes hawks in flight and Pueblo deer dancers and tender women with their arms about their children. Naranjo's sculptures make the viewer forget they are made of bronze and stone because the figures seem so lively and pliable. Looking at his work, you might think this sculptor had spent his whole life enfolded in the peace and beauty of Santa Clara, close to the seasons' rhythms of planting, tending the crops, and reaping the harvest. But that isn't the case. Michael Naranjo is blind, and his loss of sight came about in the nightmare of war in Vietnam. Perhaps it is his knowledge of pain and death that enables him to make sculpture so full of living energy.

Even though he has drawn much strength from his Pueblo roots, war and conflict touched Mi-

266

chael Naranjo's life early on. Santa Clara Pueblo lies just off the main road to Los Alamos, New Mexico. At the time of Naranjo's birth on August 28, 1944, Los Alamos was a newly built laboratory town hidden in the Jemez Mountains. Scientists and engineers from many different countries gathered there to design and build the first atomic bomb. Los Alamos was built on lands that traditionally belonged to the pueblos of Santa Clara and San Ildefonso. Near the bunkers and quonset huts where scientists still experiment with nuclear power lie many sacred shrines. One nearby hunting shrine, for example, is a big stone gently shaped to suggest crouched twin mountain lions. Pueblo people have visited holy places like the mountain lion shrine for many generations. At the shrines, they leave prayer sticks, corn pollen, and other offerings, and give thanks for good crops, successful hunts, and harmonious lives. It is ironic that the nuclear bomb, a weapon that could easily destroy all life on earth, was invented in a beautiful place where people have been praying for thousands of years for peace and well-being.

Naranjo's father, Michael Naranjo, Sr., like many other New Mexicans who were not scientists, was employed at Los Alamos during World War II. He was a skilled carpenter helping to build labs and equipment sheds and dormitories. Carpenters, electricians, machinists, cooks, and many other workers were much needed at this secret humming city that arose overnight amid

the ponderosa and aspen forests and abandoned cliff dwellings. Few knew that an atomic bomb was the goal of the people at work on "The Hill," but just about everybody in New Mexico could figure out that something top secret having to do with weapons and war was going on up there.

Meanwhile, down below at Santa Clara Pueblo in the fertile valley of the Rio Grande, in many ways life went on as it always had. Michael Naranjo's mother Rose was deeply part of the Pueblo. At Santa Clara, women have always been the equals of men, and in each generation a few women like Rose Naranjo are especially respected. These women are given the informal title of *gia* [*gee' ah*]. In the Tewa language spoken at Santa Clara, *gia* has a number of meanings. *Gia* is the Tewa name for Earth herself, the great Mother who gives all beings life. It also means "mother" — any mother. But there are older women who are motherly toward others beyond their own family, women who have proven themselves to be caring and wise. At Santa Clara, these women gradually come to be called *gia* in a special, reverent way by everyone in the village. These special *gias* are women who remind people of the earth because of the way they endure and nurture others. About six or seven women in every generation at Santa Clara gradually become identified as special *gias*. These women are not elected formally. Over time, it just becomes clear to the community that these women have that sort of goodness and quiet power that marks a *gia*. Though they may not necessarily be governors or sit on the tribal council, these women have a great influence on decisions that are made around the pueblo. Michael Naranjo's mother Rose is one such woman. Because of her kindness and her strong character, she is known as a special *gia* to others in the pueblo.

Like many generations of her family before her, Rose Naranjo is a noted potter who works closely with clay that comes from the earth. Santa Clara pottery is famous for its gleaming black glaze with figures and designs carved into the clay. As Rose Naranjo's ten children grew, they learned about making pottery by watching her. Certain days, for example, are better than others for digging the clay. Partly, it is a matter of weather, but mostly it is about how the clay-digger is feeling inside. People's minds and hearts should be peaceful whenever they go to dig clay. When they approach the clay-pit, they need to thank the spirit, Clay-Old Woman, with the proper prayers for her gift of her body. Later, as they prepare the clay by picking out rocks and twigs, sifting it, and mixing it with volcanic ash, people should also feel patient and hopeful.

Rose Naranjo never said that any of her children should become potters like her. That isn't the way most Pueblo Indian parents teach. Instead, she just encouraged them to play with the clay as they sat beside her at her work table. Some of Michael Naranjo's earliest memories are of pinching lumps of clay into the shapes of bear or deer. If he made a piece especially well, Rose would help him to polish it with a smooth rubbing stone after it was dry. Then she would fire it along with her pots to make the little clay animal hard and enduring. Michael still keeps on his mantelpiece a few of the tiny animal figures he made in childhood.

After the war, Michael's father decided he wanted to become a Baptist minister. In order to do that, he had to leave Santa Clara to study in Berkeley, California. There were too many Naranjo children for all of them to squeeze into the tiny apartment the family would have to live in, so only Rose and Dolly, the baby, accompanied Mr. Naranjo to Berkeley.

Even though Michael missed his parents, he was surrounded by family. His teenaged brother Tito was especially important to him. Michael was the eighth child and second son born to the Naranjos. Tito loved his six sisters, but he was very glad to have another boy join him in the family at last, and he usually didn't mind when six-year-old Michael tagged along.

Tito and Michael both loved to follow a certain dirt road that heads northwest from Santa Clara. The road goes through pueblo fields planted with corn and squash, pinto beans and chile, before winding into the wide mouth of Santa Clara Canyon. There, it passes a place called Puyé, where bright cliffs arise on both sides of the road. The ancestors of the Santa Clara Pueblo people once lived at Puyé in stone rooms fitted neatly into natural ledges and hollows in the sandstone. The walls of the old cliff houses, abandoned for hundreds of years, still stand. When the Naranjo boys climbed up there, they could look through the same windows the people of long ago looked through to watch for enemies approaching or to spot game animals on the floor of the canyon below.

A little further on, the canyon narrows as it follows Santa Clara Creek upstream. Tall ponderosa pines with vanilla-smelling bark tower on one side of the dusty road. On the other side, the creek chuckles through little open meadows of bright green grass and wildflowers. Here, Tito and Michael loved to wade and fish. The Naranjos didn't have fancy equipment, just little poles with string lines and fishhooks, and worms for bait. Naranjo remembers how, when he was seven or eight, he had a particularly lucky day. He caught lots of fish, and he was eager to show Tito, who was fishing a little farther up the stream. Michael had no creel to put his catch in, and he was afraid if he left the fish on the bank, hungry animals would make off with them. So he just stuffed a fish into every pocket of his jeans and headed off to find Tito. Years later, he would remember that day and how comical he must have looked with his pockets crammed full of flopping fish!

Michael loved being outdoors, but he also loved just being home at the pueblo, especially on feast days, when the delicious smells of piñon wood smoke, baking bread, and roasting corn and chili hung in the air and the plaza filled up with dancers, drums, and song. Michael, Sr., did not allow his children to participate in any of the dances because they were Baptists. Even so, young Michael's blood responded to the drumbeat as he watched the long lines of friends and relatives dancing out their prayers for rain, for abundant crops, for animal life and good hunting.

In 1950, Michael's father returned to New Mexico from California after completing his training to be a minister. He was first assigned by his Baptist superiors to build the Santa Clara Baptist Mission, combining his carpentry skills with his religious work. Then, three years later, when Michael was nine and just beginning the fourth grade, the Baptist authorities transferred his father to the Baptist Mission at Taos Pueblo, some fifty miles to the northwest of Santa Clara. As at most pueblos in New Mexico, Protestants are a small minority at Taos. Taos people are usually traditional believers or Roman Catholics. The majority combine Catholicism and their Taos religion, as they have been doing for hundreds of years.

The move was a big one for the Naranjo children, especially the younger ones. It wasn't just a matter of moving fifty miles. Many people think that all pueblos in the Southwest are alike, because traditional Pueblo people all live in apartment houses of adobe brick or stone. Taos people do share many things with the Santa Claras, but the two Pueblos have a number of different celebrations and different ways of doing things. They even speak two different languages. And, while Santa Clara is famous for its pottery, Taos pottery is rather plain and not usually regarded as art. Taos, instead, is famous all over Native America for its beautiful deep-sounding drums made of hide and cottonwood.

Michael Naranjo, Sr., did not take his family to live at the Taos Pueblo itself. Instead, the Naranjos lived in a huge fourteen-room house surrounded by evergreens near the Baptist Mission. The move away from his home pueblo to Taos meant that Michael, as both a Santa Clara and the son of a Protestant minister, would always be a little bit of an outsider.

At Taos Michael grew into a handsome and well-liked teenager, in spite of the fact that he was unlike his classmates. School did not really excite him, though he worked on the yearbook and ran with the track team. One of Michael's proudest days as a teenager did not come in connection with school, but at the Taos celebration of the feast of San Geronimo, Taos's patron saint, on September 30. This day at Taos begins with a Catholic mass and saint's procession and then continues with traditional Pueblo doings like dances and a trade fair. Pueblo clowns, their bodies painted in black and white stripes, have to perform a very difficult and dangerous task on San Geronimo. In the middle of the plaza there towers an enormous ponderosa pine that has been stripped of its bark and branches. A butchered sheep and other goods are tied to a cross-piece at the top. One of the clowns must shinny up the slippery trunk and lower the food to the people waiting far below. If he succeeds, the year will be prosperous.

Another eagerly awaited event at the San Geronimo feast is the big foot race. Taos's multi-storied clusters of houses are divided by Pueblo Creek into a North Pueblo and a South Pueblo, and every year the men of North and South run a relay race against one another. One year, when it seemed as if one of the sides might be short of runners, Michael was asked to be a part of the team. Though Michael, Sr., didn't like his children to dance at either Taos or Santa Clara, he did allow Michael to participate in this ceremonial race. Michael was very honored to be dressed in the ritual way and blessed and scolded by the Taos elders, just like all the rest of the runners.

As high school came to an end, Michael had not yet really found himself. He still loved to sketch and model with clay, the way he had as a child, but there were no art classes at his school. Maybe Michael was typical of many younger children in large families of highly motivated people. His brother and his older sisters had all been eager to go to college, and all of them had done very well. Perhaps Michael just figured there wasn't much he could do to surpass all those bright siblings. He agreed somewhat listlessly to go to the small religious school his father had first attended, Wayland Baptist College in Plainview,

Texas. Bored and homesick, he barely lasted one semester. On his way home, he stopped off in Santa Fe at the Institute of American Indian Arts (IAIA), a famous boarding school for artistically gifted Native American young people from tribes all over the United States. Here, he would be able to take the art classes he had been deprived of in his schooling, and the directors told him he could enroll in a week or so for spring semester.

Even though it offered art classes and materials, talented classmates, and a campus much nearer home, IAIA and Michael were not suited to one another. Like all government-run Indian boarding schools at the time, the routine was very strict and the rate of depression and attempts to run away was very high among IAIA students. Once, barely three months after the semester had started, Michael, Sr., and Rose came to visit their son. As they were about to start back to Taos, Michael asked them to wait for a moment. He ran to his room and came back carrying a pillowcase stuffed with as many of his clothes and possessions as he could cram into it. He begged them to take him home. Deciding there was no point in leaving Michael in a place where he was so unhappy, the Naranjos did so.

After dropping out, Michael Naranjo's life began to look like the lives of many other young people in the 1960s, Native Americans and non-Native Americans alike. He worked for a while at various jobs with the Santa Clara Pueblo road and campground crews, and made another try at college, this time at Highlands University in Las Vegas, New Mexico. At first, he received high grades, especially in art classes, but his work fell apart after he joined a fraternity and began to party heavily. He was soon suspended and told he couldn't return until he was serious about college. In May of 1966 he and a white girlfriend drifted into a marriage, though neither person knew the other very well. Naranjo worked on construction at Los Alamos and was absent from their home for long periods. The marriage was over by the fall of that year, when Naranjo left his wife for even longer periods to go deer hunting. The young couple separated and later divorced.

By the spring of 1967, the war in Vietnam was not going well. Many in the United States were against the war. People who were high officials in government, like Robert MacNamara, then Secretary of Defense, have since admitted that they knew very well the war against Communism in Vietnam was neither wise nor necessary. Vietcong guerrillas, fighting in the jungle terrain where they had lived all their lives, were able to outmaneuver the United States Army platoons again and again. Vietnamese village people, living in the middle of the fighting, suffered terribly, too.

In the United States, the army was drafting healthy young men who had no family obligations and who were not in school. Michael Naranjo was a divorced man with no children, and

he was no longer a student. He was working part-
time as an aide in the Taos Bureau of Indian Affairs elementary school. He could probably have
served in the National Guard and avoided the
draft that way, but he hated the strict routine he
had already experienced at religious colleges and
government boarding schools. The National
Guard would be sure to offer even harsher regi-
mentation, and like many young men, Naranjo
had just shrugged and taken his chances. In many
ways, Vietnam and the war seemed very distant
to him. On June 17, 1967, he was drafted.

The first part of Naranjo's military experience
involved training camps in the most humid parts
of the southern states, where the army hoped the
new soldiers headed for Vietnam might get used
to a climate faintly like Southeast Asia. As he
expected, Naranjo hated the discipline, but he
didn't have much choice. In the army, you
weren't suspended or expelled if you didn't behave. Instead, you were jailed or court-martialed.

Some of Naranjo's training camp experience
was actually fun, in a strange way. Toward the
end of his training, he was sent to Fort Knox,
Kentucky, to learn how to drive APCs, military
shorthand for armored personnel carriers, or armored cars. The way they learned to operate
them was by running the vehicles all over the
beautiful wooded hills and meadows around the
base. They would spot herds of deer and give
chase. Naranjo remembers well the picture of the
lumbering APCs following large herds of white-

tailed deer as the little animals bounced easily ahead of the machines.

At the end of basic training, half of the trainees went to Germany, the other half to Vietnam. Naranjo went to Vietnam, where he did not end up driving APCs. Instead, he was an ordinary foot soldier in the countryside east of Saigon. Soon after his arrival, he became disturbed by something about the faces of the men he saw who had been there for a while. He has said:

> They weren't simple, soft, tender people anymore. There was a harshness about them, a cold callous kind of feeling that came across the way they went about doing things. . . . I thought it was kind of sad when you looked at them and then you looked at the new ones coming in. After a couple of weeks of being there, all of a sudden I noticed I had slowly started becoming hard like that. . . .

Naranjo did not commit deliberately mean acts as some of the other men did, but he recognized the growing coldness in himself. During the Vietnamese War, the military taught U.S. soldiers to mistrust everyone. Even small Vietnamese children might be Vietcong, concealing a grenade or luring Americans toward an ambush. Once, Naranjo's squad was supposed to look for enemy soldiers or weapons in a tiny settlement in the jungle. The village appeared deserted, but Naranjo had a tight grip on his M16 as he checked

inside the empty huts. Suddenly, an unexpected
sight met his eyes. In one darkened hut there sat
an old man brewing tea on a little stove. He broke
into a big smile and pointed toward a cup, then
at Naranjo. There was no mistaking his invitation
to join him in a cup of tea. In the middle of this
terrible war, he saw himself as a host, and Michael Naranjo as his guest.

But Naranjo could hear in his head the voices
of the instructors at the military training camps
warning him not to take food from any Vietnamese people unless those who offered it tasted it
first themselves. They'll try to poison you, the
instructors warned. Looking around nervously
for anyone who might be coming up behind him,
Naranjo gestured brusquely with his rifle at the
cup, and then at the old man. *You drink it, old
man.* The man seemed puzzled, but he did as he
was told. And then Naranjo backed out of the hut
and fled, leaving the old man staring sadly after
him.

Michael Naranjo was shaken badly by this en-
counter. What was happening to him? The old
man had reminded him so much of the kind elders
he had known back at Santa Clara and Taos. He
should have at least accepted a cup of tea, especially after he had made the old man drink
some to prove that it was wholesome. But no, all
he could do was point a gun and snarl like an
animal. This war was killing his humanity.

About a month after he landed in Vietnam, Naranjo found himself deep in the swampy regions

of the Mekong Delta. The soldiers occupied an old fort the French had built when they occupied the country. On Christmas Day, 1967, and again on January 7, 1968, French Fort was shelled by mortar fire coming from an unknown place. Naranjo's squad, led by a Navajo Indian, a Sergeant Yazzie, was airlifted by helicopter in the direction of the shelling and set down in a dry rice field. At this season, the paddies were drained of water. The squad's mission was to locate the site of the enemy mortars. Suddenly, Vietcong opened rifle and machine-gun fire on them from a nearby grove of palm trees. During the skirmish that followed, Naranjo and Yazzie, sheltered by the low dike wall of the paddy, crawled to within fifteen feet of the grove and then made a break and ran into the trees. They hoped to sneak up through the trees to the machine-gun nest and destroy the enemy. Suddenly, Naranjo and Yazzie were face-to-face with Vietcong soldiers, no more than a few yards apart. One lobbed a hand grenade toward the two Native American soldiers. It rolled directly into Naranjo's right hand. As he raised his arm to throw it back at the VC, the grenade exploded, driving shrapnel deep into his face and his right arm and side. For some reason, the enemy stopped shooting and allowed Yazzie to drag Naranjo back to safety. Perhaps they were astonished to see in American uniforms black-haired dark-skinned people who looked not unlike themselves.

At the moment of the blast, Naranjo thought

himself dead and prayed only that his death not
be too hard on his parents. Then he heard Yazzie
asking if he was okay, and he knew he was still
alive. From that moment on, he says, he fought
to live. He was airlifted quickly to an evacuation
hospital nearby, and soon to a full army hospital
in Japan. Physical therapy would give him back
a lot of the use of his right arm and hand, but no
operation could restore his eyesight.

Many veterans in Michael Naranjo's condition
were swept by bitterness and despair. Naranjo
says he experienced bitterness at the very first.
When a fly landed on him in the ward in Japan
he would think, Even that fly can see, and I can't.
But he was quickly aware of how many people in
the hospital were worse off than he. He began to
think, All right, I'm blind, and I've got one good
hand. "I just couldn't lie there," he recalls, "I had
to do something." When a volunteer in the Japanese hospital asked if she could bring him anything, he requested modeling clay. He began to
shape tiny figures, as he had when he worked
beside his mother during long summer Santa
Clara afternoons. Slowly, they accumulated on
his bedside tray: a fish, a snail, a person. Ward
visitors began to stop to admire the little creatures. "I got started, and that's all it took," he
says now. At that moment in the Japanese hospital, his good hand immersed in a lump of
children's bright turquoise Play-Doh, Michael
Naranjo was connecting with his past and beginning to shape his future.

In October of 1968, after further rehabilitation at a Denver army hospital and some months at the Veterans' Administration School for the Blind at Palo Alto, California, Naranjo found himself back in Taos, about a year and a half after he had first left for basic training. In many ways, the past few months at home in the States had been exciting. At the Denver hospital, he had gained more and more use of his right hand and arm. There, he had begun working with oil-based clay, molding larger and more complex figures — an Indian man riding a horse at full gallop, a grizzly bear catching a salmon. Now he was grateful for the times he had spent cleaning fish and dressing out the deer he had had hunted in the mountains around Santa Clara and Taos with his father and brother. He found his fingers remembered what his eyes could no longer see, and he had a good grasp of the basic anatomy of animals and fish.

At the Palo Alto school, he decided against working with a Seeing Eye dog, choosing to try and get along with just a cane. He began to learn the many tricks of getting along as a blind person in the seeing world — how to organize a kitchen and a clothes closet, how to operate simple machines like can openers, ovens, tape recorders, and telephones. He learned to read Braille. All the while, he continued to model in clay. A story about him and his sculpture on a news service wire brought national attention to his work. People were beginning to buy his pieces. At Denver and Palo Alto, where his work was being recognized, and where he was surrounded by other veterans and medical people who were used to problems like his, Naranjo was feeling more and more like a capable person who was ready to get on with his life. Leaving the sheltered veterans' hospital environment and coming home was a big shock.

Back in Taos, Naranjo was alarmed when he walked the streets of the small town. Total strangers would approach him, start sobbing, and hurry away without even telling him their names. For a while he stopped going outside at all. He didn't know how to handle all the strange pity and guilt people seemed to feel when they saw him.

Naranjo's parents had gone to see him when he first arrived at the Denver hospital. They had walked right past his bed, not recognizing this scrawny, scarred person as their son. Now that he was home for good, it was impossible for his parents not to show their grief over their son's injuries or their worries about how he would get along in life. Sometimes Naranjo could sense that his father was just sitting there looking at him, weeping quietly. The family could not help being overprotective. One day in December, after Naranjo had been at home for about two months, the family was eating dinner. Naranjo was trying to locate a piece of meat on his plate with his fork. His father could not bear to watch him groping around, and he reached over and guided his son's hand to spear the meat.

Somehow, that did it. Naranjo sat patiently at the table until the meal was over. Then he explained to his parents that he would be moving out in a month, after the New Year. His sister Rina would help him find an apartment in Santa Fe. He loved all of his family, but he had to be on his own. In the months to come, Naranjo would eat a lot of TV dinners, have many small accidents, make many mistakes. But he was on his way to an independent full life as an artist and a man.

In the quarter-century since, Michael Naranjo's career has blossomed. There have been many shows, many awards. One of the remarkable things about Naranjo as an artist has been his eagerness to push the limits. He began with the children's modeling clay in Japan, progressing to oil-based clay in Denver. After he was on his own, installed in his own apartment in Santa Fe, he made friends with sculptors there and decided he wanted to learn how to work in wax that could then be cast in bronze. Later, he yearned to work directly on stone, something many sighted sculptors are reluctant to do. Because of flying stone chips, the work is hazardous, and stone, unlike wax or clay, cannot be fixed if the sculptor makes a wrong move. But Naranjo has learned to make massive pieces, wearing protective goggles and using a chisel powered by compressed air.

His sculptures vary in their style and subject as well as in the medium. It would be easy for someone like Naranjo to just keep making very

conventional pieces on Indian themes that all
look alike. That kind of art sells very well. But
Naranjo's work is really determined by his spirit.
Sometimes his sculptures come from an actual
vision, like his piece called *Golden Vision*, which
tries to capture a dream Naranjo once had of a
huge eagle with golden feathers perched on a
post, one wing dropped, the other raised as if to
beckon the dreamer. At other times he is moved
by a memory, as in *Room for One More*, which
depicts a Pueblo boy stuffing fish into the pockets
of his blue jeans.

In his private life, too, Michael Naranjo has
found great happiness. He and his wife Laurie
and their two daughters live near Santa Clara
Pueblo in a large sunny adobe house that Michael
designed. Several of his siblings, a number of
whom are also artists, live with their families in
adjoining houses. The Naranjo front yard always
seems to be full of sculpture and cousins big and
small. There is a lot of laughter around the Naranjo family compound.

One milestone in Michael Naranjo's life came
in 1983, when he was granted a papal audience
with Pope John Paul II. While he was there, the
Vatican granted permission for Naranjo to touch
many sculptures of Bernini, Donatello, and Ca-
nova, as well as some by Michelangelo, Naranjo's
idol. Then, in 1987, a crew from CBS came to the
Naranjo house to film the artist at home. When
they heard about his experience at the Vatican

Museum, and learned that no film had been taken
of Naranjo exploring the sculpture, they asked if
he would like to repeat the experience for their
film. Of course he said yes. When they asked what
sculpture he would especially like to touch this
time, Laurie reminded him of how Michelangelo's *David* in the Accademia in Florence, Italy,
was so huge, Naranjo had been able to reach only
the toes. Was there some way he could get access
to the whole statue?

When Naranjo and his wife walked into the
huge chamber where *David* stands, the crew led
him to a three-tiered scaffold that was carefully
built around the statue. Naranjo began touching
David's face. As his sensitive fingers and palms
moved over the statue, he was astonished by the
delicate care Michelangelo had brought to this
gigantic piece, working with only a hammer and
chisel. *David* even has tear ducts at the rims of
its eyes. Naranjo himself wept, so overwhelmed
by the sculpture and the moment that the crew
had to stop filming for a while. Then he went on,
spending nearly three hours on the scaffold. When
he stood once more on the floor of the great
echoing gallery, he could not talk. He could only
hug his wife wordlessly.

Michael Naranjo's wonderful afternoon at the
Vatican and the Accademia contrasted sharply
with a very different experience he had at the
United States' own National Gallery in 1989.
There, Naranjo had arranged for a special tour

and had requested ahead of time to be allowed
to touch certain pieces. As they began the tour,
the guide handed him a pair of gloves. Naranjo
was flabbergasted. "Give a sighted man dark
glasses, turn off the lights, and give him a tour of
paintings by Van Gogh . . . " he says, remembering what it was like. It was one of the few times
he felt deeply bitter since the first weeks following
his wounding. He barely trusted himself to talk
to the guard. Politeness and self-control are
deeply held values in Pueblo culture. He did consent to wear the gloves, just so he could get a
vague idea of the sculpture, but inside he was
furious. Museums abroad had gladly helped him
to "see" whatever he wanted, even on very short
notice, but he was forbidden to touch the sculpture belonging to the nation for whom he had
sacrificed his eyesight. When the Naranjos returned to New Mexico, they began campaigning
for the rights of the blind to be able to have access
to our national treasures. The National Gallery
and other federal institutions are now making
their policies much more flexible.

Recently, the owner of a gallery in Taos remarked on the number of Vietnam veterans who
have stopped by the gallery since it has begun to
carry Michael Naranjo's work. Some are very
quiet as they walk around the gallery. Some are
angry, and almost immediately want to talk to
her about their own experiences in the war. Most,
after a while, are drawn to sculpture. They stay

for a time and then go back into the Taos sunlight and their own lives. Perhaps they have drawn peace and life from these shapes of wood and stone and bronze that convey Michael Naranjo's unquenchable spirit.

9
Louise Erdrich

Like many Indian people today, prize-winning novelist Louise Erdrich is of mixed blood. People of all branches — white and Indian — of her North Dakota family are wonderful storytellers, and so she grew up with a double wealth of stories. From her mother's Turtle Mountain Chippewa and French-Canadian people, she heard about the Windigo, the icy flesh-eating demon who haunts the wilderness during northern winters and strikes terror in the hearts of the hunters and trappers who wander there.

She heard about the huge hairy Rugaroo, a manlike creature who crashes around in thick underbrush, and leaves his giant footprints in creekbeds. She heard about Misshepeshu, the scaly water man who lives at the bottom of certain north-country lakes, a being who can brew storms, sink boats, and drown people. She heard about the trickster hero Nanabozho, who can wriggle out of any tight situation. She heard the stories about the beginning of things, like the time Bear led the Chippewa people up from one dark world through another, and then another, until at last her great paws broke through the final crust of rock and soil, and Bear and the People emerged together onto this sunlit earth they share.

Erdrich's mother's Chippewa family were Roman Catholic, like her father's German-American people. So she also heard stories from the Bible, stories of Christian miracles, stories about the Virgin Mary appearing to people in time of trouble, and about statues of saints that wept real tears. Other stories told of droughts or hard winters or unusual storms, like the tornado that wrecked a town and yet snatched up a lighted candle from a table and set it gently down a mile away, still burning.

The stories Erdrich's family told recalled hard times and good times, births and deaths, fights and funerals. Her father recalled going up in a small plane during the Depression years with a daredevil barnstormer who had visited town; her mother told tales of how the old-time Chippewa people had endured starving winters in the bush. Through the stories Erdrich learned of the wise and foolish, the mean or kind, and of people who were a mixture of qualities. As she sat quietly listening to the grown-ups talk around kitchen

tables and on porches, those storytelling voices filled her imagination. In time, it would be her turn to become the storyteller herself. Many of the creatures and events she heard about while she was growing up would appear in her novels.

The Turtle Mountain Indian Reservation, home to Erdrich's Chippewa family, lies near the North Dakota–Manitoba border. The Turtle Mountain band of Chippewa originally lived in Minnesota. They were pushed gradually farther west into a patch of North Dakota that has been coveted by many people, white and Indian alike, for its good grasslands, thick woods, and abundant game. Here, the Turtle Mountains have eroded through the eons into soft rolling hills shaped like the arc of a box turtle's shell. At their feet lies a countryside of flat grassy plains crossed by sloughs and dotted with marshes. Redwing blackbirds teeter and trill from the cattails. Meadowlarks with their yellow breasts and smart black necklaces carol from the stubble beside winding dirt roads. In autumn and spring, great migrating flocks of sandhill cranes, snow geese and Canada geese stream overhead in wide trailing V's. Once that was also the migratory route of the whooping cranes, of which only a few now remain. Even today in stories the Chippewa people recall the vast flights of those huge white birds and their ringing cries.

The Turtle Mountain Reservation is home to a mixed population of Chippewa, Cree, and French people. Many of them still speak a pidgin dialect called Michif or Mitchef, a mixture of Chippewa, Cree, and French that developed along the Canadian border. Fiddle music with an old-time French flavor is still played there at Chippewa social events. This is the land and the culture in which Louise Erdrich's family and her stories are rooted.

Erdrich's mother's father, Patrick Gourneau, served for a while as tribal chairman of the Turtle Mountain Chippewa. During his younger years, when he labored in the great golden wheat fields that stretch across Kansas and North Dakota, Pat Gourneau was a "Wobbly," a member of the Industrial Workers of the World. As a union man, he and his fellow farmworkers spoke out against big-scale farmers who provided squalid living conditions for their hired hands and paid them low wages.

Pat Gourneau was able to keep a balance between the white and the Chippewa worlds. He believed in both the Roman Catholic religion and the traditional Chippewa ways. He would attend the ordination mass for a new priest and then perform a Chippewa pipe ceremony outside the church to bless the young cleric. With his prayer bone, a deer's legbone filled with seeds and soil and other sacred things, he prayed for the Apollo 11 expedition to land safely on the moon. He loved to dance at the powwows that brought together people from many different tribes.

Patrick's daughter, Rita Joanna Gourneau, was raised at Turtle Mountain with her eleven brothers and sisters. Rita was a beautiful, bright, and loving child, and a fine storyteller in her own right. After high school, she went to work in the Bureau of Indian Affairs school system and married Ralph Erdrich, a BIA schoolteacher of German-American descent.

Ralph and his three brothers were the adopted sons of Mary Erdrich Korll, a big strong woman who ran a butcher shop in Little Falls, Minnesota. Mary Korll was not one to pet and fuss over her grandchildren. When Erdrich thinks back on her childhood visits to Little Falls, she recalls being put to work cleaning chicken gizzards and listening to Mary Korll swearing a blue streak in the back of the shop. Though she was a butcher, Korll loved animals and all growing things. Erdrich remembers how her grandmother would sneak dog biscuits to the four captive wolves someone kept caged near her home. She grew prize-winning hollyhocks and nursed her geranium plants through the winter in coffee cans she kept inside the house. Erdrich loved her grandmother for her honesty and for the way she treated children as equals.

Ralph Erdrich, Mary Korll's adopted son, grew up to be a shy, gentle, scholarly person. Like his wife Rita, he cared deeply for children. Karen Louise Erdrich, the oldest of their seven sons and daughters, was born on July 6, 1954, into this family that valued education and history. She grew up mostly in the small town of Wahpeton, North Dakota, where both her parents worked at the Wahpeton Indian School, some 250 miles southeast of the Turtle Mountain Reservation.

Ralph and Rita Erdrich recognized early that their daughter was gifted with language and a fertile imagination. Ralph Erdrich remembers a two-year-old Louise perfectly reciting a version of the Christmas story. As she grew older, she learned to love stories she found in books as well as the stories that were told to her. She loved the way books smelled and the way the paper felt beneath her fingertips. She began to read whatever came her way — *Nancy Drew*, *The Hardy Boys*, old *National Geographics* and *Reader's Digests*, field guides, and Shakespearean plays. "I remember having books splayed open," she has said, "under pillows and jackets all over the house, because as the oldest of several children I had lots of responsibility and not much time to read."

When she was still very young, she began to want to make books of her own. Her parents encouraged her to write in very direct ways. As she remembers, "My father used to give me a nickel for every story I wrote, and my mother wove strips of construction paper together and stapled them into book covers. So at an early age I felt myself to be a published author earning substantial royalties."

Erdrich's small-town childhood was largely a peaceful and happy one among her six lively brothers and sisters, surrounded as they were with love from both her Chippewa-French and her German-American relatives. Always, for her, family trips back to Turtle Mountain were exciting times. "When you go on Indian land," she has said, "[you] feel that there's more possibility, that there is a whole other world besides the one you can see and that you're very close to it. . . . There's a kind of feeling at Turtle Mountain — I guess just *comfortable* is the way to describe it. There are also places there which are very mysterious to me." She remembers walking around the land with her grandfather, who would teach her the names of places and tell her stories about different things that had happened there.

In her teenage years during the late sixties and early seventies, Erdrich began to feel lonely. She was growing into a beautiful young woman, slender and long-limbed, with almond-shaped eyes and high cheekbones. But she had always been somewhat shy, and her interests were not the same as many of her classmates. She cared about much more than dating and school sports. Wahpeton, like many small towns, expected people to behave in a certain way, to be "nice," and Louise knew that people can make life very hard on someone who does not fit in. She did the things she was expected to do in order to seem like a normal Wahpeton teenager. She got good grades and became a cheerleader for the wrestling team. Still, she expressed her individuality in small ways. She insisted on wearing her father's old army jacket instead of the bright-colored parkas the other girls chose. Instead of listening to Top

40 hits, she preferred the old ballads and protest songs of folksinger Joan Baez.

One night, feeling rebellious and depressed, she packed a sleeping bag and sneaked out to spend the night on the high school football field. A skunk came strolling across the grass, and, sensing a warm place, he curled up on top of Erdrich. At first she was frightened, but eventually, like the trusting skunk, she, too, fell asleep. Toward dawn, she awoke drenched with skunk scent, for a dog had come by to investigate and frightened her bedfellow. The young rebel walked home through the early morning streets of Wahpeton, reeking of skunk.

Always, Erdrich kept diaries and journals, scribbling her thoughts and feelings, descriptions of what she saw and heard around her, and ideas for stories and poems. However sad or different she might feel, in the world of her writing she could be herself.

Erdrich's parents were very intelligent, but neither they nor her teachers knew a great deal about colleges and universities beyond North Dakota. As Louise's senior year drew near, everyone saw that this bright young woman should go to college, but no one was quite sure where it would be best for her to go. One day when Rita Erdrich picked up a copy of *National Geographic*, an article about Dartmouth College in Hanover, New Hampshire, caught her eye. There were pictures of slalom races, bobsled runs, and the elaborate floats and giant ice sculptures Dartmouth students created to celebrate their traditional Winter Carnival. But the article also told how the men who founded Dartmouth had originally intended to offer a free education to Indian people. That aim had been forgotten for a long time. Now, in 1971, the college was starting a Native American Studies program and trying hard to recruit Native American students. It was also changing from an all-male college and accepting its first women students.

Wouldn't this college be a good place for Karen Louise? Rita wondered. She was right. In the autumn of 1972, Erdrich found herself amid the green lawns, scarlet maples, and the neat wooden-and-brick colonial buildings of Dartmouth. One of fifteen Native American freshmen, she was more than 1,500 miles from home.

A new teacher had just come to Dartmouth that same year, a young part-Modoc Indian anthropologist named Michael Dorris. He was handsome, energetic, and very smart. He had been hired to supervise the new American Indian Studies program. At a welcoming picnic for Native American students and faculty, Erdrich struck up a conversation with him and his four-year-old adopted son, Abel. The Dorrisses had brought their Siberian husky Skahota with them. The big dog looked like he could use a romp, and Erdrich offered to take him for a run. Dressed stylishly in a miniskirt and cowboy boots, she was not ready for Skahota's muscle, and he eagerly dragged her around the park as she stumbled behind him. It was not a very dignified introduction, but in a few years' time Dorris and Erdrich would come to mean much to one another. Since their senses of humor would help to bring them through many hard times later on, it is fitting that laughter marked their first meeting.

Erdrich made the most of her four years at Dartmouth. She majored in English and creative writing and won prizes for her poetry. When she enrolled in one of Dorris's Native American Studies seminars, she asked if she could write a story instead of doing an ordinary research paper. When he agreed, she wrote a story based on what had actually happened when the Swedish colonizers first encountered the Delaware Indians. The vain colonial governor thought he would really impress the Delaware people if he had a whole suit of clothes made out of wampum, the lustrous pieces of shell Eastern Native Americans used for money. The Delaware made the suit for him, but the governor was very fat, and as soon as he took a deep breath the whole suit burst apart! Even as a young woman, Erdrich had a great talent for envisioning the real human beings, the comedy and the tragedy behind the dry facts of history.

After Erdrich graduated from Dartmouth in 1976, she wanted more than anything else to be a writer. Most authors do not make their living just from their writing. They support themselves at other jobs and write in their spare time. Many choose to go to graduate school in English or creative writing and find work as college teachers. But Erdrich thought that she was not cut out to be a teacher. During her high school and college summers, and after her college graduation, she took many odd jobs. At various times she picked cucumbers, hoed sugar beets, sold popcorn, life-guarded, and waitressed. She was a Kentucky Fried Chicken clerk and a short-order cook. She worked on a road construction crew and at a truck weighing station. Still later, she was a North Dakota poet-in-the-schools, an advertising manager, and an aide at both a psychiatric hospital and a senior citizen center. These jobs may have been hard and boring work at the time, but later on, her experience would find its way into her novels. When one of Erdrich's characters works as a restaurant cook or lives at a home for the elderly, what happens to them seems very true-to-life.

In 1978, after many such jobs, Erdrich decided that graduate school might be a good thing after all. In 1979 she earned a master's degree in creative writing from Johns Hopkins University in Baltimore. After graduating, she taught at the university for a year and then returned to New England to work as the writer and editor for *The Circle*, the newsletter of the Boston Indian Council. In May of 1979 she was invited back to Dartmouth to give a reading of her poetry. It was a very important homecoming. Michael Dorris, her former professor, sat in the audience. He and Erdrich had kept in touch with postcards and an occasional phone call over the years since she had graduated, but they had not spent a lot of time thinking about one another. Now, in a soft, vibrant voice, Erdrich read her poems about North Dakota men and women, about life in small towns on the Great Plains, about Chippewa heroes and monsters. Dorris was overwhelmed by Louise Erdrich's poems and by her quiet beauty.

After the reading, Dorris drove Erdrich back to the house where she was staying. He wanted to ask her then and there in the dark car to marry him, but he didn't dare. By now he was the single father of three adopted children, and he and his family were about to leave for a year in New Zealand where Dorris was to do research. Erdrich and Dorris exchanged addresses and promised to write. After he drove away, Erdrich went inside the house and telephoned her mother in North Dakota. "You won't believe this," she told Rita Erdrich, "but I've met the man I'm going to marry!"

While Dorris was abroad, Erdrich continued with her writing. She won prestigious fellowships to the MacDowell Colony and the Yaddo Colony. Both of these institutions give writers a room and meals and a quiet and beautiful place to work uninterrupted. From the MacDowell Colony, Erdrich mailed to Dorris, halfway around the world in New Zealand, an envelope full of red-and-gold autumn leaves. For seven months, Erdrich and Dorris exchanged letters. They shared the stories and poems they were writing with one another.

Though they had known each other for some time, they felt as though at last they were really getting to know one another through those letters. When Dorris's New Zealand visit came to an end in December, he was eager to get back to New Hampshire. One reason was that Erdrich had been invited back to Dartmouth to be a visiting writer, starting in January. Both wondered what the future would hold, now that they would once again be living in the same town.

When Dorris picked Erdrich up at the airport after her flight from North Dakota, he brought his three adopted children with him. They were Abel, 13; Sava, also called Jeffrey, 9; and Madeline, 6. It was important to both Erdrich and Dorris that she should get to know the children if they were to be more than friends. Erdrich, coming from a large family, felt very easy around children. But Dorris's family was not average. All three were Sioux children whose alcoholic families were unable to care for them. Abel, the oldest, was a special challenge. He was a very loving boy, but he had many problems. He was very small for his age. He often had epileptic seizures. Abel also had trouble learning in school. Unless someone was there to remind him, he would forget to do the things he needed to do, even simple things like brushing his teeth or eating his lunch.

No doctor or teacher or counselor could seem to figure out what was wrong with Abel. Certainly, he had not had a good start in life. He had been born prematurely to an alcoholic mother who neglected him. She often forgot to feed him, and when she wanted to go out, she would tie him to the bars of his crib and leave him for hours. Social workers took Abel away from her. The little boy lived in state hospitals and foster homes until he was three, when Dorris adopted him. Everyone agreed that those first three years probably slowed Abel's development. But whatever was wrong, the ten years of loving care Dorris had given Abel in the meantime, and all the doctors and the special schooling Dorris had arranged for him, had made no difference.

That first night in New Hampshire when Dorris met Erdrich at the plane, he drove her to her new apartment. They stayed up until early morning talking eagerly about their writing and their experiences, while Abel, Sava, and Madeline fell asleep on her bed. In the days to come, it seemed as if there was never enough time to say all the things they wanted to say to one another. On October 10, 1981, with all three Dorris children there, Louise Erdrich and Michael Dorris got married at Dorris's eighteenth-century farmhouse, which Abel had named Pumpkin Pond Farm. It was a beautiful day of gray and blue sky and brilliant autumn colors. The bright leaves Erdrich had mailed to Dorris in New Zealand might have been an omen of this wedding day. Standing before a few friends and relatives beneath two willow trees, Erdrich and Dorris vowed to love and respect one another. Then the parents and the children all promised to be good to one another. Now they were a family.

Erdrich had taken on a big job. Abel was a loving boy, but because he could not reason well, he could make even the most patient person angry.

Learning to be a mother to a difficult family was not the only thing going on in Erdrich's life. She was beginning to create an imaginary world in stories and poems. This world centers around the shores of Matchimanitou Lake, where a number of Chippewa people live, and nearby Argus, North Dakota, a small northern-prairie town of people of German and Polish descent. Before her marriage, Erdrich had begun to write a novel about several Chippewa families in the years between 1912 and 1924 who are threatened by hardship, epidemics, and the loss of their land, but she was having trouble seeing just where the book was going. After her marriage, she put that novel aside and began working on a series of short stories that are set in those same fictional North Dakota places.

In 1982, one of Dorris's aunts read an announcement that *The Chicago Tribune* was offering the $5,000 Nelson Algren award for the best short story submitted to them. She told Erdrich and Dorris about the contest. Erdrich had an idea for a story she was planning to write, but she didn't feel she had much of a chance of winning any contest. Besides, the deadline was only twelve days away! But Dorris urged her to try, and so she went off to a corner of their kitchen and quickly wrote down the story she had been thinking about. When she finished the first draft, she and Dorris went over the manuscript carefully together, adding some things, changing others. They talked out and argued over their ideas about what different characters might say and do. Finally, when they agreed on every word, Erdrich mailed off her entry.

The story, "The World's Greatest Fisherman," is about a mixed-blood Chippewa family in 1981. Albertine, a college nursing student, tells about returning to the reservation for a visit home. June, Albertine's favorite aunt, has recently died after getting drunk and becoming lost in a snowstorm. As Albertine and her relatives fix big family meals, visit old graveyards, drink, and gossip, we learn a lot about them. Many emotions come out, especially when they start talking about the different ways they felt toward June. At last, the reunion ends up in a big fight.

The story is sad and funny at the same time. The characters are Chippewa and part-Chippewa, and some of what happens to them is very much a part of being Native American and living on a reservation in the northern Midwest. But the story has also reminded many people, Indian and non-Indian, of their own families. Many families have secrets they keep from one another. People often don't want to talk about the things that have happened in their family that they think are shameful, things like alcoholism or babies born to mothers and fathers who aren't married. It is hard to admit that you might feel closer to an aunt than to your own mother, or that you love deeply a person whom everyone else considers a disgrace. But these sorts of things happen everywhere. Even people from Denmark, Russia, and Italy have seen in Erdrich's story many things families everywhere have in common.

When the judges at *The Chicago Tribune* awarded "The World's Greatest Fisherman" the Nelson Algren Prize, Erdrich and Dorris felt very encouraged. They saw that their way of helping one another to write really seemed to work. They also began to see how other stories Erdrich had written might fit together to make a whole novel about Albertine and her family and community. Erdrich began to imagine what might have happened in her characters' earlier lives to cause that fight to break out. She began to think about what might happen to them in the years after that family reunion. And she and Dorris suddenly realized that the people she had been trying to write about in her unfinished novel, set in the first part of the twentieth century, might be the ancestors or the younger selves of some of the characters in "The World's Greatest Fisherman."

In 1984 Erdrich published a book of poems, *Jacklight*, and her first novel, *Love Medicine*, which immediately became a best-seller, like all her novels that would follow. "The World's Greatest Fisherman" is the first chapter of *Love Med-*

icine, which won the National Book Critics' Circle
Award and the American Book Award. In 1986
she followed with *The Beet Queen*, mainly about
German-American and Polish-American families
in Argus. One of them is a tough, eccentric woman
who runs a butcher shop, much like Erdrich's
grandmother Mary Korll. But these white characters also figure into the lives of the Chippewa
families of *Love Medicine*. Dot, the beauty queen
of the book's title, is half Chippewa, and related
to Albertine's family. *Tracks*, Erdrich's third
novel, which came out in 1988, is based on that
first novel she had once given up writing. It
gives the early history of many of the characters
in the two previous novels, as it tells of Chippewa
families who fight to keep their land and others
who are content to sell out to the government and
to big lumber companies. That novel made the
New York Times Best-Seller List. In *The Bingo
Palace*, published in 1994, she takes her characters into the 1990s, when operating legal gam-
bling casinos on reservations has become a way
for many tribes to get back some of what they
have lost.

One of the main Chippewa families whose stories are told in these four novels is the Nanapush
family. Their name comes from Nanabozho, the
Chippewa trickster of the old-time stories, who
always manages to stay alive no matter what
trouble he gets himself into, no matter how others
try to get the better of him. In Erdrich's books,
many bad things befall the different generations

of Nanapush family members. But even in the 1990s they are still very much around, laying plans and hatching schemes and figuring out how to keep going. One of the main themes of Louise Erdrich's work is how, with courage and laughter, American Indian people survive, just like the trickster of the stories from long ago.

While Erdrich was publishing her novels about intertwined Chippewa and white families, she was working with Dorris on his books as well. They continued their method of going over every draft together and talking out their ideas about their characters on the long walks they took together around their farm. It has always been hard for some people to believe that Louise Erdrich and Michael Dorris write their books in the way they say they do. They both insist they really write together every book either one of them produces. Many critics scoff that two people can't really work so closely and harmoniously together. But Erdrich and Dorris just smile, as if to say, Who knows better than us how we work?

During these years, Erdrich gave birth to three daughters, Persia, Pallas, and Aza, adding to their adoptive family. In *The Blue Jay's Dance*, her book of essays published in 1995, she tells many wonderful stories about what it has been like for her to be both a mother and a writer. Family life has been very full for Erdrich and Dorris, but despite their joy in their children, it has not been at all easy. Through his teens, Abel continued to have difficulty at the most ordinary tasks of living.

Suddenly, as they neared adolescence, the two younger adopted children began to fail in school and seriously misbehave.

In 1982, around the time Erdrich won the Nelson Algren Prize, Dorris first learned what was really wrong with Abel. On a visit to a treatment center for addictive teenagers at the Pine Ridge Sioux Reservation in South Dakota, Dorris walked into a recreation room where three boys sat watching TV. They reminded him powerfully of Abel. It was not only that his son and these boys were all Sioux Indian teenagers. Like Abel, they were small for their age, and their heads seemed slightly too small for their bodies. Their noses were short, their upper lips were thin, and the little dimple most people have between the bottom of their nose and the bow of their top lip was not clearly marked. But more than their physical features caught Dorris's attention. Like Abel, these boys did not seem to notice or care about most of the things that were going on around them. As they stared intently at a cartoon program on TV, their mouths hung slightly open. Dorris thought they could almost be Abel's twin brothers. He showed a photo of Abel to the director of the center. The man nodded. "FAS, too, huh?" he asked.

At that time, Dorris did not even know those initials stood for the words Fetal Alcohol Syndrome. FAS is an untreatable condition that can affect children whose mothers drink while they are pregnant.

Every FAS child has his or her own story, but many parts of the story are sadly the same. These children are likely to have many physical ailments: epilepsy, curvature of the spine, and heart trouble are a few. More tragically, they are usually slow learners, and they are usually not able to understand that doing certain things might be unsafe. They have very bad judgment. If they grow up and become pregnant, they often give birth themselves to FAS children, since they can't understand that a drinking binge in June might result in an FAS child born a few months later.

Almost all Abel's problems could be traced to FAS. Moreover, it became clear that the family's two younger adopted children, who had also been born to drinking mothers, had a milder form of the condition, called Fetal Alcohol Effect, or FAE. Their physical and mental problems were not as obvious as Abel's, but as they grew older, they, too, seemed more and more unable to look out for themselves or make wise decisions.

Dorris wanted to tell Abel's story, in hopes he might spread the word about FAS and FAE and what can happen to the babies of mothers who drink. Erdrich supported his plan and helped him write *The Broken Cord*, the story of their family and especially of Abel. It was very hard for the whole family to reveal so much about their private lives, but they all thought it would be worth it if the book made readers more aware of FAS and FAE. Abel also agreed to tell his story in his own words for the book. It was probably the hardest thing he ever did. He did not write easily, and he was usually not good at sticking to tasks. But his account of his own life is included in *The Broken Cord*, which was published in 1987. A few years later, Abel would barely remember he had written his autobiography. In 1987, Dorris also published *A Yellow Raft in Blue Water*, his first novel.

In 1992, despite their children's problems, things seemed to be going very well for Erdrich and Dorris. They had just published *The Crown of Columbus*, a fat novel that carried both their names. They had a lot of fun writing this love story about two college professors who research together the real story of Columbus's first days in the Bahamas. The book was scheduled to come out in time for the quincentennial, the five hundredth anniversary of Columbus's landing. At the same time, a network TV film was being made of *The Broken Cord*. But just at this time of so many blessings, terrible news came to them. One night in September, while walking to his job at a truck stop, Abel was struck by a car. He had severe internal injuries, and never regained consciousness. He died about two weeks after the accident.

After a year of mourning, Erdrich and Dorris buried their oldest son's ashes on a little hill Abel had loved overlooking Pumpkin Pond. Then Erdrich, like her husband, went on with her work of writing and raising her children.

Storytellers and writers like Louise Erdrich are

heroes in a different way from many of the people in this book. They do not fight battles like Weetamoo and Geronimo or lead their people in making political decisions like Ben Nighthorse Campbell or Wilma Mankiller. They don't perform for cheering crowds like Will Rogers, Jim Thorpe, and Maria Tallchief. Mostly what they do is sit and write. But Erdrich is a hero nonetheless. Her rich books have given many people, American Indian and white alike, as much pleasure as has any performer. In telling the stories of land loss, alcoholism, injustice, and prejudice that American Indian people have endured, her novels are also powerful weapons of the truth. They present Native American history in a way that makes many people eager to read it. Erdrich is not afraid to talk about sorrow or about how through love and courage people can endure terrible loss and grief. Like the old-time storytellers, Louise Erdrich teaches us how to survive.

Selected Bibliography

(starred items are written especially for younger readers, or else are very accessible)

Weetamoo

Bourne, Russell. *The Red King's Rebellion: Racial Politics in New England 1675–1678*. New York: Atheneum, 1990.

Church, Colonel Benjamin. *Diary of King Phillip's War, 1675–1676*. Alan and Mary Simpson (eds.). Tiverton, RI: Lockwood Publications, 1975.

Horowitz, David. *The First Frontier: The Indian Wars and America's Origins 1607–1776*. New York: Simon and Schuster, 1978.

Kolodny, Annette. *The Land Before Her: Fantasy and Experience of the American Frontier, 1630–1860*. 1984.

Leach, Douglas. *Flintlock and Tomahawk: New En-*

gland in King Phillip's War. New York: W.W. Norton, 1966.

Malone, Patrick M. *The Skulking Way of War: Technology and Tactics Among the New England Indians.* Lanham, MD: Madison Books, with Plimouth Plantation, 1991.

* Peters, Russell M. *Clambake: A Wampanoag Tradition.* Minneapolis: Lerner Publications, 1991. *Photo-essay.*

* Roman, Joseph. *King Philip, Wampanoag Rebel.* New York: Chelsea House Publishers, 1992.

Rowlandson, Mary. *Narrative of the Captivity and Restoration of Mrs. Mary Rowlandson.* In *The Meridian Anthology of Early American Women Writers.* ed. Katherine M. Rogers. New York: Meridian, 1991.

Russell, Howard. *Indian New England Before the Mayflower.* Hanover, NH: University Press of New England, 1980.

* Simmons, William S. *Spirit of the New England Tribes: Indian History and Folklore, 1620–1984.* Hanover, NH: University Press of New England, 1986.

* Weinstein-Farson, Laurie. *The Wampanoag.* New York: Chelsea House Publishers, 1989.

* Wilbur, C. Keith. *New England Indians.* Chester, CT: The Globe Pequot Press, 1978.

Geronimo

Ball, Eve. *Indeh: An Apache Odyssey.* Norman: University of Oklahoma Press, 1988.

———— *In the Days of Victorio.* Tucson: University of Arizona Press, 1970.

Betzinez, Jason, with Wilbur Sturtevant Nye. *I Fought With Geronimo.* Lincoln: University of Nebraska Press, 1987.

Debo, Angie. *Geronimo: The Man, His Time, His Place.* Norman: University of Oklahoma Press, 1976.

Geronimo, with S.M. Barrett. *Geronimo's Story of His Life.* Williamstown, MA: Cornerhouse Publishers, 1989.

Roberts, David. *Once They Moved Like the Wind: Cochise, Geronimo, and the Apache Wars.* New York: Simon and Schuster, 1993.

Wetherill, Marietta. *Marietta Wetherill: Reflections on Life With The Navajos in Chaco Canyon.* Kathryn Gabriel, ed. Boulder, CO: Johnson Books, 1992.

Jim Thorpe

Hahn, James. *Thorpe! The Sports Career of James Thorpe.* Mankato, MN: Crestwood House, 1981.

Nabokov, Peter. *Indian Running.* Santa Fe, NM: Ancient Cities Press, 1987.

Newcombe, Jack. *The Best of the Athletic Boys: The White Man's Impact on Jim Thorpe.* Garden City, NY: Doubleday, 1975.

* Oppenheim, Joanne. *Black Hawk: Frontier Warrior.* New York: Troll Associates, 1979.

* Rivinus, Edward F. *Jim Thorpe.* Austin, TX: Steck-Vaughn Company, 1992.

* Van Riper, Guernsey, Jr. *Jim Thorpe, Olympic Champion.* New York: Aladdin Books, 1986.

Will Rogers

Brown, William R. *Imagemaker: Will Rogers and the American Dream.* Columbia: University of Missouri Press, 1970.

Byers, Chester. *Cowboy Roping and Rope Tricks.*

Mineola, NY: Dover Publications, 1966.

Day, Donald. *Will Rogers: A Biography*. New York: Van Rees Press, 1962.

Ketchum, Richard M. *Will Rogers: The Man and His Times*. New York: American Heritage Publishing Company, 1973.

Rogers, Betty Blake. *Will Rogers: His Wife's Story*. Second Edition. Norman: The University of Oklahoma Press, 1979.

Sterling, Byran B. and Frances N. *Will Rogers and Wiley Post: Death at Barrow*. New York: M. Evans and Co., Inc: 1993.

———— *The Best of Will Rogers*. New York: M. Evans and Company, 1979.

———— *Will Rogers' World*. New York: M. Evans and Company, 1989.

Yagoda, Ben. *Will Rogers*. New York: Alfred A. Knopf, 1993.

Maria Tallchief

Garis, Robert. *Following Balanchine*. New Haven: Yale University Press, 1995.

* Gridley, Marion E. *Maria Tallchief: The Story of an American Indian*. Minneapolis: The Dillon Press, 1973.

Mason, Frances, ed. *I Remember Balanchine: Recollections of the Ballet Master by Those Who Knew Him*. New York: Doubleday and Company, 1991.

Mathews, John Joseph. *The Osages: Children of the Middle Waters*. Norman, OK: The University of Oklahoma Press, 1961.

* Myers, Elisabeth P. *Maria Tallchief: America's Pre-*

miere Ballerina. New York: Grossett and Dunlap, 1966.

Rautbord, Sugar. "Maria Tallchief." *Interview* 17, March 1987, 60–63.

* Sonneborn, Liz. "Maria Tallchief" in *American Indian Lives: Performers*. New York: Facts on File, Inc., 1995.

* Tobias, Tobi. *Maria Tallchief*. New York: Crowell Company, 1970.

on film:

Belle, Anne, Producer. *Dancing For Mr. B: Six Balanchine Ballerinas*. Los Angeles: Direct Cinema, Ltd. Videotape, 1989.

Ben Nighthorse Campbell

Connell, Evan S. *Son of the Morning Star: Custer and the Little Big Horn*. New York: HarperCollins, 1984.

Viola, Herman J. *Ben Nighthorse Campbell: An American Warrior*. New York: Orion Books, 1993.

Welch, James. With Stekler, Paul. *Killing Custer*. New York: W.W. Norton and Company, 1994.

Michael Naranjo

* Nelson, Mary Carroll. *Michael Naranjo*. Minneapolis: Dillon Press, 1975.

Swentzell, Rina, and Naranjo, Tito. "Nurturing: The *Gia* at Santa Clara Pueblo," *El Palacio*, Volume 92, Number 1, Summer/Fall 1986, 36–39.

* ———— *Children of Clay: A Family of Pueblo Potters.* Minneapolis: Lerner Publications, 1992.

on film:

Kamins, Michael, producer. *Michael Naranjo: A New Vision.* Albuquerque: KNME TV and Native American Public Broadcasting, 1991.
Hal Rhodes, producer. *Images of War.* Albuquerque: KNME-TV, 1985.

Wilma Mankiller

Awiakta, Marilou. "Rebirth of a Nation." *Southern Style*, September-October, 1988.
———— *Selu: Seeking the Corn Mother's Wisdom.* Golden, CO: Fulcrum Publishing, 1993.
Fortunate Eagle, Adam. *Alcatraz! Alcatraz!* Berkeley, CA: Heyday Books, with the Golden Gate National Park Association, 1992.
Mankiller, Wilma Pearl, and Wallis, Michael. *Mankiller: A Chief and Her People.* New York: Saint Martin's, 1994.
* Rand, Jacki Thompson. *Wilma Mankiller.* Steck-Vaughn, 1993.
Steinem, Gloria. *Ms.*, January, 1988.

Louise Erdrich

Dorris, Michael. *The Broken Chord.* New York: HarperCollins, 1992.
———— *Paper Trail.* New York: HarperCollins, 1994.
Erdrich, Louise. *The Blue Jay's Dance: A Birth Year.* New York: HarperCollins, 1995.

Chavkin, Allan R. and Nancy F., eds. *Conversations with Louise Erdrich and Michael Dorris*. Jackson: University of Mississippi Press, 1994.

on film:

Bill Moyers, producer. *Searching For a Native American Identity: Louise Erdrich and Michael Dorris*. Princeton, NJ: Films For The Humanities, 1994.

Index